What people ar

"John Alexander has utilized both research and experience in the process of writing about the Ten Commandments. Academic preparation, decades of pastoral work, and years of real-life experiences come together creating a 'timeless' document both challenging us and inspiring us to trust again in the essentials of Christian living in a post-Christian culture—the Ten Commandments. *Timeless* is a relevant read for anyone seeking to find practical application for their Christian faith. *Timeless* is also an incredible help for pastors and Christian leaders searching for teaching and sermon material."

Fred Garmon, Ph.D.
Executive Director, People for Care and Learning
President, LeaderLabs, Inc.

". . . I read a great deal of wisdom in [Dr. Alexander's] writing, most wholesome common sense, and deep morality. . . . This is a very important work. . . . It is written . . . with numerous examples from everyday life, and consequently is very readable to a broad public persuasion. . . . Be assured of the importance and validity of the writing. . . ."

Rabbi Daniel Sperber
Professor and President of The Ludwig and Erica Jesselson Institute for Advanced Torah Studies

"Dr. Alexander is a gifted and talented pastor, teacher and author. His genuine love for God His church and His people is the motivating factor in the life and ministry of John and Lori Alexander. In the pages of this book Dr. Alexander gives insight, wisdom and enlightenment concerning the relevance of the Ten Commandments in the life of the modern day believer. I highly recommend this book to all who desire a deeper knowledge of God and His Word as revealed to us in the Ten Commandments."

Bishop Kevin Taylor
District Bishop of the East Houston District of the Church of God
Senior Pastor of Victory Temple in Houston, Texas for over 20 years

JOHN L. ALEXANDER, PH.D.
Foreword by Dr. Mark L. Williams

TIMELESS

The Ten Commandments Today

ISBN: 978-1-59684-781-1

@Copyright 2013 by John Alexander
All Rights Reserved

Printed by Derek Press, Cleveland, TN

Dedication and Acknowledgements

This book is dedicated to . . .

God, my Father, and His Son, Jesus Christ, who by the Holy Spirit has enabled me to do those things that would, without Him, be far beyond my grasp. All honor, glory, and praise be unto your name, O Lord, in all things and at all times, for You are my eternal hope.

My lovely wife, Lori, who has been my lifelong friend, encourager, and support in everything I've been fortunate enough to accomplish in life. She is God's gift to me for any success I may have achieved in life. Thank you for your patient and supportive love. This book is a credit to your steadfast love and ongoing assurances to what we can do together in Christ and by His grace. What I do, I do because of you . . . thank you!

My children, Dustin and Ashley, for whom my love has always motivated me to work hard to set a godly example and to encourage them to do their best in all they set their mind to do. They are the two best children I could have ever asked God for. Serve the Lord with all your strength.

Sanctuary Church and my church family, you have been tremendously supportive and encouraging to me on this journey. Thank you for your patience and understanding.

Foreword

Through this book, Dr. John Alexander aims to help readers understand that the Ten Commandments are not antiquated laws hopelessly outdated for the contemporary world, but absolute essentials for Christian living that bring the law of God and the grace of God together for the people of God to live an abundant life in Christ.

I believe he has succeeded admirably.

It is a notion commonly accepted by many that the Ten Commandments were abolished by Christ when a new era of grace was ushered in by His death on the cross. In defense of this idea, His words in Matthew 5:17 (KJV) are often quoted, "Think not that I am come to destroy the law, or the prophets: I am not come to destroy but to fulfill," with "fulfill" erroneously interpreted to mean "do away with because it is no longer necessary." An excellent version that accurately captures the sense of the word *fulfill* is the New Living Translation, which renders Matthew 5:17 as follows: "Don't misunderstand why I have come. I did not come to abolish the law of Moses or the writings of the prophets. No, I came to accomplish their purpose."

That is precisely what Jesus did. In His own life experience, He observed the Ten Commandments and completely *filled full* their meaning. He also showed their deeper spiritual intent, explaining for example, that unjustified anger equated murder and lust is mental and emotional adultery. Jesus *filled full* God's commandments through His teachings, expanding their intent.

If we can recognize that the Ten Commandments recorded in the Old Testament are repeated in the thinking and practice of Jesus and throughout the New Testament—the age of grace—we can move toward an understanding that they are eternally contemporary. The Giver of the commandments voiced His desire that they be eternally kept in Deuteronomy 5:29 (NKJV), "Oh, that they had such a heart in them that they would fear Me and always keep all My commandments, that it might be well with them and with their children forever!"

These guidelines for living were given by God so individuals, families, and whole societies would understand how they should conduct themselves. The Creator Himself knows best how people should live. Obeying His commands results in His blessing, but also ensures that we are pleasing the Lord. Jesus said, "Whoever has my commands and keeps them, he is the one who loves me" (John 14:21 NIV).

The *Midrash* preserves an ancient Jewish tradition that when God's mighty voice spoke the Ten Commandments it had no echo. An echo occurs when sound encounters resistance, striking an impenetrable barrier. God's voice had no echo, they believe, because it penetrated not only the desert mountains, but also the human heart. Nothing or no one could block the voice out. The Ten Commandments are to be internalized, guarded, and practiced until the end of time.

Dr. John Alexander has discussed in depth the definition and implications of each of the Ten Commandments. I commend these writings to your attention and to your careful consideration. My prayer is that you will come away from this reading with a new and sincere appreciation for the significance and eternity of God's law.

—Dr. Mark Williams
  Presiding Bishop/General Overseer
  Church of God International Cleveland, Tennessee

Table of Contents

Chapter One: Introduction 11

Chapter Two: The First Commandment Only You 17
- God Deserves My Undivided Attention 19
- God Desires My Undivided Affection 23
- God Demands My Undivided Allegiance................ 28

Chapter Three: The Second Commandment
The Right God, the Wrong Way 33
- A Created God Limits Real Worship 35
- A Created God Leads to False Worship 38
- The Creator God Liberates True Worship............. 43

Chapter Four: The Third Commandment
You Give God a Bad Name............................. 51
- Be Careful How You Treat God's Name............... 53
- Be Thoughtful About Where You Take God's Name 61
- Be Faithful About How You Trust in God's Name...... 63

Chapter Five: The Fourth Commandment Rest Assured 69
- What Is the Sabbath? 70
- When Is the Sabbath? 76
- How Do We Keep the Sabbath Day Today?............. 78

Chapter Six: The Fifth Commandment
The Key to Success and Long Life..................... 87
- The Prominent Importance of the Fifth Commandment... 88
- The Principle Interpretation of the Fifth Commandment .. 90
- The Indisputable Purpose of the Fifth Commandment.... 94

Chapter Seven: The Sixth Commandment Pro-Life............. 105
- The Abomination of Murder......................... 105
- The Analogy of Murder 108
- The Anatomy of a Murderer 110
- The Antithesis of Murder 117

Chapter Eight: The Seventh Commandment Sex Offenders 121
- God's Plan Concerning Sex 122
- Man's Problem With Sex 127
- A Biblical Prevention Plan for Man 133
- God's Power to Restore Sex Offenders................ 141

Chapter Nine: The Eighth Commandment
The Possession Paradox 145
- I Want What I Want and Will Take What I Want 146
- I Want What I Want and Will Work for What I Want 157
- I Want What I Want and Will Trust God for What I Want . 161

Chapter Ten: The Ninth Commandment The Lying Truth 165
- Lying Dishonors God 167
- Lying Deceives Others 170
- Lying Destroys Character 175

Chapter Eleven: The Tenth Commandment Enough Already...... 179
- The Price We Pay When Enough
  Is Not Enough Already 181
- The Problems We Encounter When Enough
  Is Not Enough................................... 184
- The Process We Engage in Practicing a
  Life of Enough Already 188

Chapter Twelve: Epilogue................................. 195

About the Author... 197

End Notes 201

CHAPTER ONE

INTRODUCTION

Are the Ten Commandments Antiquated Laws of Contemporary Irrelevance or Timeless Essentials for Christian Living in a post Christian culture? In the post Christian culture of today most people have little or no regard for the Ten Commandments because they are unaware of their New Testament relevance. This book will establish an understanding of these laws as Timeless and absolute essentials for life today.

Although Jesus has fulfilled the law, according to Matthew 5:17: "Do not think that I have come to abolish the Law or the Prophets; I have not come to abolish them but to fulfill them,"[1] it does not mean we are to forsake the law. Jesus also said concerning the law, in verse 18: "For truly I tell you, until heaven and earth disappear, not the smallest letter, not the least stroke of a pen, will by any means disappear from the Law until everything is accomplished."[2] As Christians we must discover how to rightly divide and apply the Word of God in its entirety to today's living.

The U.S. Supreme Court has outlawed the displaying of the Ten Commandments on any government building and has forbidden their display in public schools as well. Yet, they are the law of God for all generations without exception. The morality of our society has greatly diminished in recent years, and many Christian leaders believe it is a direct result of our shift from the laws of God (specifically the Ten Commandments). Former president James Madison said, "The structure of our government and society to morally prosper is built on the Ten Commandments."[3] In order for our society to morally prosper there must be a return to the Ten Commandments, and it begins with the Christians of our society. Until the Christians (the Church) can understand, through proper biblical analysis, the New Testament application of these Old Testament laws, they will continue on a divergent course from God.

The Ten Commandments hold the secret to our world's survival. These are not God's recommendations; they are God's *commandments*. To reject them is to reject Him. To reject Him is to guarantee our moral destruction. The key is to learn to understand these Ten Commandments through the lens of God's love and New Testament grace, and then to follow them.

In studying the contemporary relevance of the Ten Commandments, one must discover the correct interpretation of their meaning and how they apply in Christian living today. Much of our society has created a culturalization of the Ten Commandments that has left us with the belief that they are irrelevant to Christian living today, and I believe that even most Christians have a wrong interpretation and understanding of their original intent. Believers and nonbelievers alike must understand that God has, out of love, outlined these commands as the disciplines of a right relationship with Him and with mankind.

It's amazing the responses people give when asked about heaven and why they believe they are going there. Some say, "I'm a good person; I help people." And one of the more common reasons people give is "I try to keep the Ten Commandments." We have created the idea that they were given so that we might have a relationship with God. But God did not give them as rules in order for us to have a relationship with Him; rather, to obey them is a reflection of a relationship we already have with God. They were not given so that we might have the hope of heaven, but because we have heaven's hope in our hearts. They are not rules for religious people but guidelines for God's family. Those who try to obey God out of a mere sense of obligation end up becoming legalistic or hypocritical. The Ten Commandments aren't meant to enslave us but to enrich us, to free us into God's fullness.

Some may ask, "Why do we need such commandments?" Ted Turner has declared the Ten Commandments obsolete:

> We're living with outdated rules. The rules we're living under are the Ten Commandments, and I bet nobody here even pays much attention to them because they're too old. When Moses went up on the mountain, there were no nuclear weapons, there was no poverty.

CHAPTER ONE:
INTRODUCTION

Today, the Ten Commandments wouldn't go over; nobody around likes to be commanded. Commandments are out![4]

Today, in America, many believe that there are no moral absolutes. Many hold to a philosophy of moral relativism. We have often heard statements like these: "What's right for you may not be right for me" or "If it feels good, do it" or "Anything goes" and, finally, "Nothing is right or wrong; there are just different opinions." All of this is the result of the feeling that there is no absolute truth—that you are entitled to your truth, and I am entitled to mine. Ted Koppel of *Nightline* said, "Our society finds truth too strong a medicine to digest undiluted."[5] A recent poll found that sixty-seven percent of Americans do not believe in moral absolutes. Among "Baby Busters," those born between 1965 and 1983, the percentage was even higher at seventy-eight percent. Even sixty-two percent of professing Christians said that there was no absolute standard of right and wrong.[6] According to James Patterson and Peter Kim in their book *The Day America Told the Truth*, they report that . . .

> 74 percent of Americans will steal from those who won't miss it, and 64 percent will lie for convenience as long as no one is hurt. Most Americans (93 percent) say they alone decide moral issues, basing their decisions on their own experience or whims. 84 percent say they would break the rules of their own religion. And 81 percent have violated a law they felt to be inappropriate. Only 30 percent say they would be willing to die for their religious beliefs or for God.[7]

Yet this nation was founded on biblical principles of right and wrong. James Madison, the fourth president of the United States said this:

> We've staked our future on our ability to follow the Ten Commandments with all of our heart. We have staked the whole future of American civilization, not upon the power of government, far from it. We've staked the future of all our political institutions upon our capacity . . . to sustain ourselves according to the Ten Commandments of God. (1778 to the General Assembly of the State of Virginia)[8]

God gave the Ten Commandments as a way of helping people lead a life of practical holiness. The law of God is given as an insight into the holiness, truth, and love of God for man. Mature believers delight to obey the commands of God as a way of expressing their love for their heavenly Father. God is not simply interested in outward obedience, but love from a pure heart, a good conscience, and a sincere faith. His commands give us guidelines to know the ways that we can please the Lord and bear fruit in every good work as we increase in the knowledge of Him.

The Ten Commandments do not stand as rungs on a ladder to climb for salvation. They stand as barriers erected by God to help us live lives that glorify His Name. They are relevant today, not to restrict us but to release us into the fullness and the freedom of what God has for His children.

What Moses brought down from Mount Sinai were not the "Ten Suggestions"; they are *commandments.* Can you imagine a world without rules and the chaos that would ensue? No laws would lead to no freedom of life and the imploding of any sense of a moral code or ethics. Today's society has reduced the potential for a fuller and more complete life by limiting their approach to the Ten Commandments. Israel illustrates this well in Judges 21:25 as they threw off restraints, when the people of the nation did what was right in their own eyes: "In those days Israel had no king; everyone did as they saw fit."[9] Life became dysfunctional for the nation. And so it is for America today when we disregard the Decalogue as archaic rules of irrelevance. Remember the words of David in Psalm 11:3: "If the foundations are destroyed, what can the righteous do?"[10]

Many believe the law has been fully abrogated by Christ, but that is not what He came to do. In returning to Matthew 5:17-18, remember that Jesus stated His intent was not to end the Law but to fulfill the Law. In fact, Jesus would transform the Law from a requirement of outward obedience to inward obedience. It would be no longer a covenant of work but rules for life and the ongoing work of sanctification in us. The problem is religion has created thousands of rules to enforce Ten Commandments.

CHAPTER ONE:
INTRODUCTION

Think about it: instead of thinking of them as rules of irrelevance, what if everyone recognized the Ten Commandments as absolute essentials for life and relationships? There would be no more abortion, rape, or murder; the moral change would drastically reduce disease; and the death rate would decline exponentially. Wealth would increase as prices would go down when stealing and cheating cease. Can you imagine what would happen in Washington alone? The law of God is not out-of-date, as some suggest, but it has never been more current and needed in America than right now in 2012.

The Old Testament law of God was an expression of His holiness and man's duty to follow it. Nothing has changed concerning God's holiness and His desire for us to be holy, as we read in Hebrews 12:14: "Be holy; without holiness no one will see the Lord."[11] Listen to the words of the apostle Paul in 2 Corinthians 7:1: "Having therefore these promises, dearly beloved, let us cleanse ourselves from all filthiness of the flesh and spirit, perfecting holiness in the fear of God."[12]

The law was spoken out of God's love to care for, protect, and show mercy to His people. That has not changed for us as New Testament believers. Too often people think of the law as a series of negative commands. What must be seen is that every negative command has a positive implication for the protection of life and for healthy living in relationships. When parents tell their child not to play in the street, it has a positive implication that because of their love for that child, they don't want their child to be hit by a car. The command is for the child's protection. Where God forbids sin, it is to protect the nation and the people from the destructive consequences of sin.

The Ten Commandments were to give man an outline of reverence for God and respect for one another. After thirty-five hundred years the need hasn't changed; there is perpetuity to the Ten Commandments. We must realize that God has not changed, and His expression for obedience has not been rewritten. Man's need for moral law and God's demand for obedience to His law are both absolute.

The law of God is not encumbering but liberating. The apostle Paul said in Romans 7:14: "For we know that the law is spiritual . . ."[13] The law is spiritual as it proceeds from God for the fulfillment of His purposes and use. That has not changed except for a higher demand of internal obedience that is made possible through our relationship with Jesus Christ and His Spirit dwelling in the heart of every believer.

To abandon the Ten Commandments as antiquated laws of irrelevance is to shatter the mirror of righteousness that God gives us through His Word to examine the condition of our lives. The whole of the Scriptures is but a commentary on the Ten Commandments of God for us. Jesus said, in the Gospel of Matthew, the whole law could be summed up in two commandments: to love God with our whole being and to love our neighbors as ourselves. They are summed up, not removed; even then, love for both will ultimately lead us to perfect obedience to the Ten Commandments.

Some claim the New Testament is about grace and the Old Testament is about law and that we live under grace. Think of it like this, the law needed love, and grace needs guidelines of moral structure. Together they complete us in Christ. This book will guide and direct its readers to understand that the Ten Commandments are not antiquated laws of contemporary irrelevance but absolute essentials for Christian living that bring the law of God and the grace of God together for the people of God to live an abundant life in Christ.

CHAPTER TWO
The First Commandment
ONLY YOU

Exodus 20:1-3
I am the Lord your God who brought you out of Egypt, where you were slaves. Worship no god but Me.

God spoke, and these were his words: "I am the Lord your God who brought you out of Egypt, where you were slaves. Worship no god but Me."[14] Anne Graham Lotz, the daughter of Billy Graham, wrote this in her book *God's Story*:

> A young boy spent many hours building a little sailboat, crafting it down to the finest detail. He then took it to a nearby river to sail it. When he put it in the water, however, it moved away from him very quickly. Though he chased it along the bank, he couldn't keep up with it. The strong wind and current carried the boat away. The heartbroken boy knew how hard he would have to work to build another sailboat. Farther down the river, a man found the little boat, took it to town, and sold it to a shopkeeper. Later that day, as the boy was walking through town, he noticed the boat in a store window. Entering the store, looking at it closely, he told the owner that the boat belonged to him. It had his own little marks on it, but he couldn't prove to the shopkeeper that the boat was his. The man told him the only way he could get the boat was to buy it. The boy wanted it back so badly that he did exactly that. As he took the boat from the hand of the shopkeeper, he looked at it and said, "Little boat, now you're twice mine. I made you and I bought you."[15]

In the same way, we belong twice to God: He both created us and paid a great price for us. With the blood of His Son, we have been redeemed and reunited with Him. His Son gave His life to get us back, yet so often we show such little gratitude for what He has done for us. The Word states in 1 Peter 1:18-19: "For you know what was paid to set you free from the worthless manner of life handed down by your ancestors. It was not something that can be destroyed, such as silver or gold; it was the costly sacrifice of Christ, who was like a lamb without defect or flaw."[16]

Before giving the Ten Commandments, God said this: "I am the Lord your God who brought you out of Egypt, where you were slaves." He was reminding them that not only did He create them, but He also redeemed them. He gave them life, and He gave them freedom. That's the relationship that God had with Israel, and it is the relationship He has with us. We are His because He created us. And we are His because He bought us out of slavery to sin. He created us, and He redeemed us. And that relationship is the basis for the commands that God gave to Israel.

"You shall have no other gods before me," or as the *Good News Translation* states it: "Worship no god but Me." The words demanded that God's people worship, and love, and serve only the one true God. With this first commandment, God makes it clear that His people are to have an exclusive relationship with Him.

Oswald Chambers wrote, "Let me fix my heart on gain and I do not see God. If I enthrone anything other than God in my life, God retires and lets the other god do what it can."[17]

There's room for only one throne in your life. The first commandment defines all others to follow, for in it God defines Himself, establishing His identity and His right to speak commandments for us to obey.[18] To worship the Lord your God and Him only is the fabric of both New and Old Testament alike. The first commandment establishes there can be only one God in our lives, and that can only be Jehovah God. The Bible is permeated by this truth that there is only one true God. Jesus echoed this in Matthew 22:37: "You must love the Lord your God with all your heart, all your soul, and all your mind."[19] The apostle Paul offered reference to this as well in 2 Timothy 2:4: "No one serving as a soldier gets entangled in civilian affairs, but rather tries to please his commanding officer."[20] The first commandment is the highest duty of man, placing

God first in every area of our lives. The first commandment requires us not only to love God, but also to be loyal to Him, and Him only, in a totally monogamous relationship with Him as a demonstration of our ongoing worship of Jehovah God.

Here are three things to note concerning the first commandment and its instructions that we are not to worship any other god but Jehovah God.

God Deserves My Undivided Attention

The first command teaches us to worship God and God only. Thirty-five-hundred years ago God took Israel out of bondage from Egypt. He freed them and made them a promise: "If you'll love Me and obey Me I'll make you a great nation, I'll bless you . . . prosper you . . . protect you . . . and give you a land that is full of My favor. Look at Deuteronomy 28:1-14:

> If you fully obey the LORD your God and carefully follow all his commands I give you today, the LORD your God will set you high above all the nations on earth. All these blessings will come on you and accompany you if you obey the LORD your God: You will be blessed in the city and blessed in the country. The fruit of your womb will be blessed, and the crops of your land and the young of your livestock—the calves of your herds and the lambs of your flocks. Your basket and your kneading trough will be blessed. You will be blessed when you come in and blessed when you go out. The LORD will grant that the enemies who rise up against you will be defeated before you. They will come at you from one direction but flee from you in seven. The LORD will send a blessing on your barns and on everything you put your hand to. The LORD your God will bless you in the land he is giving you. The LORD will establish you as his holy people, as he promised you on oath, if you keep the commands of the LORD your God and walk in obedience to him. Then all the peoples on earth will see that you are called by the name of the LORD, and they will fear you. The LORD will grant you abundant prosperity—in the fruit of your womb, the young of your livestock and the crops of your ground—in the land he swore to your ancestors to give you. The LORD will open the heavens, the

storehouse of his bounty, to send rain on your land in season and to bless all the work of your hands. You will lend to many nations but will borrow from none. The LORD will make you the head, not the tail. If you pay attention to the commands of the LORD your God that I give you this day and carefully follow them, you will always be at the top, never at the bottom. Do not turn aside from any of the commands I give you today, to the right or to the left, following other gods and serving them.[21]

Notice also Exodus 20:2: "I am the Lord your God who brought you out of the land of Egypt, out of the house of slavery." In other words, God was saying: "Even before I'm giving you these laws, I've delivered you, and I've made you My people. I'm not giving you this law so you can earn that privilege. I'm giving it to you because I love you and I'm committed to you and I want you to live the good life. I didn't bring you out of slavery to put you under a whole new kind of slavery. The laws of God are liberating not legalistic." Eerdman's Dictionary of the Bible has this to say:

> The Ten Commandments reflect the insight that the God of Israel is a God who governs all spheres of human life and that this God requires obedience. Still, it is essential to see the commandments in context of Israel's covenant with God. The obedience that God requires of Israel flows from God's liberating action on Israel's behalf. Freeing the Hebrew slaves from Egyptian bondage established a relationship between them and their God. The Ten Commandments are the means by which ancient Israel was to maintain that relationship. Finally, the individual stipulations that make up the Ten Commandments show that the status of Israel's relationship with God was a by-product of harmony within the Israelite community."[22]

God brought Israel out in a powerful display of His mighty hand and brought them to the edge of Mount Sinai, where He could reveal His heart, mind, and will to His people. Now, in Exodus 20:1-3, for the first time ever in history, God spoke to a nation and called them His own: "I am the Lord your God." This speaks of two things that are important to recognize—the sovereignty of God and the salvation of God.

CHAPTER TWO:
The First Commandment
ONLY YOU

The Sovereignty of God. Before God told them what He wanted them to do, He first told them who He is: "I am the Lord." He was saying, "There is only one God and I am that One; one God—almighty, sovereign, glorious—and I am all that and more." Don't pass over the statement "I am the Lord!" It's a statement about *who* God is. Remember when God appeared to Moses in the burning bush and Moses asked God what His name was, God answered with this statement: "I am the Lord. I am Yahweh." In other words: "I am the sovereign ruler of the universe; I made it all; I sustain it all; I control it all; I'm not limited by time; I AM."

At that time Egypt was the world power. The Pharaoh was viewed as a god. He was seen as all-powerful. But Yahweh came along and said, "Let Me show you who is in charge." Remember the ten plagues? Remember how he opened up the Red Sea and let the Israelites pass through and then, after they made it safely through, all the waters came down and drowned Pharaoh and his army? What a display of power! Always His power will be thus. He is the Lord, the only true God.

The Salvation of God. Look again at verse 2: "your God." We need to examine three areas pertaining to these words, "your God." First, He is *personal*. Not only is He Sovereign God, but he is also a personal God. That's why He said, "I am the Lord *your* God." When He said, "*your* God," he used the singular form of the pronoun. He was talking to individuals—to you and me personally. He is not only the God of the past generations, but of every individual soul in each generation."[23] He's not a God that exists way out there in the recesses of the universe and has no time for or interest in you. Remember what is written in Jeremiah 33:3: "Call to me and I will answer you, and will tell you great and hidden things that you have not known."[24] He's not a distant, unapproachable king. He's a personal God. He knows you, and He wants to be known by you. We see this invitation again in Matthew 11:28: "Come to Me, all who are weary and heavy-laden, and I will give you rest."[25] That's beyond believing in a god or the God, but that the Lord God is my God and that He wants a personal relationship with *me*.

Second, He is *powerful*. His relationship with us is a saving relationship. In verse 2 we have seen who is He; now we will see what has He done. "I am the Lord God who . . . let me remind you of what I've done before this." Most people see the Old Testament as only about the *law* of God and the New Testament as the *grace* of God. Yet the first commandment is all about grace. God was giving freely and abundantly. Before giving the Ten Commandments, God said, "I am *the* Lord *your* God, who brought you out of Egypt, where you were slaves." He was reminding them that not only did He create them but that He had also redeemed them. God also spoke to Israel this way in Isaiah 43:1-3: "But now thus says the LORD, he who created you, O Jacob, he who formed you, O Israel: Do not fear, for I have redeemed you; I have called you by name, you are mine."[26] What we are reading here is this: "I did for you what you could not do for yourselves. Now, go with Me to the shores of the Red Sea, where, after ten plagues and by miraculous means, I took you through the sea. I made bitter water sweet, I brought water out of the smitten rock, I fed you with heavenly bread . . . I protected you . . . I supplied answers to every need you had. Now here is what I require." It was only after God first gave His love through grace that He gave His law.

Third, He is *practical*. This is the divine order of God: He revealed Himself, delivered the people, and then gave them instruction. Before He gave the Ten Commandments to live by, He gave His loving grace to establish a personal relationship with them. Salvation both in the Old and New Testaments is by grace. We don't keep the law to earn grace, but out of His grace we are able to keep the law. The law He has given is for those He redeemed, those in relationship with Him. Not everyone hears His voice and obeys it, but His sheep do, according to the statement of Christ in John 10:27: "My sheep hear my voice, and I know them, and they follow me."[27] Out of this relationship He gives rules for guidance. Rules cannot establish relationship. A good example of this is how kids will rebel against our rules unless we first build a loving relationship with them. Andy Stanley said in his book *The Grace of God*: "Rules without relationship lead to rebellion."[28] But this is the way God establishes relationship (just as He did with the people of Israel): First,

He initiates love, and then He gives law. *He deserved their attention, and He certainly deserves ours as well.*

God Desires My Undivided Affection

The Ten Commandments are not about the *law* of God but the *love* of God—His love for us and our love for Him. He is one Lord, and He wants our single-hearted love—fully and completely devoted to Him.

It starts with relationship: The whole Bible can be boiled down to one word, *relationships*. The Bible focuses on two types of relationships—our relationship with God and our relationship with other people. From Genesis to the end of Revelation, the Bible focuses on how to have a close, intimate relationship with a holy God; and out of that relationship, we can have healthy relationships with others. In the first nineteen chapters of Exodus, He establishes a relationship of love to lead us—love then and love now. Out of this love for us, He says, "All I want is to be your one and only." He demands to be our first love and our most loved—not just *the* God, but *our* God; not just *a friend* but our *closest friend*; not just *a* Father but *our* Father; not just a help but *our* helper. And He wants us to be not just *a* family but *My* family, not just *a* people but *My* people.

God is too often seen as a God of law, rules and regulations, do's and don'ts, and "thou shalt nots." Yet that's not what the Bible teaches us. God is love, not law, and He wants us to love Him and to love others as He has loved us. When Jesus stepped to the forefront of ministry in what we know as the Sermon on the Mount (recorded in Matthew 5), He turned our attention from law to love by offering us the intimacy of a true relationship. It was relationship first . . . so it is that He came to us when we couldn't come to Him . . . laid down His life . . . and told us what to do, but He also empowered us to be able to accomplish it by His Spirit. Almost fifteen hundred years after God gave the laws, Jesus upheld them, calling them the "commandments" and listing five of them for the rich young ruler (Matthew 19:16-19). And in the Sermon on the Mount, Jesus showed that His coming had not canceled the commandments. He specifically mentioned the laws against killing (5:21) and committing adultery (v. 27). Jesus actually placed these laws on a higher plane by demanding that the spirit as well as the legal aspects of the law be kept (vv. 17-28). Jesus placed His eternal stamp of approval on the law by declaring: "Do not think that I came to destroy the Law or the Prophets. I did not come to destroy but to fulfill" (vv. 17-19)."[29] You cannot separate the love of God from the law of God: "Those who accept my commandments and obey them are the ones who love me. My Father will love those who love me; I too will love them and reveal myself to them."[30] To the degree that I bring my life in conformity to the law of God demonstrates the level of my love for Him. The measure of our love for God is seen in our obedience to God's laws. Look at Matthew 7:24: "Everyone then who hears these words of mine and acts on them will be like a wise man who built his house on rock."[31] The story of an attorney seeking to discredit Jesus and confronting Him is told in Matthew 22:36-40:

> "Teacher, which is the great commandment in the Law?" And He said to him, "'YOU shall love the lord your god with all your heart, and with all your soul, and with all your mind.' This is the great and foremost commandment. The second is like it, 'you shall love your neighbor as yourself.' On these two commandments depend the whole law and the prophets."[32]

Jesus said, "Love the Lord your God with all . . ." This is the number one commandment, to love God, and the second is to love your neighbor as yourself. At that moment everything changed, much like the message in the Sermon on the Mount. Serving God and pleasing Him is about relationships and not religious ritual—a totally new perception about God and life and our approach to Him. The people of God (the Jews) had perfected the art of living the law and beyond it. They were the epitome of *law-abiding citizens*. There were 613 laws in the Old Testament,[33] and they had followed the law until it sickened God . . . He was worn out with their religious acts.

> "What makes you think I want all your sacrifices?" says the Lord. "I am sick of your burnt offerings of rams and the fat of fattened cattle. I get no pleasure from the blood of bulls and lambs and goats. When you come to worship me, who asked you to parade

through my courts with all your ceremony? Stop bringing me your meaningless gifts; the incense of your offerings disgusts me! As for your celebrations of the new moon and the Sabbath and your special days for fasting—they are all sinful and false. I want no more of your pious meetings. I hate your new moon celebrations and your annual festivals. They are a burden to me. I cannot stand them! When you lift up your hands in prayer, I will not look. Though you offer many prayers, I will not listen, for your hands are covered with the blood of innocent victims. Wash yourselves and be clean! Get your sins out of my sight. Give up your evil ways. Learn to do good. Seek justice. Help the oppressed. Defend the cause of orphans. Fight for the rights of widows. "Come now, let's settle this," says the Lord. "Though your sins are like scarlet, I will make them as white as snow. Though they are red like crimson, I will make them as white as wool. If you will only obey me, you will have plenty to eat."[34]

Now God says it's not about law but about love; it's not the rules you keep but the relationship you reflect because of your love for Me. As earlier stated, the Sermon on the Mount (Matthew 5—7) beautifully reflects this; in that dissertation, Jesus boiled the Ten Commandments down to two. The whole law and the words of the prophets are summarized by these commandments: "You shall love the Lord your God" and "your neighbor as yourself." According to the commentary *Exploring the Old Testament*, "Jesus made a distinction between the duties to God and duties to man when He summarized the commandments in Matthew 22:37-40."[35] First, we are to love God and put Him first as the Lord said in Matthew 6:33: "But seek first the kingdom of God and His righteousness, and all these things shall be added to you."[36]

The first four Commandments tell about our duty to God. The first commandment concerns the person of Jehovah and only Him: "Honor Me, Worship Me, don't misuse My name, and set aside a day to worship Me." The Ten Commandments start with the vertical, our relationship with God. Only after we get that right can we turn to the horizontal—our relationship with other people. Commandments five through ten then tells us to love others by not stealing, honoring our parents, not lying, not killing, not cheating, not wanting things that aren't ours, and being true to our spouse. The Bible is really one command—love in two parts: God is love, and we are to love Him and others as He has loved us. We are told in 1 John 4:11: "Dear friends, since God so loved us, we also ought to love one another."[37]

Review God's message in Exodus 20: "I am the Lord your God . . . I've redeemed you, I've rescued you, I've cared for you, I've helped you, I've supplied for your every need, and all I want you to do is love Me with your undivided affection." What is our undivided affection? According to verse 37, it's loving God more than anything else, and following are four areas that show this quite clearly:

The Great Commandment, which is to love God with all every part of who we are, according to Mark 12:30 is this: "Love the Lord your God with all your heart, all your soul, all your mind, and all your strength."[38] This speaks of our loving God with our complete selves. It is loving God with a *sincere love*—from the heart out. This speaks of the reality of our love for God. Is Jesus real to you? Does your heart burn within you with love for Him and in awe of His love for you? True love from the heart out is this kind of love. There are too many phonies that turn people off to God and Christianity by speaking of loving God but not demonstrating love. There is an awakening story about a young Jewish boy in Germany who watched his father practice their faith. One day after they had moved to England, he would watch his father join the Lutheran Church. The young boy asked, "Dad, why did you do this?" "Son," explained his father, "we live in a different place; it would be good for business." At that point the boy who once had a strong interest in God and religion lost it all. His name was Karl Marx, who wrote the *The Communist Manifesto*, from which we remember this quote: "Religion is the opium of the people."[39] In Matthew 15:8, Jesus spoke of those who had head knowledge without heart knowledge: "'These people, says God, honor me with their words, but their heart is really far away from Me.'"[40]

The Great Commandment speaks of loving God with a *selfless love*— with all of your soul. This is to be our responsiveness. The soul is our

CHAPTER TWO:
The First Commandment
ONLY YOU

self, and to give our whole self, our total self, because He has given His all to us, is what He requires. Romans 12:1-2 teaches us this biblical truth:

> So here's what I want you to do, God helping you: Take your everyday, ordinary life—your sleeping, eating, going-to-work, and walking-around life—and place it before God as an offering. Embracing what God does for you is the best thing you can do for him. Don't become so well-adjusted to your culture that you fit into it without even thinking. Instead, fix your attention on God. You'll be changed from the inside out. Readily recognize what he wants from you, and quickly respond to it. Unlike the culture around you, always dragging you down to its level of immaturity, God brings the best out of you, develops well-formed maturity in you.[41]

No area is off-limits to God. How can the world believe there is one Lord unless they see in us a single-hearted love, a sincere and selfless love? God gave us all His love, His everything, and we are to return His love in our dedicated relationship to Him by giving ourselves completely to Him. The Great Commandment speaks of loving God with a *sensible love*, that is to say, with your entire mind, which speaks of reasonableness. The apostle Paul instructs, in Philippians 2:5, that we are to seek the mind of Christ: "Let this mind be in you, which was also in Christ Jesus:"[42] The Great Commandment also speaks of loving God with a *strong love*, all my strength. This is our resourcefulness—every fiber of our being, emotional, intellectual, financial, physical, and temporal. Many say, "I love God, but I'm not faithful to Him." But our love for God is measured in our obedience and sacrifice to Him. Look closely at John 14:23: "Jesus answered him, 'If anyone loves me, he will keep my word, and my Father will love him, and we will come to him and make our home with him.'"[43] Dr. Doug Stringer states, "Those who truly love God will view obedience to His commandments as a joy and gateway into intimacy."[44]

The Great Commitment is the second area that demonstrates our undivided affection to God. If we love Him, we'll follow Him as He taught in Luke 9:23: "If anyone desires to come after Me, let him deny himself, and take up his cross daily, and follow Me."[45] Notice four areas Jesus communicated the extent of what commitment really is by His use of four simple words:

1. *Come* speaks of our availability, whereby we offer ourselves fully to Him.
2. *Deny* speaks of the expendability of our lives for Him.
3. *Cross* speaks of our responsibility, for it must be our job to carry the cross.
4. *Follow Me* speaks of our accountability to the call and the work of Christ.

The Great Compassion is the third area. If we love God, then we'll love our neighbor as ourselves, as stated in Mark 12:31: "The second is this: 'Love your neighbor as yourself.' There is no commandment greater than these."[46] Jesus was never too busy to love people and to care for them.

The Great Commission is the fourth area through which we show our undivided affection to God. Jesus said in Matthew 28:18-20 that we are to go and reach the world with the gospel message: "Then Jesus came near and said to them, 'All authority has been given to Me in heaven and on earth. Go, therefore, and make disciples of all nations, baptizing them in the name of the Father and of the Son and of the Holy Spirit, teaching them to observe everything I have commanded you. And remember, I am with you always, to the end of the age.'" It has been said, "The Ten are built of the first, love for God."[47] Ask the Lord to help you to keep the commandments out of love for God instead of out of a begrudging sense of obligation. It's all about love and not law.

God Demands My Undivided Allegiance

"You shall have no other gods before Me." *No other gods* makes it clear that we are to have an undivided allegiance to God alone. Who is He? He is the Great I AM. What has He done? He has delivered us. What does He want? No other gods before Him. It cannot get any simpler than that. He is to be . . .

CHAPTER TWO:
The First Commandment
ONLY YOU

The God of our faith. The words of the first commandment demand that God's people worship, love, and serve only the one true God. The *Good News Bible* translates the command, "Worship no god but me." With this first commandment, God also makes it clear that His people are to have an exclusive relationship with Him. God sees our relationship with Him much like a marriage relationship.[48] Read and compare what Ephesians 5:22-32 says to us about our relationship with God:

> For wives, this means submit to your husbands as to the Lord. For a husband is the head of his wife as Christ is the head of the church. He is the Savior of his body, the church. As the church submits to Christ, so you wives should submit to your husbands in everything. For husbands, this means love your wives, just as Christ loved the church. He gave up his life for her to make her holy and clean, washed by the cleansing of God's word. He did this to present her to himself as a glorious church without a spot or wrinkle or any other blemish. Instead, she will be holy and without fault. In the same way, husbands ought to love their wives as they love their own bodies. For a man who loves his wife actually shows love for himself. No one hates his own body but feeds and cares for it, just as Christ cares for the church. And we are members of his body. As the Scriptures say, "A man leaves his father and mother and is joined to his wife, and the two are united into one." This is a great mystery, but it is an illustration of the way Christ and the church are one.[49]

As our wedding vows are more than "You'll be my favorite girl [or guy]" but is, rather, "forsaking all others," which speaks of complete loyalty and devotion to the other, in much the same way God demands that we serve Him *only*. When this commandment was made, no other nation prohibited the worship of other gods. There was no such thing as "monotheism." Nobody had just one god. All of Israel's neighbors were pagans—that is, they worshipped lots of different gods. People believed that certain gods ruled certain geographic areas or natural phenomena. There were "national gods": The Philistines had Dagon; the Moabites had Chemosh: the Ammonites had Molech. They also had fertility gods, storm gods, sun gods, sea gods, etc.[50] There were all kinds of gods, and the people believed they all had to be kept happy. And while a person or nation might have a favorite god, they certainly wouldn't think of narrowing their worship to just one god. They could worship whomever they chose and as many as they chose. God said there is only one God, and I am He! He is absolutely intolerant to the worship of anyone or anything else.

"You shall have no other gods before me," which is to say, the Lord is the only true God. M. Cherif Bassiouni has been a law professor at DePaul University College of Law for over thirty years. He is one of the world's leading authorities on international criminal law and human rights. In 1999, he was nominated for the Nobel Peace Prize for his role in establishing the International Criminal Court. At a January 4, 2000, interfaith dialogue near Chicago, Bassiouni said this: "All religions lead to God using different paths . . . judgment is not by the choice we make, but by how we pursue the path of the choice we make. Different religions and cultures are equal in the eyes of God and should be seen as equal in the eyes of man."[51] The most common way to be "spiritual" now is to take the parts of a religion you like and to leave the parts you don't like. It's like a faith buffet; you get to pick and choose. There is only one God, however, and His name is not Allah or Zeus or Hermes or any other name that might be chosen. This one God demands to be worshipped exclusively. In an interview with *Rolling Stone* magazine, Steven Van Zandt, guitarist in Bruce Springsteen's E Street Band, said, "I am a reformed Taoist, part-time Buddhist, Hindu, animist, pagan, Jewish mystic, and Christian. I always got along great with priests and rabbis and mullahs and gurus, even though I spend most of my life constructively criticizing them."[52] John Lennon said, "Whatever gets you through the night. . . ."[53] That's sort of the American ideal of religion, that you can have it all and you can believe it all, God is what you want Him to be, you can have it your way, whatever it takes as long as you benefit. Actress Sarah Michelle Gellar said this: "I consider myself a spiritual person. I believe in an idea of God, although it's my own personal ideal. I find most religions interesting, and I've been to every kind of denomination: Catholic, Christian, Jewish, Buddhist. I've taken bits from everything and customized it."[54] Geller and Van Zandt don't worship God; they worship "Franken-god," not the God who *is*, but a god they've invented from pieces of other gods.

People today attempt to make God into what they want Him to be and put that before God. Their attitude is "Who are you to say that your way is the only way? That is so narrow-minded." But Jesus said in John 14:6 His way was the only way: "I am the way, the truth, and the life; no one goes to the Father except by me."[55] People will say, "Well, I don't believe in a god who would send someone to hell" or "I don't believe in a god who would say homosexual behavior is wrong." That's strange, considering that they believe it's okay because the president says it's acceptable. Last year Franklin Graham (son of Billy Graham) was soundly criticized by the media because he declared that Islam was not the way to God but that Jesus was the only way. In an interview with National Public Radio, he said: "This whole notion of tolerance. They say, 'Well, you Christians are narrow-minded. You say Jesus is the only way. You're not tolerant of other religions.' Well, if other religions are not tolerant of us, I'm not putting down their faith system; it's just not what I believe. And I don't accept their way as truth. They don't accept my way. That's fine. But don't ask me to believe that their way to God is a valid way. I don't believe that."[56] Leo Tolstoy, the Russian novelist and philosopher, said, "To know God and to live is one and the same thing. God is life."[57]

Some believe "It doesn't matter what we believe; as long as we're sincere, we'll be okay." That may sound really good, but think about it in any other context. Let's say I have a bottle of arsenic in my medicine cabinet, and you come over with a terrible headache and say, "Hey, do you have any aspirin?" So I open up the medicine cabinet and say, "I'm all out of aspirin, but, hey, these arsenic pills look like aspirin! As long as I say it's aspirin and you believe it's aspirin, it'll be fine. After all, what's important is the sincerity of your faith, right?" What's important is not the faith. What's important is the object of your faith. The arsenic is going to affect you like arsenic regardless of what you think those little pills are.

He is to be the God of our faith, and He is the God of our function. "No other gods before Me. . . ." It's about both what we believe *and* what we do—our position and our practice. This question has probably already crossed most people's mind: Why did God put this commandment first? God knew our greatest challenge would be to put God where He belongs, as God, the only true God, and as our personal God through relationship. We can always have some reason/excuse why He is not first in our lives. Too often we are busy *doing* (perhaps even doing good things for God) rather than *being* what God wants us to be. Yet He said, "no other gods of faith or function." Our greatest challenge as believers is to model what it means to put God first in our life.

Here are three phrases that best frame the meaning of "before me." *Instead of Me*—we substitute something else for God. People today create gods in their lives. I have heard it said, "It's not that people don't want God; it's that they've found something they want more."[58] *In front of Me*—we snub God and make Him an afterthought in our everyday lives. *In addition to Me*—we crowd God out, as shown us in Matthew 6:24-25: "You can't worship two gods at once. Loving one god, you'll end up hating the other. Adoration of one feeds contempt for the other."[59] God is saying, "I don't want to be just first in your life: I want to be the hub of your life that everything else comes from, and if I'm not Lord of all, then I'm not Lord at all." Isaiah 42:8 states; "I am the LORD; that is my name! I will not yield my glory to another or my praise to idols."[60]

How do we give glory to another? By sharing our allegiance with another. We find another god instead of the one true and eternal God—like the god of pleasure, the god of possession, the god of each person, the god of play, and the god of position. God doesn't fit until God is first because that's where He belongs.

CHAPTER THREE
The Second Commandment
THE RIGHT GOD, THE WRONG WAY

Exodus 20:4-6

You shall not make for yourself an idol, whether in the form of anything that is in heaven above, or that is on the earth beneath, or that is in the water under the earth. You shall not bow down to them or worship them; for I the Lord your God am a jealous God, punishing children for the iniquity of parents, to the third and the fourth generation of those who reject me, but showing steadfast love to the thousandth generation of those who love me and keep my commandments.[61]

The first commandment is "You shall have no other gods before me." The second commandment appears to be very similar: "You shall not make for yourselves an idol." The two appear to be the same. Both of these commands have to do with idolatry. Both of them tell us to keep our relationship with God pure. But they're dealing with two entirely different problems. The first commandment tells us not to worship false gods. The second is concerned with worshipping the true God falsely: "Don't make for yourselves an idol." The first is about worshipping the right God; the second is about worshipping the right God in the wrong way. The first forbids false gods; the second forbids false worship. The first is about *whom* we worship; the second is about *how* we worship. When God forbade false worship, He was commanding true worship, much like the command we have all heard from our parents, "Don't stay outside," which actually means to come inside. God's laws are given to us for positive instruction for our lives that we may live a healthy life spiritually, physically, and emotionally.

God's laws are not temporary. It is important that we realize that the Ten Commandments are just as active, alive, and contemporary as the day they were given. They are for all people of all times. Eighteen hundred years after the Ten Commandments were given, one of the New Testament writers restated this second commandment: "Dear children, keep yourselves from idols."[62] Jesus said in Matthew 5:18: "Till heaven and earth pass away, one jot or one tittle will by no means pass from the law till all is fulfilled."[63]

God's laws are not arbitrary. It is also important to understand that God's laws are not arbitrary. Although man's laws often have a reactionary and arbitrary element to them, God's laws are not open to man's individual discretion. Here is a sample of just a few of man's laws on the books in our country:

> A recently passed anti-crime law in Texas requires criminals to give their victims 24 hours' notice, either orally or in writing, and to explain the nature of the crime to be committed. It is illegal to flirt or respond to flirtation using the eyes and/or hands: San Antonio, Texas. It is illegal for children to have unusual haircuts: Mesquite, Texas. It is illegal for one to shoot a buffalo from the second story of a hotel. It's illegal to go to church in disguise.[64]

God's laws are not too difficult. Examine what the apostle John stated in 1 John 5:3: "For our love for God means that we obey his commands. And his commands are not too hard for us."[65] It is necessary to look at what John said of Jesus' words in John 14:15-16 as well: "If you love me, you will keep my commandments. And I will ask the Father, and he will give you another Helper, to be with you forever."[66]

Here are the two most important questions for everyone to answer: Will you worship the right God, and will you worship the right God in the right way? Answer that, and the Bible tells us the future of our life and family in Deuteronomy 30:19-20:

I am now giving you the choice between life and death, between God's blessing and God's curse, and I call heaven and earth to witness the choice you make. Choose life. Love the Lord your God, obey him and be faithful to him, and then you and your descendants will live long in the land that he promised to give your ancestors, Abraham, Isaac, and Jacob.[67]

In order to understand the contemporary relevance of the second commandment, following are three statements this commandment teaches us about how we should worship God today.

A Created God Limits Real Worship

Idolatry is the attempt to represent a supernatural God in a natural way by reducing God to the human level. Psalm 34:3 is an interesting scripture concerning this thought: "O magnify the LORD with me, and let us exalt His name together."[68] Truly we cannot magnify God to make Him bigger, but we can magnify Him in how we see Him. If we can see Him bigger in our own eyes, then we can also make Him smaller in our eyes. Idolatry limits the divine relationship of God until He is just another god. Idolatry is the greatest of all sins, because the greatest commandment is to love God as Jesus said in Matthew. William Barclay stated: "The very essence of idolatry is that it is the worship of a thing instead of the worship of a person; the dead idol has taken the place of the living God."[69]

Idolatry is a remuneration of life, meaning that out of that concept comes the offering of oneself instead of God for the reward of life. Acts 17:28 states: "For in him we live, and move, and have our being."[70] Idolatry finds its being in self instead of in God. It is "me-ology" instead of theology, because by it God is made small. And here is the problem, when you try to worship God through an image or picture it would be like having a picture of your wife and loving her through the picture, spending more time with the picture than with her, prioritizing the picture. That is not the kind of relationship that God wants with us. Yet this is exactly what the Israelites did in Exodus 32, when they became impatient while Moses was on Mount Sinai. They told Aaron to make them a god they could see and touch. And so Aaron melted down their jewelry and made a golden calf. But listen to what he said: "This is your god, O Israel, who brought you up from the land of Egypt." What was Aaron saying? "This is the same God as before; the only difference is, we now have an image of Him. We have something we can see and touch; He's been reduced to human level so we can relate in our own way with Him."

When we reduce God to the human level, we distort the reality of God. John Calvin wrote:

> A true image of God is not to be found in the entire world; and hence ... his glory is defiled, and his truth corrupted by the lie, whenever he is set before our eyes in a visible form.... Therefore to devise any image of God is itself impious, because by this corruption his majesty is adulterated and he is figured to be other than he is.[71]

The problem is, the Almighty is made merely mighty, and this distorts the reality of God. Any image or likeness of God we create falls short, distorting the glory of God and misleading people as to what He's really like and who He really is. This puts God on the level of other gods, which, of course, are no gods at all—only false gods. To try to fully explain God borders on idolatry, because He is inexhaustible and unexplainable. Why, then, did Israel desert the eternal God for a diminished temporal god? They did it for the same reason we do so today. It's a lot easier to worship a god that appeases the flesh over one for which we must crucify the flesh. It takes less faith to worship the tangible idol than it does to worship the eternal God. That's why we must walk by faith and not sight, according to 2 Corinthians 5:7: "For we walk by faith, not by sight."[72]

Idolatry, which reduces God to the human level, limits our faith in God, while also limiting the God of our faith. Anyone can have faith in a god you can see. But if you can see Him, you've cut him down to your size. What is forbidden in this commandment is creating images of God that serve as objects or aids to worship. In Exodus 20:4 God covered it all: "No carved gods of any size, shape, or form of anything whatever, whether of things that fly or walk or swim."[73] Yet today we don't think that way.

> Most of us haven't spent a Saturday afternoon fabricating statues or images for the purpose of worship—objects such as a rabbit's foot, a horseshoe, or a four-leaf clover; however, much of today's New Age groups . . . have created objects of overt worship such as crystals, pyramids, and rainbows.[74]

Not only does idolatry reduce God to a human level, but *idolatry also reaches to the heart level.* Not all idols are a figure or image; an idol can be anything we worship with our heart and with our mind. Martin Luther said: "Whatever the heart clings to and relies on, that is your god. Anything you love, serve, or value more than God is your god."[75] This is also idol worship when we worship things not created by our hands but worship instead the idols we create in our hearts. These are not idols made of metal but idols that are mental. Notice what Ezekiel 14:6-7 says:

> Therefore say to the people of Israel, "This is what the Sovereign Lord says: Repent! Turn from your idols and renounce all your detestable practices! When any of the Israelites or any foreigner residing in Israel separate themselves from me and set up idols in their hearts and put a wicked stumbling block before their faces and then go to a prophet to inquire of me, I the Lord will answer them myself."[76]

Where did the Israelites get the idea for creating God into something tangible? In answering that, we first need to consider where they had lived. The Israelites had been living among the Egyptians for 432 years. The Egyptians worshiped hundreds of different gods. The second fact to consider is with whom did they now live—a mixed multitude and, undoubtedly, a bad influence. Look at Exodus 12:38 to see this: "A mixed multitude went up with them also, and flocks and herds—a great deal of livestock."[77]

A created god limits real worship because *idolatry regards God at a dishonored level.* Remember that idolatry creates a god that limits true worship. With this in mind, we must recognize the many ways by which people dishonor God in how they refer to Him, such as, the man upstairs god; a gimmee god, which makes Him into some sort of Santa Claus; a doctor god, because we want Him to make us feel better, and that's when we recognize our need for Him and go to Him; our errand god, if we see Him as being there to get us what we want in life; a saccharine god, because He makes everything sweet. A saccharine god is one who allows nothing bad to ever happen, nothing is wrong, there is no hell, and everyone is going to heaven. At this dishonored level, we are saying, "Any faith will do, just have faith." The problem is that in your mind, you've made God into something He isn't and then worshiped Him as the image you have created in your mind, and that is an idol. By this process, we create an emotional and intellectual image and made that our god. We've dishonored the true God by making the infinite God finite, and a finite god infinite; the invisible God visible; the omnipotent God impotent. Additionally we've made the omnipresent God local, the eternal God temporal, the heavenly God earthly, the living God dead, and the spiritual God material. God said we are to have no idols, because they limit real worship!

A Created God Leads to False Worship

Not only does a created god limit real worship, but a created god also leads to false worship. A created god is any god that is not the true God; an idol is creating God to be anything more or less than who He is. We should all take caution against this by the words of John the Revelator in Revelation 22:18-19:

> And I solemnly declare to everyone who hears the words of prophecy written in this book: If anyone adds anything to what is written here, God will add to that person the plagues described in this book. And if anyone removes any of the words from this book of prophecy, God will remove that person's share in the tree of life and in the holy city that are described in this book.[78]

In understanding that a created god leads to false worship you must first discover that *an improper concept of God causes us to worship the right God in the wrong way.* This is false worship. Remember that an idol is when a physical image is used to represent the spiritual God.

Christ said in John 4:24: "God is Spirit, and those who worship Him must worship in spirit and truth."[79] *The Handbook on the Gospel of John* states:

> As . . . [in truth] seems to refer to the "true revelation about God," it is possible to translate it "will worship the Father as he truly is" or "will worship the Father as the one who he truly is." Offering him the true worship that he wants may require restructuring, since it may not be possible to speak of "offering worship" or even of "true worship." The closest equivalent may be "worshiping him in the true way, the way that he wants" or "worshiping him genuinely, just as he wants to be worshiped." In some languages true worship is equivalent to "worship in the way in which one should." In other words, it is equivalent to "right worship."[80]

Isaiah 40:25 shows us that no one who can compare with God: "'To whom will you compare me? Or who is my equal?' says the Holy One."[81] In life one man can be compared to another, one car may be like another, and one house can be like another, but there is only one God, and no one and nothing else is like Him or can be compared to Him. Just as He can't be compared, neither can He be explained: "Nothing like Me." What if a woman came home and found her husband and another woman kissing. And suppose that at that moment her husband said to his wife to justify his actions, "She is so beautiful that she reminded me of you." Who would buy it? God won't buy it either. "God, this just reminded me of You, so I'll just love on You by loving on the things that reminds me of You."

There are four ways a created god leads to false worship. First of all, we worship the right God in the wrong way whenever we worship God's creation above God, the Creator. Idolatry is the worship of a god we create instead of the God who created us. We worship one of two gods, the God who made you or the god you made; the Creator or the one you created. Jeremiah 14:22 says, "None of the idols of the nations can send rain; the sky by itself cannot make showers fall. We have put our hope in you, O LORD our God, because you are the one who does these things."[82] Romans 1:20-23 adds well to this:

> Ever since God created the world, his invisible qualities, both his eternal power and his divine nature, have been clearly seen; they are perceived in the things that God has made. So those people have no excuse at all! They know God, but they do not give him the honor that belongs to him, nor do they thank him. Instead, their thoughts have become complete nonsense, and their empty minds are filled with darkness. They say they are wise, but they are fools; instead of worshipping the immortal God, they worship images made to look like mortal human beings or birds or animals or reptiles.[83]

They worshipped the creation instead of the Creator.

Second, a created god leads to false worship whenever we worship the right God in the wrong way by worshipping God for some of his attributes but not all of them. Some people want a God of love. So they focus on his love, compassion, and mercy, but leave out things like His holiness, His justice, and the reality of both heaven and hell. We tend to elevate what we like about God and limit what we don't like about God. We make God into what we want God to be instead of allowing God to make us into what we're supposed to be.

Third, a created god leads to false worship whenever we worship the right God in the wrong way by making the expression of worship more important than the essence of worship. Expressions of worship have to do with style; the essence of worship has to do with God. We all have preferences in worship styles. Across the nation churches have been divided over this issue.

Whenever our focus shifts from the person of God to the style of worship, we're in danger of breaking the second commandment. Whenever we exalt a style to the point that we say, "I just can't worship unless it happens in this way," then something is wrong. God is bigger than any worship style. Whatever our preference is, as long as it exalts the true God and focuses our attention and adoration on him, we should thank God for it.

Finally, a created god leads to false worship whenever we worship the right God in the wrong way by divorcing our concept of God from the conduct it produces in our lives. Worshipping God in the right way impacts the way we live our lives. When one looks at the sixth chapter of Isaiah, we see Isaiah in the Temple worshipping God. It is out of this worship that he experiences an introspective moment that is seen in verse 4: "Woe is me, for I am undone! Because I am a man of unclean lips, and I dwell in the midst of a people of unclean lips; for my eyes have seen the King, The LORD of hosts."[84] Worship brings us into an encounter with the living God, and that encounter will change us if it's authentic. We live in a country where scores of people would claim to have a relationship with Jesus Christ, but when asked about how that relationship really impacts their lives and their decisions, they are silent. Too many can simply go to church, sing a few songs, pray a few prayers, and feel some warm feelings, maybe even be really convicted by the sermon, but then they can just go out and live the way they want to live. They may think they're worshipping the right God, but I'm not sure they're worshipping the right God at all. The danger is that the worship experience can serve to bring more pleasure to us than it does to God. There must be a proper concept of God.

To understand that a created god leads to false worship, we must see that an inappropriate creation of God causes us to worship the right God in the wrong way. Many have their own idols that break the second commandment—things they've made as gods of worship. These can be the gods of possessions, such as their house or yard. Some park their idols in a garage, dock them at a marina, or lock them up in a safe. Others have made their families their gods and make statements like these: I love them, I adore them, or I worship the ground they walk on. There should always be a willingness to sacrifice for our family and loved ones, but they must never become our gods. I often hear people make this statement: "My family comes first." If this is true in the strictest sense, then their family is an idol that is before God. In Matthew 10:37, Jesus said: "If you love your father and mother more than you love me, you are not worthy of being mine; or if you love your son or daughter more than me, you are not worthy of being mine."[85] Why did He say this? Because He knew what is highly important could easily become wholly important if we aren't careful. To put God first doesn't mean we love our families less; it actually means we love them more, because we know that when God is first, He'll bless the rest when our lives line up with His Word. And only when we have a right relationship with God and love Him supremely do we have the God-given ability to love our families and others as we should with a high and selfless godly love.

There are the gods of pleasure that are wrongfully worshipped as well. The apostle Paul referred to these in 2 Timothy 3:4 when speaking of the last days: "They will be treacherous, reckless, and swollen with pride; they will love pleasure rather than God;"[86] Notice how today's culture is consumed with sports, gambling, Hollywood, and the entertainment industry. Today's sports figures are like idols. America has too many idols and not enough heroes. God is not against our having pleasure. He wants us to enjoy life—in the right way, to the right extent, and always after Him. But He is against our placing anything before Him. If any other things come first, we are then idolaters, according to the Word of God.

There are also the gods of money. It has been said, "Our god is gold, our creed is greed, and our theology is 'get all you can.'" People worship at the shrine of materialism. Covetous people will not inherit the kingdom of God according to God's Word in 1 Corinthians 6:9-10: "Or do you not know that the unrighteous will not inherit the kingdom of God? Do not be deceived; neither fornicators, nor idolaters, nor adulterers, nor effeminate, nor homosexuals, nor thieves, nor the covetous, nor drunkards, nor revilers, nor swindlers, will inherit the kingdom of God."[87] How can we know if money is our idol? Do you see money as your money to spend as you chose or as God's money to be used as He directs? Job understood this when he wrote Job 31:24, 28: "I have never trusted in riches or taken pride in my wealth. . . . Such a sin should be punished by death; it denies Almighty God."[88]

There are so many kinds of idols, each unique to a particular person. The question is not are there idols, but what is your idol? Who or what is your god? The following two questions will answer that first question: What do you love the most? If it's anything but God, that's your idol. The second question is this: What do you trust the most? Is it security, your job, medicine? What you put your trust in becomes your idol by default. If you're not sure of the answer to either of the two, all you need to do is to look at two books—your checkbook and your date book (calendar/i-pad/smart phone). People can say what they want, but these two tell the truth. How do you spend your money and your time? A created god does indeed lead to false worship.

The Creator God Liberates True Worship
The passionate cry of God is to liberate us into true worship. The psalmist calls out in Psalm 107:8: "Oh that men would give thanks to the Lord for His goodness, and for His wonderful works to the children of men!"[89] Jesus spoke of true worship in John 4:23-24: "But an hour is coming, and now is, when the true worshipers will worship the Father in spirit and truth; for such people the Father seeks to be His worshipers. God is spirit, and those who worship Him must worship in spirit and truth."[90] Let's re-read Exodus 20:5: "You shall not worship them or serve them; for I, the Lord your God, am a jealous God."[91] He is a jealous God, and *A Handbook on Exodus* explains what that means for us:

> A jealous God uses a word meaning to be envious of or zealous for someone. The root meaning of "red" may suggest the color of one's face produced by deep emotion. It is a human emotion, to be sure, but it is used here to describe the intense reaction of a holy God who demands unqualified loyalty from his chosen people. Jealous in modern English usually carries negative overtones that may seem inappropriate in reference to God. However, the emphasis here is on Yahweh's righteous anger in response to any who violate their pledge not to bow down or serve any other god.[92]

Jealous means to burn. God burns with jealously when you put anything before Him. God's jealousy is a hard concept to understand, because we think of jealousy in such negative terms. But we all know that while some jealousy is indeed rooted in selfishness, there is an appropriate kind of jealousy that's rooted in passionate love. Deuteronomy 32:21 makes this clear: "They made me jealous by what is no god and angered me with their worthless idols."[93] This kind of jealousy is fiercely protective of one's rights or possessions, demanding faithfulness and exclusive worship.

The emphasis of jealousy here is on Yahweh's righteous anger in response to any who violate their pledge not to bow down or serve any other god. Exodus 34:14 declares: "Do not worship any other god, because I, the Lord, tolerate no rivals."[94] He is an impassioned God that says, "I will not tolerate your worshipping other gods." God will not give his glory to another, as stated in Isaiah 42:8; 48:11: "I am the Lord; that is my name. I will not give my glory to anyone else or the praise I deserve to idols. . . . Why should my name be dishonored? I will not give my glory to anyone else."[95] Deuteronomy 4:24 confirms this same thought: "Because the Lord your God is like a flaming fire; he tolerates no rivals."[96]

It is important to note that God's jealousy is not the insecure, insane, or the possessive human jealousy we all disdain, but rather it's the intensely caring devotion he has to the objects of his love. A God who isn't jealous over his people is as contemptible as a husband who doesn't care when his wife is unfaithful to him. God is jealous for us, as I'm jealous for my family; I want what's best for them, and God wants what's best for us.

The persuasive communication of God liberates us in true worship. It is the promise of a curse or a blessing as in Exodus 20:5-6: "Never worship them or serve them, because I, the LORD your God, am a God who does not tolerate rivals. I punish children for their parents' sins to the third and fourth generation of those who hate me. But I show mercy to thousands of generations of those who love me and obey my commandments."[97] Wrong worship is iniquity that corrupts the minds of the children and shows up in the grandchildren. God will not visit the *guilt* of the parent's sin but the *results* of it upon their posterity to the third and fourth generation. *The New American Commentary* addresses the issue in this way:

> God is jealous . . . punishing the children for the sins of the fathers, has been widely misunderstood. It does not represent an assertion that God actually punishes an innocent generation for sins of a predecessor generation. . . . Rather, this oft-repeated theme speaks of God's determination to punish successive generations for

committing the same sins they learned from their parents. In other words, God will not say, "I won't punish this generation for what they are doing to break my covenant because, after all, they merely learned it from their parents who did it too." Instead, God will indeed punish generation after generation. . . . if they keep doing the same sorts of sins that prior generations did. If the children continue to do the sins their parents did, they will receive the same punishments as their parents.[98]

Look at the curse that is stated in verse 5 and recognize that if you don't obey, you'll curse your family to the third and fourth generation by way of perpetuating the curse through learned behavior that creates wrong worship. Your kids will likely worship the gods you worship, and so they will also likely perpetuate your actions all the way down to your great-grandkids. God said if you do it wrong, you will affect many generations to come. As a parent, the greatest and most important thing you can do is to teach your children to worship the right God in the right way. If you don't, you'll ruin them with the curse of worshipping the right God the wrong way. John Calvin stated, "The curse of the Lord righteously rests not only on the person of the impious man, but also on the whole of his family."[99] It's interesting to note that the punishment here is placed not only upon the fathers, but also upon the children. Fathers in this case is not intended to be exclusionary of mothers as is clarified in the New Revised Standard Version: "punishing children for the iniquity of parents."[100]

In the Old Testament Book of 2 Chronicles, chapters 26—28 illustrate the digression from worship in a family and how one parent's failure had an exponentially sad effect on his posterity. In 2 Chronicles 26:16, Uzziah the king loved God, but became prideful, and he worshipped God his own way. He worshipped God the wrong way; he went into the Temple to burn incense, which was wrong and unacceptable before God, and Azariah the priest, along with eighty other priests, rebuked him for his wrong action (v. 18). God also was not pleased and the king was cut off from the Lord for his actions and died of leprosy. He worshiped the right God the wrong way. Uzziah's son Jotham would then become king at the age of twenty-five (v. 21). The digression would now continue in 2 Chronicles 27:1-2. Jotham was a good man (v. 2): "He did what was pleasing to the LORD, just as his father had done; but unlike his father he did not sin by burning incense in the Temple. The people, however, went on sinning."[101] Notice that the "the people went on sinning." This passage parallels with 2 Kings 15:34-35: "Jotham did what the LORD said was right, just as his father Uzziah had done. But the places where gods were worshiped were not removed, and the people still made sacrifices and burned incense there."[102] Jothan was a good man who learned from his father Uzziah's example, both the good and the bad, and because of it, he chose not to worship falsely. Still his father's failure had an effect on him. Though Uzziah performed in a sinful way as he worshipped God falsely, Jotham permitted sin in the way that the people worshipped falsely. Uzziah's egregious sin of offering incense unlawfully would cause a recompense of leprosy on the King, and Uzziah would be legally kept from the Temple for his condition. Jotham allowed the false worship of his people to continue unabatedly, and the people kept on sinning. What Uziah did Jotham allowed, and we learn in a few verses that his son Ahaz would affirm the sin.

What a horrible digression from father to son to grandson. Jotham's father did not worship God in a proper way and was cut off from God. Jotham didn't correct his people, and they would be cut off from God. Is that not the climate that many parents have set for their children today? They fail in worship and now their children fail for a lack of correction and conviction. How sad that we seek to give our children everything we didn't receive, while failing to give them what we did receive as children, a sincere worship and commitment to God. Yes Jotham was a good man before God in his worship, but look at all those he failed by not exerting any influence over them to encourage an end to their sinning through false worship.

Going back to the Old Testament story, the digression continues in 2 Chronicles 27:9. Now Uzziah's grandson Ahaz reigned at the age of twenty years. In chapter 28:1, Ahaz turned from the ways of God completely: "Ahaz became king at the age of twenty, and he ruled in Jerusalem for sixteen years. He did not follow the good example of his ancestor King David; instead, he did what was not pleasing to the LORD."[103] In verse 2 we discover that Ahaz was worshipping Balaam, (demon sex god) and making idols. *The Teachers Bible Commentary* states:

> The rule of Ahaz was marked by wickedness, shame, and defeat for Judah. Though his reign was no longer than that of his father Jotham, it was much more eventful. The Chronicler first treats the spiritual apostasy of Ahaz. There was nothing good that could be said for him as a spiritual leader. Rather than following the ways of David he lived like the kings of the apostate Northern Kingdom. He worshiped almost all of the foreign deities with which Judah had any contact whatever.[104]

In 2 Chronicles 28:24, the grandson of Uzziah, Ahaz, was worshipping the wrong gods in the wrong way; Uzziah was cut off from God for worshipping the right God in the wrong way. He had a performance problem in his worship, and it's called idolatry, which is self-worship. Idolatry is the secularism of today, whereby people are inclined to lift up self over the Savior. Uzziah's son Jotham didn't perform sin, but rather he permitted sin. He allowed sin by not stopping the people from worshipping falsely. When we don't at least warn the people about their wrongdoing, we become compliant to the performance of their sins. That which we fail to do rightly will ultimately lead others wrongly.

Now Uzziah's grandson Ahaz was worshipping idols, he cut up the vessels of the house of God, and nailed the door shut. Go back for a moment and look at the digression from the right God but the wrong way to the wrong god in any way, and now we come to the most detestable sin of all (2 Chronicles 28:3-4): "He burned sacrifices in the Valley of Ben Hinnom and sacrificed his children in the fire, engaging in the detestable practices of the nations the LORD had driven out before the Israelites. He offered sacrifices and burned incense at the high places, on the hilltops and under every spreading tree."[105] Uzziah's great-grandchildren were offered to the demon gods of the heathen, the god of Moloch, in whose belly was fire. He offered his babies to Moloch, which would cause the loss of generations of life.

Uzziah loved God but worshipped in a wrong way; he had a worship performance problem. Jotham loved God, but failed to warn the people of their sins through false worship, which demonstrates he had a permissive problem. Ahaz hated the house of God and offered his children to be sacrificed to a demon god. We can clearly see he was now guilty of promoting sin as a wicked king. I wonder if Jotham had warned the people, and if Uzziah had showed the people a lifelong commitment to God and His laws and had continued to worship correctly, if we would even be talking about Ahaz in such a horrible and deplorable context.

That's what will happen in America if we don't get back to the true worship of God. America today has an unstated philosophy: "Do what you want if it doesn't hurt others." But sin never hurts just one person; it always shows up in their children. Because of what one performed and another permitted, their posterity reaped the sad consequences for their failure to do right before God in the beginning. This is the digression of failed worship.

God not only warns of the generational curse for wrong worship, but He as well promises blessings to those who honor Him with right worship: "But I show my love to thousands of generations of those who love me and obey my laws."[106] The generation of the upright shall be blessed if only that generation will obey His laws and live according to His commands. Mark Rooker writes: "Whereas man's sin may have negative repercussions unto the fourth generation, God's faithfulness extends to a thousand generation."[107] By obeying and worshipping God correctly, we can bless thousands of generations. The New Testament passage in 2 Timothy 1:5-6 is a great illustration of generational blessing:

> I remember your true faith. That faith first lived in your grandmother Lois and in your mother Eunice, and I know you now have that same faith. This is why I remind you to keep using the gift God gave you when I laid my hands on you. Now let it grow, as a small flame grows into a fire."[108]

Eunice, Lois, and now Timothy—from grandmother to daughter to grandson, the legacy of blessing continues. May the Lord help us to

CHAPTER THREE:
The Second Commandment
THE RIGHT GOD, THE WRONG WAY

start a fire to future generations that will bless our posterity for many generations to come. This is the hope of America.

The greatest gift we can give our children is to teach them to worship. Blessings or curses will follow by the legacy we leave them. A woman asked her pastor, "When should I start religious training for my children—at four, five, or six?" The pastor responded, "With grandparents."

Why are the first two commandments first? Why no other gods before Me, and you shall not make any idols? Because God is not about rules but relationships! If we put Him first, everything else will come together. That is what Jesus was saying as well in Matthew 6:33: "But seek first His kingdom and His righteousness, and all these things will be added to you."[109] The interesting thing about this Old Testament commandment is that the God who told us not to make an image of Him has, in fact, given us an image of Himself in the New Testament to worship. Colossians 1:15 tells us, "He is the image of the invisible God, the firstborn of all creation."[110] The writer of Hebrews says Jesus is the exact representation of God's nature: "The Son is the radiance of God's glory and the exact representation of his being, sustaining all things by his powerful word."[111] And Jesus himself said in John 14:9, "Whoever has seen me has seen the Father."[112] Now we don't know what Jesus looked like, and we don't worship a physical image of Jesus, but in order to worship the right God in the right way, we need to focus on the person of Jesus. When we focus on the person of Jesus, we find ourselves becoming more and more like him. When we worship the right God in the right way, our worship will be centered on the person and work of Jesus and that will lead to a transformed life. This is the true contemporary approach to the historical laws of the Ten Commandments. Edmund Clowney stated, "The coming of Jesus transposes the second commandment into specific adoration for the one who is the image of the Father. That same miracle of grace also draws us to praise God for the imaging of Christ in the lives of those brothers and sisters in whom the Spirit works."[113]

CHAPTER FOUR

The Third Commandment

YOU GIVE GOD A BAD NAME

Exodus 20:7

"You shall not misuse the name of the Lord your God, for the Lord will not hold anyone guiltless who misuses his name."[114] What's the big deal about a name? A name is just a name, right? In Shakespeare's *Romeo and Juliet*, Juliet says, "What's in a name? That which we call a rose by any other name would smell just as sweet."[115] In other words, it doesn't matter what you call something or someone because the name doesn't matter. What matters is the thing itself, the flower or the person represented by the name. In ancient Hebrew culture, however, a name was everything. A name represented the very essence and presence of a person. A person's identity was bound up in his name. A name contained power, and, in truth, nothing's changed.

"In any culture, modern or ancient, a name is a verbal symbol for a person or thing, and the ancients in particular obviously appreciated the way names connoted the very value, character, and influence of a person or thing. To speak Yahweh's name was to recognize his awesome power and holiness and even to invite his response to one's particular situation at the moment."[116]

Names still hold power today. What comes to mind when I say the names Mother Theresa, Adolph Hitler, Steve Jobs? People change their names because of what their names might convey. Marian Michael Morrison became John Wayne because you can't be a cowboy with a name like Marian!

You get your identity from your name. Why did your parents choose your name? Who would you be without your name; who would you be if no one knew what to call you, if you didn't know what to call yourself, if you didn't know your own name? In Bible times a name was more than a label; it had meaning that revealed the character of a person. A name was used to represent character and virtue; it was who you were. "A good name" was everything in Solomon's estimation. According to Proverbs 22:1, "A good name is to be chosen rather than great riches, and favor is better than silver or gold."[117] God is concerned about His name, Alan Cole said: "The whole of the Ten Commandments is really the explanation of the third commandment: God's name."[118] You shall not misuse the name of God. We've dumbed down the commandment; as long as we don't use it in a way to profane it, we feel we're okay. Not so; God takes His name seriously, and it is in the top three commandments that He says, "Don't take My name in vain; don't misuse it in any way." The *UBS Handbook on Exodus* says:

> Since the name of any deity was considered sacred, any careless use of that name was to "misuse" it (NJB, CEV), or "abuse" it (Childs). 20:7 TEV interprets it to mean "for evil purposes," and 20:7 NRSV has "make wrongful use of." TAN gives it an even narrower meaning, in the sense of invoking the name in an oath: "you shall not swear falsely by the name." It is better, however, to give it the broader meaning of "abuse" or "misuse."[119]

In Leviticus 24:10-16, a man was using God's name in vain, and the people were ordered to put him to death for his transgression of the commandment:

> There was a man whose father was an Egyptian and whose mother was an Israelite named Shelomith, the daughter of Dibri from the tribe of Dan. There in the camp this man quarrelled with an Israelite. During the quarrel he cursed God, so they took him to Moses, put him under guard, and waited for the LORD to tell them what to do with him. The LORD said to Moses, "Take that man out of the camp. Everyone who heard him curse shall put his hands on the man's head to testify that he is guilty, and then the whole community shall stone him to death. Then tell the people of Israel that anyone who curses God must suffer the consequences and be put to

death. Any Israelite or any foreigner living in Israel who curses the LORD shall be stoned to death by the whole community.[120]

Praise God for the New Testament; though it forbids such behavior, it does offer grace whereby we can repent and live.

Today we have laws against slander because it damages character, a person's name. To slander someone's name would mean you have slandered the person. Jesus had something to say on this; remember when the disciples asked Jesus for a lesson on prayer and He gave them the answer in Matthew 6:9: "Pray like this: Our Father in heaven, may your name be kept holy."[121] He was teaching them to revere and respect God's name and not to slander His name. The problem is, we've given God a bad name in our speech, our actions, and our attitudes, and God said it will not go unpunished. Dr. D. James Kennedy said, "In America, a country born out of trust for God, how could it come to pass that a people have so little respect for His name?"[122] Here is how a person can avoid giving God a bad name and avoid misusing His name.

Be Careful How You Treat God's Name

People hurt God's name when they mishandle His name; so the question begins with "What is God's name?" The Lord thy God as well as Jehovah and El—both include the Trinity and are representative of the fullness of God and who He is.[123] They speak of His character and nature while representing His relationship with us. His name speaks of personality, for He is a real person. The following, taken from a sermon by Dr. Raymond Culpepper, former general overseer of the Church of God, Cleveland, Tennessee, is an overview of the names of God and how they relate to us:

> *Elohim: The creator God, 2,700 times in the Bible. It means the plural God of Father, Son, and Holy Ghost. The creator God who spoke the world into existence.*

Jehovah: *6,800 times in the Bible. It means Covenant God, the One who has made a promise and agreement with us. He is....*
- Jehovah Jireh—My provider
- Jehovah Nissi—You are my banner
- Jehovah Ropheh—You are my healer
- Jehovah Rohi—You are my shepherd
- Jehovah Tsidkeneu—You are my righteousness
- Jehovah M'kiddesh—You are my sanctifier
- Jehovah Shalom—You are my peace
- Jehovah Shammah—The Lord is there
- Jehovah Saboth—The Lord of Hosts/Commander

> ***EL means God: Look at the Suffix and Prefix***
> - EL-ELYon—Most High God
> - EL-Olam—The Everlasting God
> - EL-Shaddi—The God who is sufficient for the needs of His people; All-sufficient One
> - EL-Roi—God who sees
> - EL-Gibhor—The mighty God[124]

Edmond P. Clowney states: "It is impossible to dissociate God's name from His person, identity, and character."[125] Notice the phrases, The Lord thy God: "Lord" is *Jehovah,* and "thy God" is *Elohim* in the Hebrew text.[126] "I am a person, this is who I am, and my name tells of my personality and what I'm like." Jehovah is who God is, and His name tells of who He is. He is the everlasting God, who is a covenant keeper; and thy God, *Elohim,* speaks of His being "the Mighty One," our Creator.[127] His name says, "I am a covenant-keeping God who has power to perform His Word." And He is telling people not to take His name in vain.

There is power in God's name. The Bible is replete with references of the power in His great name. Consider the story of David against Goliath. David invoked the name of God against His enemies as they came against the armies of Israel (1 Samuel 17:45): "Then David said to the Philistine, 'You come to me with a sword, with a spear, and with a javelin. But I come to you in the name of the LORD of hosts, the God of the armies of Israel, whom you have defied.'"[128] How did this deliverance happen in God's name? In His name there is power. Jesus himself said in John 14:14: "If you ask me for anything in my name, I will do it."[129] A close look at Colossians 3:17 illustrates the thought of using God's name: "Everything you say or do should be done in the name of the Lord Jesus, giving thanks to God the Father through him."[130] Do it all in His name because there is power in God's name. We should be careful to understand that when we profane God's name, we make it common and reduce it to the level of mere man.[131] His name is powerful.

There is *protection* in God's name. Solomon stated this in Proverbs 18:10: "The name of the LORD is a strong tower; the righteous man runs into it and is safe."[132] *Strong tower* indicates that people can take refuge in God's name.

There is *provision* in the name of God. In John 16:23-24, Jesus spoke about this provision to those who believed: "When that day comes, you will not ask me for anything. I am telling you the truth: the Father will give you whatever you ask him for in my name. Until now you have not asked for anything in my name; ask and you will receive, so that your happiness may be complete."[133] In 1 John 5:14, John declared God's provision for His people when they pray according to His will: "And we have this confidence in him, that if we ask anything according to his will, he hears us. And if we know that he hears us in regard to whatever we ask, we know that what we have asked him for is ours."[134] In other words, "If you can sign My name to it, I'll do it."

There is *praise* in the name of God. Psalm 8:1 is a good example of this: "O LORD, our Lord, your majestic name fills the earth."[135]

Remember that God commands us not to use His name in vain. This brings one to the question "What does *vain* mean?" J.I. Packer says *vain* is "any use or involvement of God's name that is empty or insincere."[136] The Hebrew word for vain is *Shâv*; it means both "vanity" and "falsehood."[137] It has the implications of using the name meaninglessly, carelessly, and thoughtlessly, empty of content. The *New International Version* of the Bible translates the command this way: "You shall not misuse the name of the Lord." The intention and indication of the passage is "Do not use His name in a careless or thoughtless way. Don't give God a bad name." The problem is that most people don't take His name seriously, not like in Bible times. Whenever a scribe was transcribing the Bible and he came to the name Yahweh (Lord), he would put his pen down, take his clothes off, take a bath, put on fresh clothes, burn the old pen, take a new pen, and write the name God. He would then continue his writing until the next time he came to the name of God, then he would repeat the process over and over again.[138] Jewish tradition believes and declares that anything His name is written on makes that document holy.[139] Maybe people should reconsider their approach to American currency, which has on it "In God we trust." The rabbis teach that one should be very careful even speaking the name of God, while some stricter beliefs held to the notion that God's name was not to be spoken outside of any direct reference to His person and holy character. Judaism so feared misusing the name of God that the Jews permitted only the high priest to speak the name, and only on the Day of Atonement.[140] Most would agree that things have changed; most people don't pay much attention to the mishandling of God's name.

Below are five areas whereby people mishandle God's name:

Profanity is mishandling God's name. William Barclay said the Lord's name is used in vain through swearing in the sense of bad language.[141] The term comes from the Latin word *pro*, which means, "out of" and *fain*, which means "temple"; thus it literally means "out of the temple." When someone takes God's name in a profane way, they are taking His name out of His holy temple and dragging it through the filth of this world. One of the main ways Americans use and misuse God's name is by using it essentially as a cuss-word.[142] It's the devil's work, and we have a responsibility to remind ourselves of the sin of profaning God's name. Jesus stated in Matthew 12:36: "I can guarantee that on judgment day people will have to give an account of every careless word they say."[143]

When a person does this, it is an insult thrown into the face of God and is inexcusable. When we profane God's name with our language,

CHAPTER FOUR:
The Third Commandment
YOU GIVE GOD A BAD NAME

we are blaming God and making Him responsible for our own actions, behaviors, and bitter disappointment of our choices.[144] There is a temporary reward in breaking many of the commandments—steal, and you have something to show for it; cheat, and maybe you get away with it to somehow better yourself; commit adultery, and you have temporarily satisfied the flesh; kill, and you've fulfilled your angry heart's intent; but the only reward for misusing God's name is judgment. What an ignorant and foolish thing to do, for it only demonstrates contempt before God. Never use His name profanely; profanity is ignorance and shows two things: an empty head and a wicked heart. One person said profanity is a feeble mind trying to express itself.

Profanity really says something about the person who uses it. William Ward said, "Profanity is the use of strong words by weak people."[145] Jesus said in Luke 6:45: "Good people do good things because of the good in their hearts. Bad people do bad things because of the evil in their hearts. Your words show what is in your heart."[146] Remember, the words we use expose what's on the inside of us, not only the obvious but also those that are oblivious.

Even the euphemism of our vernacular is contemptible to God, words such as *gosh*, *gee*, *darn*, and similar variations. Be careful of the secondhand cursing of God.[147] The attitude with which His name is spoken can be another way people profane God's name, such as saying "dear Lord" as a byword. Others use His name in a flippant way. "Good God," "Oh, my God," "Sweet Jesus," and "Oh, God" are all flippant uses of His name. When people casually toss out His name to fill in their verbal gaps, that's profanity. Profanity occurs when someone takes something sacred, like the name of God, and treats it irreverently. Any use of God's name that is misused or wrongly used is the abuse of His name! What would happen if we treated God's name the same way a businessperson treats that precious, moneymaking brand name? It is interesting to read what one writer had to say about that:

> One way for a modern American to begin to understand this command is to treat God's name as a trademarked property. In order to gain widespread distribution for His copyrighted repair manual—the

Bible—and also to capture greater market share for His authorized franchise—the Church—God has graciously licensed the use of His name to anyone who will use it according to His written instructions. It needs to be understood, however, that God's name has not been released into the public domain. God retains legal control over His name and threatens serious penalties against the unauthorized misuse of this supremely valuable property. All trademark violations will be prosecuted to the full limits of the law. The prosecutor, judge, jury and enforcer are God.[148]

God has given us the use of His name, not for our own purposes, but to fulfill His purposes. He has not "released His name into the public domain." That is, only His followers or those who desire to become His followers are given the right to use His name. And there are rules about how we use it. What does it mean to use God's name according to His written instructions? First, it means not using God's name lightly and carelessly.

Foolishness takes God's name in vain. God's name is taken in vain by us when we use it without due consideration and reverence.[149] Laughing at God, joking about God, not taking God seriously, that is, to trivialize God or to take His name carelessly or lightly are all a part of profaning His name. Notice what the apostle Paul said about this in Ephesians 5:3-4: "Don't let sexual sin, perversion of any kind, or greed even be mentioned among you. This is not appropriate behavior for God's holy people. It's not right that dirty stories, foolish talk, or obscene jokes should be mentioned among you either. Instead, give thanks [to God]."[150] Foolish jesting is little sayings about God, and when people entertain jokes that bring His name into them, they are profaning His name. There are too many "witticisms" today, like "Bless him, Lord" and foolish stories of Jesus or God or His Word. To trivialize the name of God is to diminish His person and His glory while showing the utmost disrespect for the God to whom we owe everything.[151]

Associating filth with God, His purity, and His holiness and treating lightly that which is holy are all a part of profaning God. God's name should never be used, except to honor Him or to bring Him glory. Look at Ephesians 4:29: "Watch the way you talk. Let nothing foul or dirty come out of your mouth. Say only what helps, each word a gift."[152] Also we should examine Colossians 3:8: "But now is the time to cast off and throw away all these rotten garments of anger, hatred, cursing, and dirty language."[153] These command believers who name the name of Christ to clean up their life and lifestyle.

Hypocrisy is another way to profane God's name. The quickest way to turn others away from God is through hypocrisy. The word *hypocrite* comes from an ancient Greek word once used to describe stage actors.[154] Those who use His name without having a true relationship with Him are hypocrites, or pretenders. Brennan Manning said, "The greatest single cause of atheism in the world today is Christians who acknowledge Jesus with their lips, then walk out the door and deny Him by their lifestyle. That is what an unbelieving world simply finds unbelievable."[155]

Consider the Word of the Lord in Isaiah 48:1-2:

> Listen to this, you descendants of Jacob, you who are called by the name of Israel and come from the line of Judah, you who take oaths in the name of the Lord and invoke the God of Israel—but not in truth or righteousness—you who call yourselves citizens of the holy city and claim to rely on the God of Israel—the Lord Almighty is his name:[156]

One area of hypocrisy is a false claim to worship, as seen in Luke 6:46: "Why do you call me 'Lord, Lord,' and do not do what I tell you?"[157] And also in Matthew 15:8: "These people draw near to Me with their mouth, and honor Me with their lips, but their heart is far from Me."[158] Edmund Clowney said, "The testimony of a believer should be backed up in his godliness by the testimony of God Himself."[159]

A second area of hypocrisy is falsely using God's name in service (Matthew 7:22-23): "When Judgment Day comes, many will say to me, 'Lord, Lord! In your name we spoke God's message, by your name we drove out many demons and performed many miracles!' Then I will say to them, 'I never knew you. Get away from me, you wicked people!'"[160]

A third area of hypocrisy is falsely praying in Jesus' name. Matthew 7:21 states, "Not everyone who calls out to me, 'Lord! Lord!' will enter the Kingdom of Heaven. Only those who actually do the will of my Father in heaven will enter."[161] Acts 19:15 speaks of how an evil spirit didn't even recognize these so-called followers of Jesus, "One day the evil spirit answered them, 'Jesus I know, and Paul I know about, but who are you?'"[162] When you pray, don't attempt to justify your insincere prayer by adding "in Jesus' name" at the end. Instead, pray honestly and sincerely to the Father in Jesus' name. All of these are examples of how people can profane God's name through hypocrisy.

Forgery profanes God's name as well. Forgery is when a person signs another's name to get what they want, and it's a felony in America. Stephen Carter, author of *Taking God's Name in Vain*, says this:

> In truth, there is probably no country in the Western world where people use God's name quite as much, or quite as publicly, or for quite as many purposes, as we Americans do—the third commandment notwithstanding. Few candidates for office are able to end their speeches without asking God to bless their audience, or the nation, or the great work we are undertaking, but everybody is sure the other side is insincere. . . . Athletes thank God, often on television, after scoring the winning touchdown, because, like politicians, they like to think God is on their side. Churches erect huge billboards and take out ads in the paper. . . . God's will is cited as a reason to be against gay rights. And a reason to be for them. . . . Everybody who wants to change America, and everybody who wants not to, understands the nation's love affair with God's name, which is why everybody invokes it.[163]

People mishandle His name when they "sign His name" to an action He wouldn't sign off on. J.H. Hertz stated: "The third commandment forbids us to dishonor God by invoking His name to attest what is untrue, or by joining His name to anything that is frivolous or insincere."[164] There is a lot of spiritual forgery today by invoking what is sometimes called the God clause and by attributing divine authority to human ideas. "God told me . . ." is too often used, when the truth is, God hasn't told that person anything at all. The Talmud says that whoever says a blessing that is not necessary transgresses the third commandment.[165] Dr. Laura Schelessinger states: "The prohibition of Leviticus 19:11-12 forbids us to invoke the name of God as a reference for our personal honesty, our product, our service, our property, and so on."[166] Yet we see it all the time from corrupted evangelists who claim to hear God more clearly than the rest of the church world and from those who seek to advantage their view or opinion by using God's name as the authority for their words. This is a reckless proclaiming of what God will do, a prostitution of His promises, and it is inconsistent with His Word. Those who do such are failed ambassadors because of their misrepresentation of God's name, and today's ministries who do such should be held accountable. We must make all efforts to refrain from misusing God's name because the Lord will punish anyone who misuses His name.[167] God's Word has said, "I will not hold you guiltless," so be careful how you treat God's name.

Be Thoughtful About Where You Take God's Name

People hinder the positive impact of God's name when they misrepresent it. You can misuse and abuse God's name not only by what you say but also by how you live. Perhaps you have never thought much about this one, but how you live your life is an indicator of how you dishonor God or honor Him. Remember, everything is based on the belief system that God created you and that He sets the rules for how you are to live. The Westminster Shorter Catechism states: "The chief end of man is to glorify God."[168] If you believe in God as creator, then you must accept that He knows best and that when you live contrary to His plans, principles, and even rules, you are dishonoring your Creator.

People can honor God when they "wear His name." That is, when they live their Christian lives in the manner seen in 2 Timothy 2:19: "Everyone who confesses the name of the Lord must turn away from wickedness."[169] Acts 11:26 illustrates how people can interpret people by the way they wear the name of Christ: "It was at Antioch that the believers were first called Christians."[170] Luke refers to Christians as "believers," "disciples," or "brothers." *Christians* was an outside nickname, possibly given in derision. It means "Christ followers" or "people of Christ's party."[171] The new moniker speaks of the witness of those who profess to be disciples of Christ. From the inception of salvation, a Christian should be a twenty-four-hour billboard of Jesus and His name. The question is, as a follower of Jesus, "Where do Christians take His name?" The answer is "Everywhere!" When you claim to be a follower of God and don't back it up with your life, you're misusing God's name and misrepresenting Him. When you wear the name, you must also "walk the walk." Remember who you are and whose you are. The apostle Paul reminds us in 1 Corinthians 6:19-20: "You should know that your body is a temple for the Holy Spirit who is in you. You have received the Holy Spirit from God. So you do not belong to yourselves, because you were bought by God for a price. So honor God with your bodies."[172]

The two reasons most people don't become a Christian are (1) They never met a Christian who explained the gospel to them, or (2) they discover that with most of the Christian people they've met their walk is not commensurate with their talk. Therefore, the non-Christians aren't impressed. Why would they want Jesus if your walk doesn't match your testimony of what Christ has done for you? Then you've just done some bad advertising for God, because it speaks of inconsistency between your words and your deeds.

Remember that your character affects people's view of God's credibility, so be careful where you take His name. The words you say shape other people's opinion about God's reputation; everything you do and say demonstrates whether your conduct and your speech line up to magnify the name of the Lord. The casual manner in which some Christians use the name of the Lord can be a stumbling block to nonbelievers and hinder them from giving serious consideration to the gospel message.[173] The way you live can be a smear on the name of God. Isaiah 5:20 reads, "Woe to those who call evil good, and good evil, who change darkness into light, and light into darkness, who change bitter into sweet, and sweet into bitter!"[174] Speaking to religious hypocrites, Paul wrote in Romans 2:21-24:

> Well then, if you teach others, why don't you teach yourself? You tell others not to steal, but do you steal? You say it is wrong to commit adultery, but do you commit adultery? You condemn idolatry, but do you use items stolen from pagan temples? You are so proud of knowing the law, but you dishonor God by breaking it. No wonder the Scriptures say, "The Gentiles blaspheme the name of God because of you."[175]

He also stated in Titus 1:16: "They claim that they know God, but their actions deny it. They are hateful and disobedient, not fit to do anything good."[176] There is a story of Alexander the Great that brings great understanding to this thought:

> Alexander the Great was one of the greatest warriors of all time, gaining a larger empire than Rome in a very short time. Apparently, during one particular battle, one of his soldiers got cold feet and stayed hidden from the fighting. He was caught by the others and brought before Alexander. As the soldier stood trembling, Alexander asked him what his name was. The soldier very meekly replied "Alexander." Alexander the Great couldn't believe what he'd just heard and asked him again to hear the same reply. You could hear a pin drop in the room. Alexander the Great was incensed and everyone thought he would give the order to have the man killed. Instead, with great anger, yet contained, he looked at the man and said: "Either change your name, or change your ways."[177]

God wants you to look at this change. Look at what you're doing, where you're going, what you're saying, where you're hanging out; stop and change your direction or change your name. Be thoughtful in where you take God's name, and be careful in how you treat God's name.

Be Faithful About How You Trust in God's Name

To trust God's name is to honor Him. You can do two things with God's name: the first is to take His name in vain; the second is to take His name in victory.

Here is how someone can take God's name in victory: Colossians 3:17 states: "Everything you say or do should be done in the name of the Lord Jesus, giving thanks to God the Father through him."[178] This is taking His name in victory! The last name used for God in the Bible is Jesus. *Jesus* means "Jehovah saves" and is a beautiful picture of God's grace. Jesus fulfills the promise of the Old Testament names of God.[179] All the names of God are compressed in the one name of Jesus (Savior). He is the One in whom we trust, and by this we take His name in victory.

People honor God's name by how they share His name. Malachi 3:16 speaks of how God honors those who honor His name: "Then those who feared the LORD spoke with one another. The LORD paid attention and heard them, and a book of remembrance was written before him of those who feared the LORD and esteemed his name."[180] God has three books: the "Book of Revelation," which is the Word of God; the "Book of Redemption," or the Book of Life; and the "Book of Remembrance," which is spoken of here in Malachi. God sees and remembers those who fear and remember His name. There are three areas this passage speaks about concerning God's name.

The first is the character of a person as seen in those who fear the Lord. Why do people take His name in vain? No fear? The beginning of knowledge comes to those who fear the Lord. A nation is on a crumbling foundation when it no longer fears God. The second is the contemplation that people should have; they thought upon His name (meditated). We should learn and teach the name of God, teaching others to think on the name of God. Psalm 9:10 tells us what happens when you know God's name: "And those who know Your name will put their trust in You." The third speaks of their conversation; they spoke one to another about God. Looking at the Old Testament passage in Psalms, let us exalt His name together. And considering the New Testament passage in Hebrews 10:25 to exhort one another, we can see the importance of communicating God's name to others. God's name is to be shared with the world we live in.

People heed God's name by how they bear His name. The name of Jesus is both loved and hated more than any other name on earth. In fifty-one countries the name of Jesus is banned from being spoken.[181] To bear His name speaks of two things: First, be fruitful in your trials for His name. In Acts 5:40-42 a powerful story is recorded about the disciples having been beaten and then commanded not to speak in Jesus' name. But they *rejoiced* "that they were counted worthy to suffer for His name." Though there is a concerted effort in many places and nations to stop the name of Jesus from being uttered, we should never be ashamed of that name. Jesus tells us in Mark 8:38, "For whoever is ashamed of me and of my words in this adulterous and sinful generation, of him will the Son of Man also be ashamed when he comes in the glory of his Father with the holy angels."[182]

The second thing bearing His name speaks of is being faithful in your trust of God's name. Psalm 9:10 indicates how we know if we trust God: "And those who know Your name will put their trust in you, for you, Lord, have never forsaken those who seek you."[183] Psalm 33:21 tells what happens when we trust: "Our heart is glad in him, because we trust in his holy name."[184] He'll save us and give us joy as we trust His name. Look at Isaiah 50:10: "All of you that honor the Lord and obey the words of his servant, the path you walk may be dark indeed, but trust in the Lord, rely on your God."[185] Psalm 20:7: "Some trust in chariots and some in horses, but we trust in the name of the Lord our God."[186] Both of these illustrate the thought of being faithful in our trust in God's name.

Why did God give us His name? To have a personal relationship with Him, to know Him on a first-name basis when we talk to Him. This does not occur by our being in school, or in the courtroom, or in graduate school, or in most offices, but God wants us to have a personal relationship with Him and to call Him by name. The story is told of William Booth while he was on his deathbed. With his family and an attorney there, the family asked the attorney to sign a document. "Please help us by signing this," they requested. He did, and then Mr. Booth signed. Later when they looked, they discovered that Mr. Booth had signed "Jesus," because that is what was most on His heart.[187] Who is it that is most on your heart? We should put on attitudes of the heart and deeds of obedience that bring honor to His name.[188]

When we misuse God's name, we forget two things: who He is and who we are. He is a holy, perfect, righteous God, and we are imperfect, unrighteous sinners. We should go through every day with that in mind.

The greatest thing any of us will ever teach our kids is respect for God's name. How can you teach them to respect you if they don't respect God? How can they respect others if they can't respect God? But if you teach them how worthy God's name is to be respected, then they can respect others as well.

God's name is so big a deal that one day every person who will ever live will say four words: "Jesus Christ is Lord," according to Philippians 2:9-11: "God raised him to the highest place above and gave him the name that is greater than any other name. And so, in honor of the name of Jesus all beings in heaven, on earth, and in the world below will fall on their knees, and all will openly proclaim that Jesus Christ is Lord, to the glory of God the Father."[189] How big a deal is it? What we do with His name will determine where we spend eternity! God's name is the only name that can take us to heaven. Romans 10:13 tells us: "Everyone who calls on the name of the Lord will be saved."[190] When people hear the name Trump, they think of money; when they hear the name Einstein, they think of intelligence; when they hear the name Michelangelo, they think of art; but when they hear the name of Jesus, they think of salvation. In Acts 4:12 we discover that only His name brings salvation: "Nor is there salvation in any other, for there is no other name under heaven given among men by which we must be saved."[191] Why did Peter say no other name? Because there is only one Lord, and His name is Jesus Christ.

Victory begins with receiving Him as our Savior. To truly represent God and honor His name, we are to stand out as beacons of light through our words and deeds. Jesus said in Matthew 5:16: "In the same way, let your good deeds shine out for all to see, so that everyone will praise your heavenly Father."[192] When a person uses or abuses God's name, it reveals whether or not that person is converted, whether the person is a Christian, or whether the person has been saved, that is, been born of the Spirit of God and transformed.[193]

Calvin said, "The end of this precept is that the Lord will have the majesty of His name to be held inviolably sacred by us. Whatever we think and whatever we say of Him should savor of His excellency, correspond to the sacred sublimity of His name, and tend to the exaltation of His magnificence."[194] If we take the name of God seriously, the people around us will too. Do not misuse God's name but be careful how you treat God's name. To properly honor God, be thoughtful about where you take God's name, and be faithful in how you trust God's name.

CHAPTER FIVE
The Fourth Commandment
REST ASSURED
Exodus 20:8-11

Remember the Sabbath day by keeping it holy. Six days you shall labor and do all your work, but the seventh day is a sabbath to the Lord your God. On it you shall not do any work, neither you, nor your son or daughter, nor your male or female servant, nor your animals, nor any foreigner residing in your towns. For in six days the Lord made the heavens and the earth, the sea, and all that is in them, but he rested on the seventh day. Therefore the Lord blessed the Sabbath day and made it holy.[195]

A photographer was snapping pictures of first graders at an elementary school, during which he was making small talk to put the kids at ease. "What are you going to be when you grow up?" he asked one little girl. "Tired," she said. Will Rogers said, "Half our life is spent trying to find something to do with the time we have rushed through life trying to save."[196] And we fool ourselves if we think this nonstop pace makes us more effective. Technology hasn't fulfilled its promise; we are now only faster at being busy! If computers and electronics were made to save time, why are we so far behind? All we've added is speed and noise. We get there faster, yet we're worn out. We have less time, a shortage of time, to do all the things we expect we ought to get accomplished, and apparently there is no rest for the weary. God has a cure you can rest assured in, found in Exodus 20:8. The fourth commandment is probably left out of our thinking, culture, and way of life as much as any. The average person today sees Sunday as a fun day and off day, so much so that we call it part of the weekend. God sees it as the week beginning and a holy day unto the Lord. Yet we've made it everything but God's day.

Not only do we not fully honor the Sabbath day as a day of rest, but most are not sure or fully know what it is and what its purpose is. According to Rabbi Joseph Telushkin, "The Sabbath is one of the Bible's revolutionary innovations."[197] Remember when we honor God it doesn't make Him more holy; it makes us more holy. Remember too that all of these commands were made for *us*. God's laws are for our welfare to live a better life. Though many may think this fourth commandment is antiquated and irrelevant, the following subheads pose three questions that will give understanding of the fourth Commandment as being contemporarily applicable. Because of the fourth Commandment we can all "rest assured."

What Is the Sabbath?

"Sabbath" is the English reflex of a common Hebrew word (*šabbāṭ*) meaning "stopping/stoppage/cessation." The Sabbath is the "stopping day," the day on which one's regular work ceases both for the sake of giving laborers a break from their daily routine and for the sake of providing a focus on God that is periodically (weekly) heightened.[198]

In the Bible, the principle is laid down that one day in seven is to be observed as a day holy to God. It is the Lord's day, a day of rest and blessings. We are commanded to take a day off and focus on the Lord. There are three rest days in the Bible we will look at concerning the Sabbath.

The first rest day is Creation rest. The fourth command is the oldest of origin and goes back to the Creation: "Thus the heavens and the earth were completed in all their vast array. By the seventh day God had finished the work he had been doing; so on the seventh day he rested from all his work. Then God blessed the seventh day and made it holy, because on it he rested from all the work of creating that he had done."[199] God rested on the seventh day from finishing the creation of all life and the universe. He rested on the seventh day and blessed that day. This is the first time you will read in the Bible of God's blessing something or someone, and He chose to bless a day.

Why a rest day? Was God tired? Not according to Isaiah 40:28: "Have you not known? Have you not heard? The Lord is the everlasting God, the Creator of the ends of the earth. He does not faint or grow weary"[200] There are two primary reasons that God takes a Creation rest. The first is as in music to pause for emphasis and rejoicing, reflection, and readiness for the next part that is coming. In seventy-one of the psalms, there is a closing word that is often misunderstood, which is *selah*. *Selah* is a word that simply means to take a pause and think about it, or meditate on what you've just heard—take a break. *Eerdmans Dictionary of the Bible* has this to say concerning this word, that it is "likely a musical or liturgical notation, occurring 71 times in 39 Psalms and 3 times in the psalm of Hab. 3. In the LXX Selah is rendered as Greek *diápsalma* ("pause in singing"), suggesting some type of caesura."[201] The other reason is to reveal to mankind His plan and purpose for humankind; all of life needs rest.

The second rest day is the Covenant rest. The nation of Israel was a special people, and God gave them a special day. Exodus 31:13-17 tells us to keep the Sabbath because God said it is a sign, a perpetual covenant "between Me and you."

> But as for you, speak to the sons of Israel, saying, "You shall surely observe My Sabbaths; for this is a sign between Me and you throughout your generations, that you may know that I am the Lord who sanctifies you. Therefore you are to observe the Sabbath, for it is holy to you. Everyone who profanes it shall surely be put to death; for whoever does any work on it, that person shall be cut off from among his people. For six days work may be done, but on the seventh day there is a Sabbath of complete rest, holy to the Lord; whoever does any work on the Sabbath day shall surely be put to death. So the sons of Israel shall observe the Sabbath, to celebrate the Sabbath throughout their generations as a perpetual covenant." It is a sign between Me and the sons of Israel forever; for in six days the Lord made heaven and earth, but on the seventh day He ceased from labor, and was refreshed.[202]

God gave it to the Jews as a holy day unto Him but also as a day of rest for them, which stems from God's personal relationship with them. There are those who want to keep the Sabbath as the Old Testament nation of Israel did, but that would not easily be possible; if you were to break it, you'd be put to death. Any work on that day was forbidden, not even the building of a fire. Exodus 35:2-3 states: "For six days work may be done, but on the seventh day you shall have a holy *day*, a sabbath of complete rest to the Lord; whoever does any work on it shall be put to death. You shall not kindle a fire in any of your dwellings on the sabbath day."[203] Think about it—what it takes to get to church or go to the store would be work and even starting the car would be the lighting of a fire in your engine.

The Jews had thirty-nine words that talk about the Sabbath, and they found thirty-nine ways to break it, as well as thirty-nine ways to break each of those, which totaled 1,521 ways to break the Sabbath. They turned a righteous day into a ritualistic day, a day of tradition that would serve more in separating them from God than for drawing them closer to God. Dr. J. Vernon McGee speaks of this in his writings *The Sabbath Day or the Lord's Day*:

> When you turn to the Mishnah (or text) that was combined with the commentary in the Talmud (containing the civil and canonical laws of the nation Israel), you will find that they had reduced the Sabbath day observance of Israel to minutiae, the most trifling regulations. They had 39 ways of breaching the Sabbath, and they divided each one of those 39 ways into another 39 ways, and 39 multiplied by 39 equals 1,521 ways in which one could break the Sabbath in Old Testament times![204]

He goes on to illustrate this point with several trivial ways that caused them to break the fourth commandment. If you tied a knot you broke the Sabbath. A scribe could not carry a pen, because that would be carrying a burden on the Sabbath. A person was not even permitted to kill a flea on the Sabbath. It would appear to be strange and excessively religious that a man could not kill a flea even though it was biting him. In other words, the flea had a free day on the Sabbath. A person could not wear a coat or garment over his other clothing. The thought was that the individual might become too warm, take off his coat and put it over his arm, and that would be carrying a burden on the Sabbath. A woman was not permitted to look in a mirror on the Sabbath day for she might see a gray hair and want to pull it out, and that would be reaping on the Sabbath. They had reduced it to the point that it had become all but ridiculous. I guess one had better kill all of the fleas and pull all their grey hairs on Friday so you could stay right with God. They wouldn't eat an egg laid on Saturday for fear of breaking the fourth commandment. William Barclay said, "The Jewish Sabbath had tended to become increasingly a day of restrictions and prohibitions observed in a legalistic spirit."[205]

There was no doubt that when Jesus came and healed on the Sabbath, or picked corn on the Sabbath, it most assuredly created great angst for the Jews of that day. They hated Jesus for breaking the Sabbath by going against their created interpretation of God's holy day. Mark Rooker states: "The Gospels record six occasions where there was a controversy over the Sabbath."[206] Yet Jesus maintained consistently that it was lawful to do good on the Sabbath. The blessing of the Sabbath had been turned into a burden; God's laws were meant to liberate not become a liability of frustration. The Sabbath was not about regulations and legalistic codes, but as Abraham Joshua Heschel stated: "What is so luminous about a day? What is so precious to captivate the hearts? It is because the seventh day is a mine where spirit's precious metal can be found with which to construct the palace of time, a dimension in which the human is at home with the divine: a dimension in which man aspirers to approach the likeness of the Divine."[207]

The third day of rest is Calvary rest. Calvary rest is the New Testament rest for us today. The Old Testament Sabbath prophesied of Jesus; it was a shadow that pointed to Jesus. Here is how this Calvary rest is a foreshadowing of Christ. When did God rest? After Creation. When did Jesus rest? After His new creation by the Cross. It was on the cross that Jesus said, "It is finished." What was finished? Jesus said, "I must work the works of Him who sent Me, and I must finish the works I was sent to do." Jesus came to do a work and create a new creation. This passage in 2 Corinthians 5:17 explains this work: "Therefore, if anyone is in Christ, he is a new creation. The old has passed away; behold, the new has come."[208]

What was the work? This is a new creation, as stated in Colossians 2:13-15:

> And you, being dead in your sins and the un-circumcision of your flesh, hath he quickened together with him, having forgiven you all trespasses; Blotting out the handwriting of ordinances that was against us, which was contrary to us, and took it out of the way, nailing it to his cross; and having spoiled principalities and powers, he made a shew of them openly, triumphing over them in it.[209]

The *English Standard Version* of the Bible calls this "handwriting of ordinances" our "record of debt."

In Bible times if a man committed a crime and he was adjudicated, the court desk would write his crimes on a certificate, nail the certificate of debt to the door, which would represent their handwriting of ordinances against them. The new American Commentary states:

> Two metaphors express the heart of what Christ did for believers: the handwriting of ordinances being removed ("the written code") and nailing the accusations to the cross ("nailing it to the cross"). The first is the more complicated to interpret. Literally, the handwriting is a certificate of indebtedness written in one's own hand. Taken this way, this means that there is a pronouncement that the personal note which testifies against us is canceled. Twice the word occurs . . . in a request for payment of a loan. The word and the idea it expresses must be interpreted in connection with its modifier, "in regulations."[210]

Jesus took our handwriting of ordinances and blotted them out (nailed them to the Cross) and cancelled their record of debt. Colossians 2:15-17 continues with the reference of Christ's freeing us from the rituals of bondage concerning the Sabbath:

> And on that cross Christ freed himself from the power of the spiritual rulers and authorities; he made a public spectacle of them by leading them as captives in his victory procession. So let no one make rules about what you eat or drink or about holy days or the

CHAPTER FIVE:
The Fourth Commandment
REST ASSURED

New Moon Festival or the Sabbath. All such things are only a shadow of things in the future; the reality is Christ.[211]

Let no one make a rule that Christ freed us from.

These are a shadow of Christ, of things to come, of the future. Doug Stringer stated on this subject: "The key to understanding the present and future ramifications of all holy days (including the Sabbath) can be found in the expression 'shadow of things to come.'"[212] All things point to the ultimate rest we experience through the Lord Jesus Christ. He came, and we no longer need the old shadow; we have the body, no longer needing the shadow. Yet there are those who, like a dog chasing a shadow, are determined to follow the shadow of the past instead of the person of Christ in what He's done for us in the present. Jesus is the Body, and the Old Testament Sabbath is a shadow of Jesus Christ. The Body is of Christ, and the shadow pointed to Jesus. That's why Jesus could say He would give us rest, because He is our rest. In Matthew 11:28, He bids us: "Come to Me, all you who labor and are heavy laden, and I will give you rest."[213] Jesus was and is our finished rest, and believers in Christ are new creations.

At Calvary's cross, Jesus said, "It is finished." The rest we need was accomplished through Christ, according to Hebrews 4:1-11:

> Therefore, since the promise of entering his rest still stands, let us be careful that none of you be found to have fallen short of it. For we also have had the good news proclaimed to us, just as they did; but the message they heard was of no value to them, because they did not share the faith of those who obeyed. Now we who have believed enter that rest, just as God has said, "So I declared on oath in my anger, 'They shall never enter my rest.'" And yet his works have been finished since the creation of the world. For somewhere he has spoken about the seventh day in these words: "On the seventh day God rested from all his works." And again in the passage above he says, "They shall never enter my rest." Therefore since it still remains for some to enter that rest, and since those who formerly had the good news proclaimed to them did not go in because of their disobedience, God again set a certain day, calling it "Today." This he did when a long time later he spoke through David, as in

the passage already quoted: "Today, if you hear his voice, do not harden your hearts." For if Joshua had given them rest, God would not have spoken later about another day. There remains, then, a Sabbath-rest for the people of God; for anyone who enters God's rest also rests from their works, just as God did from his. Let us, therefore, make every effort to enter that rest, so that no one will perish by following their example of disobedience.[214]

Now those who have believed enter that rest. What is the "rest" that believers have entered into? Salvation. Verse 9 says, "There remains, then, a Sabbath-rest for the people of God." Verse 10 continues by saying that anyone who enters God's rest also rests from his own work, just as God did from His creative work. The Sabbath was a foreshadowing of salvation. The psalmist points this thought out in Psalm 62:1: "Truly my soul finds rest in God; my salvation comes from him."[215] The writer of Hebrews clearly states that it was Jesus who paid the price for our rest and peace: "Christ, however, offered one sacrifice for sins, an offering that is effective forever, and then he sat down at the right side of God."[216] He sat down after His work; yet in the Old Testament Temple, the priest never sat down. Why? Because his work was never finished. Yet Jesus finished the work of salvation and purchased our peace and rest. Let no one judge you today from the Old Testament Covenant rest instead of today's New Testament Calvary rest. Those who do are only chasing shadows.

When Is the Sabbath?

In the Old Testament, it was the seventh day of the week, Saturday. It marked the end of the week. That's why we can accurately refer to it as the weekend. But today we celebrate the Sabbath on Sunday, the first day of the week. Why? For more than any other reason we keep it as our Sabbath because Jesus came out of the grave on the first day. The new beginning was on Sunday, the Lord's Day, the first day of the week.

Below are nine facts pertaining to reasons for observing the Sabbath day now on Sunday:

1. Jesus was resurrected on the first day of the week. In Mark 16:9 we read, "After Jesus rose from death early on Sunday, he appeared first to Mary Magdalene, from whom he had driven out seven demons."[217]

2. Jesus was with His disciples after His resurrection on the first day of the week, as Mark 16:12 says, "Later that day he appeared to two who were walking from Jerusalem into the country, but they didn't recognize him at first because he had changed his appearance."[218]

3. Jesus was with them eight days later on the first day of the week (John 20:19-20): "When it was evening on the first day of the week, Jesus' followers were together. The doors were locked, because they were afraid of the elders. Then Jesus came and stood right in the middle of them and said, 'Peace be with you.' After he said this, he showed them his hands and his side. His followers were thrilled when they saw the Lord."[219]

4. In John 20:21, Jesus commissioned then to preach on the first day of the week: "Jesus said to them again, 'Peace be with you! As the Father has sent me, so I am sending you.'"[220]

5. Jesus imparted to them the Holy Spirit (insufflation) on the first day of the week. "Then he breathed on them and said, 'Receive the Holy Spirit.'"[221]

6. The day of Pentecost when the Church was born was the first day of the week. "When the day of Pentecost arrived, they were all together in one place."[222]

7. In the Book of Revelation, John was in the Spirit on the first day of the week. "It was Sunday and I was in the Spirit, praying. . . ."[223] The Lord's Day never was the Sabbath of the Old Testament; any new creation came from the Calvary Sabbath.

8. The early church met for worship on the first day of the week. "On the first day of the week we came together to break bread."[224]

9. The disciples came together, Paul preached and offerings were laid up on the first day of the week. "On the first day of every week, each one of you should set aside a sum of money in keeping with your income, saving it up, so that when I come no collections will have to be made."[225] The Lord's Day is the first day of the week. Sunday is not the end of the week, it is the first day of the week, the week beginning. The Westminster Shorter Catechism states, "From the beginning of the world to the resurrection of Christ, God appointed the seventh day of the week to be a weekly Sabbath; and the first day of the week ever since . . . which is the Christian Sabbath."[226]

Jesus has taken the Old Testament Sabbath and fulfilled it and transformed it.

Creation rest, Covenant rest, but now we praise God for Calvary rest. But what is the difference? The first Sabbath, Covenant rest, speaks of the finished work of creation; Jesus speaks of the finished work of redemption, which is Calvary rest. The first deals with the natural life, the second Sabbath (the Lord's Day) deals with the supernatural life. The first deals with life in Adam, and the last deals with life in Christ. The first commemorated the work of God's hands; the latter commemorates the work of God's heart. The first displayed God's power, and today's Sabbath displays God's grace. The first is to Israel, and the last is to the Church. The first was a day of law; the New Testament Sabbath is a day of love. Those who insist on keeping the Old Testament Covenant rest are on the wrong side of Calvary, still chasing shadows.

How Do We Keep the Sabbath Day Today?

In the New Testament, there are no specific laws concerning the Sabbath Day of today. The Lord's Day is not a day of legalism—can I do this . . . that . . . or this? He just wants us to "rest assured." The Sabbath is God's maintenance plan for the human race, a way of giving us a legal and needful timeout. Everybody needs a time out to rest one day a week. God did it to establish and set an example for life, to give us "rest assured." There are three parts to every person—mind (soul), body, and spirit; this is the trichotomy of man. God made us that all three parts will need recharged and renewed on a regular basis. My grandson Tyler has an electric car that has two large batteries. These batteries allow him to run the car for up to two, or even three, hours at a time. As the batteries begin to run down, they heat up, telling us they need to be recharged. So it is for the human race; we can go only as long as the charge on our batteries allows us, and then we start heating up, signifying we need to be recharged. The day of rest is God's way of recharging us. As with Tyler's batteries, we can't charge them while the car is still running. Neither can you become recharged without stopping. How do we keep the Sabbath Day today and receive the recharging that God supplies for us?

With our minds (soul), we are to remember the Lord's Day. Exodus 20:8 says: "Observe the Sabbath and keep it holy."[227] How can we honor the Lord's Day today? We are to remember it. We remember with our minds by taking a mental break after every six days. Here are two ways we need to remember the Lord's Day: First, we need to recall what He has already taught us. When God delivered Israel out of Egypt, there were millions of Jews that came out into the wilderness. God provided food for all of them by sending manna from heaven as their daily food. Each day they were to gather enough per family to meet their daily needs. If they gathered more than their daily needs, it would spoil and rot. On the sixth day (Friday) they were to gather enough for two days, so they could rest on the Sabbath. On the Sabbath day they were "to cease" doing anything, even to supplying food for themselves. It was a holy day unto God, but it would serve to supply a recharging for them as well. God provided for them in every way; He met their needs in a trust relationship with them.

The only day the manna they had gathered the day before didn't spoil was the Sabbath. God was, in effect, saying, "If you give Me special honor one day a week, I'll make sure you get all you need in the other six days. I'll give you more in six days than you could otherwise accomplish alone in seven."

> Truett Cathy is the founder of Chick-fil-A restaurants and a successful businessman. But for many, he is even better known—and respected—for letting his faith guide his business operation. . . .

Mr. Cathy's restaurants have been closed on Sundays since 1948. The 79-year-old CEO of the nearly 1,000 Chick-fil-A restaurants doesn't mind losing millions of dollars of business to honor the Lord's Day.[228]

He recognizes that his employees need rest. He shows mercy to them by freeing them from work one day a week. Mr. Cathy did an empirical study of every mall and fast-food restaurant and said, "We do more business in six than all others in seven days."[229]

God honors His Word. If we'll set aside one day specifically for Him, He will bless the other six. Arthur DeMoss stated: "To be successful in life, give God the first of your time, the first of every dime, and the first day of every week."[230]

The second way we need to remember in keeping the Lord's Day is by honoring what He commanded us. Every year there comes an event for every married couple called an anniversary. Men are especially expected to remember it, and we do so one of two ways. We either acknowledge the moment (often too late), or we honor the moment by honoring the wife. Acknowledging the moment only recognizes it, but honoring the moment does something about it. We can simply remember it's Sunday, even to the point that we acknowledge it's the Lord's Day. But to truly honor the Lord's Day, we must determine that on this day we will honor Him—"for this is the day the Lord has made." God wants us to remember to take a mental break every week. How do we remember? Celebrate it as God intended and put your heart and emotions into it.

With our bodies, we are to rest on the Lord's Day. The fourth commandment is unique in that it's both positive and negative. The positive is that we are to honor this day; the negative aspect is that we are told, "You shall not do any work on this day." Look at the positive meaning that God intends for His children today.

Take time to be healthy and rest on this day. Though the ceremonial part is gone, the principle is still there. We should live an industrious life and work, yet we should also live a tranquil life and rest. One day a week, we are to punch out and rest; this is God's remedy for the workaholic. It's a day to catch our breath—a day not to go to work. Dr. D. James Kennedy said, "The human body is designed so that it works best if one out of every seven is given to rest."[231] Whatever your work is, stop it once a week, and relax. Slow down and enjoy life as God intended it to be, fun and full of peaceful joy.

There is a humanitarian aspect to keeping the Sabbath as well. People are more than just machines, good only for what they can produce. The Sabbath reminds us of this and protects people from being reduced to units of production. In the aftermath of the French Revolution, the Sabbath was abolished, being substituted with one day's rest in ten. Voltaire reportedly said, "We cannot destroy Christianity until we first destroy the Sabbath."[232] But apparently the experiment was a disaster; men and women crumbled under the strain, and animals literally collapsed in the streets. People need the Sabbath because they're people, not machines.

Good health comes from God's rest. God made this world in such a way that even dirt needs to rest. I'm from Indiana, where the farming industry is a vital part of their income and daily lives. One thing you will notice is, they grow different crops each year on their farms. This is called crop rotation and is done so the dirt is not drained year after year of its same nutrients. The crops are to draw from the soil but not destroy the soil. In other words, the dirt is given a rest. Here are two things that are interesting to mention: First, we are all made from dirt, according to the Book of Genesis, yet we are better than dirt. Second, if dirt needs to rest, how can we think any less of our own need to rest? Just a thought! We, from experience, recognize that our bodies need rest every day—regular nightly rest, as well as a longer weekly rest. So why not give it the rest God intended by honoring the Lord's Day?

Take time to be happy, for the Lord's Day is made for you. God gave His people this gift of a Sabbath rest: "Then Jesus said to them, 'The Sabbath was made to meet the needs of people, and not people to meet the requirements of the Sabbath.'"[233] The Sabbath was made for man, as were all of God's commandments. Instead of working, do things that refuel your body, your mind, your relationships, and your soul. If you like the movies, see a movie; if you like to ride your bike, ride your bike; if you like to hike, take a long one. If you like to read, read to your heart's desire; if you like to garden, plant some flowers. J.I. Packer says we should "choose the leisure activities that bring us closest to God, to people, to beauty, and to all that ennobles."[234] The important thing is to detach ourselves from our everyday work and be happy in life and happy in the Lord. The Sabbath is a time to say, "I'm not a human *doing* but a human *being*; I'm more than my work." William Barclay said, "In the Lord's Day the Christian has a great possession. . . . The Lord's Day is a day of rest, but rest must be interpreted according to the needs of the individual; the Lord's Day is the day of the meeting of families and friends."[235]

Creation didn't crash when God rested. The fourth Commandment, when obeyed, puts you in control of your work instead of your work controlling you. You're telling work, "I'm not your slave," and this includes your family. Exodus 20:10 tells us, no one in the household, including the servants, should work on this day. That's how to bless your house and family; teach them to take a day off and worship. God wanted everyone to rest. Eugene Peterson wrote concerning the Sabbath: "Sabbath: Uncluttered time and space to distance ourselves from the frenzy of our own activities so we can see what God was and is doing. If we don't regularly quit work one day a week, we take ourselves far too seriously. The moral sweat pouring off our brow blinds us to the primal action of God in and around us."[236]

With our spirit we are to rejoice on the Lord's Day. Go back to Exodus 20:8-11 and read it again: "Remember the day of worship by observing it as a holy day. In six days the LORD made heaven, earth, and the sea, along with everything in them. He didn't work on the seventh day. That's why the LORD blessed the day he stopped his work and set this day apart as holy."[237] Take time to worship on this day for it is a holy day unto God. The writer of Hebrews writes in 10:25: "Some people have gotten out of the habit of meeting for worship but we must not do that."[238] It's commanded not to forsake this day and to make it holy. To keep something holy in the biblical sense also means to dedicate it for worship. The Sabbath wasn't just a day to rest; it was also a day to worship, a day to replenish the soul. This is the positive side of the fourth commandment. The Sabbath is called "a holy convocation" in Leviticus 23:3, meaning it was a time for God's people to gather for worship. The Puritans called the Sabbath the "market day of the soul."[239] The other days of the week are for doing ordinary business, but this day is for spiritual business, trading in the currency of heaven. Albert Schweitzer said, "If your soul has no Sunday, it becomes an orphan."[240] So the Lord's Day is a day to meet together with God's people; it doesn't necessarily have to be Sunday, but we need a weekly rhythm in which we observe a discipline of gathering for worship. True rest comes only through relational intimacy with God during seasons of worship, not through recreation that the world offers.[241]

Too often we make this holy day into a holiday. Many equate the Sabbath with a "day off," but if it is only a day off to you, then it becomes nothing but a secularized Sabbath. The sole goal of a day off is leisure, fun, and play. Isn't it interesting that we live in a culture obsessed with leisure and recreation, but very few people are rested? We actually have a leisure industry, a very profitable one at that, and yet we have more exhaustion, fatigue, and burnout than ever before.

There's more to the Sabbath than the absence of work; there must also be worship. The day must be more than just getting off to take off; it must also be a day for honoring God. The Sabbath, our New Testament Sunday, the Lord's Day, is to drop everything and worship God. Exodus 20:10 makes it clear: "The seventh day is a Sabbath day of rest dedicated to the LORD your God. On that day no one in your household may do any work. This includes you, your sons and daughters, your male and female servants, your livestock, and any foreigners living among you."[242] God established it as a Sabbath to the Lord, which means it's His day, not yours to do as you please.

Most people on Sunday recharge their mind and body while ignoring their spirit. The problem is if all you do is work and play then you'll see life as work and play; there is more to life than the mental and physical aspect of it. Too often we hear, "It's the only time I have for myself or with my family." What could be better than going to church together to honor God?

We've lost a biblical view of rest, rest that includes a recognition and appreciation of God, rest that includes a spiritual rejuvenation that only comes through worship of the living God and fellowship with his people. Barbara Brown Taylor writes:

> Some of us have made an idol of exhaustion. The only time we know we have done enough is when we're running on empty and when the ones we love most are the ones we see the least. When we lie down to sleep at night, we offer our full appointment calendars to God in lieu of prayer, believing that God—who is as busy as we are—will surely understand.[243]

Notice, in Isaiah 58:13-14, what God said He'll do:

> But first, you must start respecting the Sabbath as a joyful day of worship. You must stop doing and saying whatever you please on this special day. Then you will truly enjoy knowing the LORD. He will let you rule from the highest mountains and bless you with the land of your ancestor Jacob. The LORD has spoken![244]

The Lord is saying, "If you'll take my day seriously and honor Me, then I will bless you with My presence and blessings." Worshipping every Lord's Day should be a regular habit, a lifestyle, and a consistent way of life before God. Isn't it amazing that we call Sunday the Lord's Day and then we use it as our own?

One of our highest priorities should be to make church attendance a regular habit. Our worship on Sunday is even more important than our work on Monday. Try out on your boss the excuses people use to not honor the Lord's Day and see how it goes over: "Company came in," "I was tired and slept in," or "I took the family to the beach today instead." What are you saying when you do this? What you are saying with your actions is that church is not important but work is! In fact, what is really conveyed is that work is more important than church and honoring the Lord's Day. Your witness speaks loudly, and it should speak these two things: "I'm faithful to work, *and* I'm faithful to honor the Lord with my best effort in worshipping Him each week." J.C. Penney said concerning honoring the Lord's Day: "If a man's business requires his time that he cannot attend Sunday morning and Wednesday evening services, of his church, then that man has more business than God intended him to have."[245] Those who honor the Lord's Day are saying, "God matters, church matters, my church family matters, and my family matters; so I take time out to be a holy worshiper unto God." Richard Clarke Cabot said, "Worship renews our spirit as sleep renews the body."[246] The psalmist celebrated his regular worship experience with this statement in Psalm 122:1: "I was glad when they said to me, let's go to the house of the Lord."[247] He was saying, "I look forward to the house of the Lord." Why? He knew the end result. The end result was mental, physical, and spiritual renewal. The fourth commandment calls for a day to offer worship and praise to God, a day set aside that we might remember His creation and redemption.[248]

The early church met on Sunday because Jesus arose on Sunday. The resurrection changed everything. Every Sunday you attend church, you're saying, "I believe Jesus is alive, and this is the day He made, and I'm going to rejoice." You're saying your worship on Sunday is more important than work on Monday. It is a day of gladness and not gloom, love and not legalism. Romans 14:17 liberates our thinking with these words: "For the kingdom of God is not a matter of food and drink, but of righteousness, peace, and joy in the holy Spirit;"[249] Families get together on this day, living and loving life. Remember to keep the day holy; it's a day of liberty wherein Jesus sets us free. Jesus is our rest, according to Matthew 11:28: "Come to me, all of you who are tired from carrying heavy loads, and I will give you rest."[250] The invitation is "Come. It's your move—now, just as you are—and I will give you rest. Don't wait for heaven; do it now." Many will have on their tombstone the words "Rest in peace," but that will only happen if they rest in Jesus by having received His "rest assured."

CHAPTER SIX
The Fifth Commandment
THE KEY TO SUCCESS AND LONG LIFE

Exodus 20:12

"Honor your father and mother, that you may have a long, good life in the land the Lord your God will give you."[251] How would you like to have a long and prosperous life? Did you know that God wants that for you? It may surprise you what is required to achieve it. There is a direct correlation of our attitude with our parents and the blessing of long life from God. Just as success with the first commandment was necessary for a healthy relationship with God, so is success with the fifth commandment necessary for a healthy relationship with others in society. Simply put, the way children relate to their parents will determine their success in how they relate to other human beings. The honor of one's parents will be rewarded by happiness and blessings in one's life.[252] The Jewish sages stated that this was to be foremost among the commandments for which man is rewarded in this world.[253] Honoring our parents will not only affect the relationship we have with other human beings, but it has a dramatic impact on our relationship with our heavenly Father as well. The fifth commandment is a promise of both prosperity and longevity in life.[254] As you treat your mother and father, God treats you. Parents are an important connection to God.[255] Plato placed honor to parents in the highest place saying that to honor parents brings blessings from the gods.[256]

There are no perfect parents in life, but if we'll honor them on this earth, then God will reward us greatly. Adam and Eve had the best shot, and they failed. The key to walking in the blessings of God and His favor is to stay under the umbrella of respect by honoring our parents and giving them the dignity they deserve.

How does this commandment speak to us today when we have broken and abusive homes? Unlike in the days when Moses first relayed these words, we have extended families that live in entirely different parts of the country. We have an entire culture that caters to youth and marginalizes those who are older. Our society worships youth, looks, power, and health, which has caused us to lose the sense that our elderly have anything to offer us. By denying their worth, we cheapen the worth of society.[257] It's easy to think of this command as coming from a bygone era that's totally out of touch with the reality of our lives. One man complained, "Youth today have luxury. They have bad manners, contempt for authority, no respect for older people, and talk nonsense when they should work. Young people do not stand up any longer when adults enter the room. They contradict their parents, talk too much in company . . . and tyrannize their elders."[258] This may surprise you, but do you know who wrote that? Socrates, who lived five hundred years before Christ! It reminds us that every generation of young people have had issues. Maybe that's why the first of the Ten Commandments that deals with family life addresses how we relate to our parents. Following are four keys to the fifth commandment and how we can have success and long life.

The Prominent Importance of the Fifth Commandment

The placement of this command shows the special importance of how we relate to our parents. When God gave His law, He wrote it down on two tablets, so the Law was divided into two parts. Traditionally the first four commandments are distinguished from the last six. The first table of the law deals with our relationship with God.[259] The second table has six commands that deal with our relationship with people. The first four teach us how to love God; the last six teach us how to love our neighbor. Love for God has to come first. We can't truly love one another unless we love God. The duty to one's parents stands next to the duty toward God.[260] It's important to notice that in telling us how to treat our neighbor, God started with our own family. Loving our neighbor starts at home, and home life starts with how we relate to our parents. This relationship is foundational to every other relationship. Augustine said, "If anyone fails to honor his parents, is there anyone he will spare?"[261]

Not only is this commandment the foundation for all our other human relationships, it's the foundation for human society as well. Our family is our first hospital, first school, first government, and first church. If we don't honor authority at home, we'll have a hard time respecting it anywhere else, and society will crumble. This law creates stability in society as it is carried out through subsequent generations, and the effect of the family will affect the entire nation.[262] Look at what the writer of Hebrews 13:17 says: "Obey your leaders and follow their orders. They watch over your souls without resting, since they must give God an account of their service. If you obey them, they will do their work gladly; if not, they will do it with sadness, and that would be of no help to you."[263] When you look at the fifth commandment, you might notice that it is unequal to all the rest. There is nothing about this one that gives a negative command. All the others also have a "thou shalt not," but not the fifth one; it is a totally positive commandment. Here we are told to do one thing and God will reward it greatly.

Sometimes we overcomplicate what God wants of us and how we can live a prosperous life. Instead of a twelve-step program to a better life, God gives us a one-step command to a long and blessed life. That one step is to honor your mom and dad. God said if you will do this correctly, He will bless you and your home and the entire nation. How will He do this? As the family goes, so goes the nation! What makes a nation great? Integrity, honesty, loyalty, courtesy, purity, morality, and all the other virtues God requires of us, and it all begins at the home. God lets us know by the prominence and importance of the placement of this commandment that it affects the person, the family, and the whole nation.

The Principle Interpretation of the Fifth Commandment

Because of its importance, we need to study this commandment carefully. The first and most important word to examine is *honor*. Webster's dictionary says, *Honor* is "to respect greatly, regard highly; treat with deference and courtesy."[264] The Hebrew word translated "honor" is *kabad*. Its basic meaning is "weighty" (that is, with dignity, respect and reverence). It's the word the Old Testament uses to describe the glory of God, the weightiness of his person.[265] The New Testament word from the Greek is "time" which basically means value or price paid. To honor another person is to value that person, to respect and esteem that individual, and to regard the importance of him or her. It is a call to recognize and esteem the value of one's father and mother. Respect for parents is among the primary human duties.[266]

To honor our parents is to give due weight to their position, to hold them in high esteem, to value them. When we give weight to something, we give it our time, energy, and attention. How much weight do you give to your work? How much weight do you give to your finances? How much weight do you give to your favorite sports team? How much weight do you give to your health or your friends? These are things to which we typically give time, energy, and attention and on which we place the most value. It is the moral obligation of every person to give filial respect, love, and reverence to their parents.[267]

> The obligation of filial respect, love, and reverence is so instinctively felt by all that the duty has naturally found a place in every moral code. In the maxims of Ptahhotep, an Egyptian author who lived probably before Abraham, "the duty of filial piety is strictly inculcated" (Birch, Egypt from the Earliest Times, p. 49). Confucius, in China, based his moral system wholly upon the principle of parental authority; and in Rome it may be regarded as the main foundation of the political edifice. In the Decalogue, the position of this duty, at the head of our duties towards our neighbour, marks its importance, which is further shown by this being "the first commandment with promise" (Eph. 6:2). It is curious that the long life here specially attached to the observance of this obligation was also believed to accompany it by the Egyptians. "The son," says Ptahhotep, "who accepts the words of his father, will grow old in consequence of so doing;" and again—"The obedient son will be happy by reason of his obedience; he will grow old; he will come to favour." Modern commentators generally assume that the promise was not personal, but national—the nation's days were to be "long upon the land," if

the citizens generally were obedient children. But this explanation cannot apply to Eph. 6:1-3. And if obedience to parents is to be rewarded with long life under the new covenant, there can be no reason why it should not have been so rewarded under the old. The objection that good sons are not always long-lived is futile. God governs the universe by general, not by universal laws.[268]

Notice this commandment includes both fathers and mothers. In other places in the Bible there is an emphasis on the father as the leader of a household. But this never meant that mothers are to deserve a smaller amount of honor than fathers. Proverbs 6:20 says, "My son, obey the command of your father, and do not disregard the teachings of your mother."[269] To include both mothers and fathers in this proverb is very unusual for an ancient culture, especially a patriarchal one. In Leviticus 19:3, mothers are even mentioned first: "You must respect your mother and father, and you must keep my Sabbaths. I am the LORD your God."[270] In certain ways, a mother can be easier for a child to take advantage of, but God says mothers deserve equal respect. And one of the ways a father leads his family is by honoring his wife and insisting that his children honor her (their mother) as well. This commandment is our training for life and it teaches us a most fundamental lesson in all our relationships, to honor our parents.

It is important to understand what honor means and how it can be applied. *First of all, honor is personal.* Honor can be bestowed only on a person. Things are not honored; only people are honored. And if we are to receive honor, it must come as a gift from another person or persons. We really cannot honor ourselves, in the strictest sense of the word. God's Word says in Hebrews 5:4, "And no one takes this honor on himself, but he receives it when called by God, just as Aaron was."[271] Honor is only honor when given by one person to another by what we do for another. Since honor, because of its very definition, is personal, it can only be given by a person or by God and received by a person or by God.

Honor means giving preference. Honoring someone means giving them preference over and above others. The question that may arise here is "Is it okay to honor someone over and above another, give preferential treatment to one, subjectively showing favoritism to that person?" It is possible to be so afraid of honoring someone above another that we fail to give just due and honor to those who deserve it most. The Word teaches us in Romans 12:10 that it's okay to honor others: "Be kindly affectionate to one another with brotherly love, in honor giving preference to one another."[272] Notice what Samuel said in 1 Samuel 2:30: "But now the LORD declares: 'Far be it from me; for those who honor me I will honor, and those who despise me shall be treated with contempt.'"[273] We are called to honor our parents by giving them preference above some of the other people that may be part of our lives.

Honor is related to position. Sometimes, we honor a person solely because of the position. As Americans, no matter what party you are affiliated with or not affiliated with, we should honor the President. This does not mean you agree with him on every issue; it is, however, respect and recognition of his position of leadership. Doug Stringer stated in his book *Living Life Well*, "If we disagree with someone in authority, it must be done with an attitude of humility and respect."[274] The Bible tells us in 1 Peter 2:17 that we are to honor our leaders, those in authority: "Show respect for everyone. Love Christians everywhere. Fear God and honor the government."[275] The apostle Paul told the Romans to submit to the authorities because God had ordained their authority. He went on to say in Romans 13:6-7: "This is also why you pay taxes, for the authorities are God's servants, who give their full time to governing. Give to everyone what you owe them: If you owe taxes, pay taxes; if revenue, then revenue; if respect, then respect; if honor, then honor."[276]

The position of authority someone has, at times, demands we honor the person holding that position regardless of whether we agree with all of their decisions. Edmund P. Clowney says, "Structure and order, whether in the home, in life, or in society, involve submission of some to others."[277] We are to honor parents, not because they necessarily deserve it in their actions, but because of the position they hold, the position of parents. So even when parents are doing their job poorly, we have an obligation before God to honor them and thus bring glory to

CHAPTER SIX:
The Fifth Commandment
THE KEY TO SUCCESS AND LONG LIFE

God. In our Western culture we think that it must be the person and their conduct that merits honor. But if you go to many Eastern cultures, you'll find there is a respect for parents and grandparents and those that are older just for the simple fact that they are elderly, and so they hold them in high regard.

Honor has to be practical. To truly honor someone, it must be more than just lip service. This was the problem for many people in Isaiah's time between the people and God. In Isaiah 29:13, we read: "The Lord says, 'These people worship me with their mouths and honor me with their lips. But their hearts are far from me, and their worship of me is based on rules made by humans.'"[278] Their actions were not commensurate with their words. To honor someone requires action, not only by feelings but also by function. To truly honor God, or any one person, honor must be sincere and be expressed in practical or visible terms, not just flattering words that have no meaning. Honor is personal, it gives preference over others, it is often related to position, and it is has to be manifested in practice, not just in insincere words without true meaning. This is important because God promises three blessings if we do.

The first promise is *longevity*. He says our "days will be prolonged." This promise is seen in national outcomes. The right kind of children becomes the right kind of citizens, and they build a great nation. God said, "If you teach your children . . . I'll bless your nation." America is not so much a product of our government and military as our families and our faith. It is not our economic strength but the character of our people that makes this nation great. Good kids make good people, and good people make a good nation.

This is a personal promise as well. If you honor your parents you'll live a long life. Ephesians 6:1 reads: "Children, it is your Christian duty to obey your parents, for this is the right thing to do. 'Respect your father and mother' is the first commandment that has a promise added: 'so that all may go well with you, and you may live a long time in the land.'"[279] The promise that was made to the people of Israel was not that if they obeyed their parents, they wouldn't die young. The promise was "so that you may live a long time in the land that I am giving you."

Many children have avoided destructive forces in their life by following their parents' example. God is teaching us that when we listen to and honor our parents, we can live a better life. Luke 15:11-24 tells the story of the Prodigal Son, who dishonored his father by demanding that his father give him his inheritance while his father still lived. As a result of his demand and the foolish way he handled the inheritance once it was given to him, the son ended up in a terrible situation. But God gives us the promise of long life if we honor our parents.

The second promise is *prosperity*, as seen in Deuteronomy 5:16: "Honor your father and mother (remember, this is a commandment of the Lord your God); if you do so, you shall have a long, prosperous life in the land he is giving you."[280] "I'll prosper you," God says, "and you'll not only avoid problems, you'll also reap blessing." When we sow faithful obedience, we reap favor and grace. When we are obedient, there is a fulfilling joy and peace about life.

The third promise God gives is *security*. He says, "I'll keep you in the land." Isaiah 41:10 tells us, "Do not be afraid—I am with you! I am your God—let nothing terrify you! I will make you strong and help you; I will protect you and save you."[281] God gives those who honor their parents a promise of His continual security in our lives. God promises us earthly blessings if we follow the conditions of the fifth commandment and assures us of our eternal happiness; otherwise this commandment would be a threat rather than a promise.[282]

The Indisputable Purpose of the Fifth Commandment

Here are three reasons we should honor our parents: The first reason is, they deserve it. We could come up with a whole list of reasons that parents deserve to be honored. They deserve to be honored because of the sacrifices they make; they deserve to be honored because of the life experience they have. They are the people God chose to give us as our parents at birth. William Barclay wrote, "A child owes a parent his life in a double sense: First he owes him his life for his birth, and second, for the care that was provided for him when he could not care for himself."[283] Proverbs 3:27 says, "Do not withhold good from those to whom it is due, when it is in your power to do it."[284] Do good things for your parents as often as you can. One word of encouragement to a lonely parent will mean more to them than a hundred flowers at their funeral. Calvin once said, "We are to reverence our parents whether they deserve it or not, for they have brought us into this life."[285]

The second reason is God declares it. We are told in Ephesians 6:1: "Children, obey your parents because you are Christians. This is the right thing to do."[286] Your obedience is not contingent upon their correctness, but God's counsel. Have you ever heard, "Because I said so"? That's what the Word is saying: "Obey your parents because I said so," and "It is right." When you do what is right, it puts the weight of the outcome on the decision to obey. We are responsible to honor through our obedience. When the police at a traffic light tells us to go on through the light with the waving of a hand, even though the light may be red, whatever may happen is their responsibility not ours; we are responsible only to obey. Colossians 3:20 states: "Children, be obedient to your parents in all things, for this is well-pleasing to the Lord."[287] What about bad parents, are we to honor them? Yes, God offers no disclaimer or appendix to problem parents. Do you honor bad judges, police, politicians, and a boss that is mean? God gave you your parents, and He said without equivocation, "Honor them." Why are we to do this? There is one reason in two parts: They are our parents, and God said honor them.

This does not mean, of course, that we are to obey if they give a directive that is in violation of any of the other nine commandments. We are to honor and obey God and His commands above all others and all else.

The third reason we should honor our parents is we're discipled by it. By learning to honor them, we learn to honor authority in general. Zacharius Ursinus, the primary author of the Heidelberg Catechism, wrote: "The design or end of this commandment is the preservation of civil order, which God has appointed in the mutual duties between inferiors and their superiors. Superiors are all those whom God has placed over others, for the purpose of governing and defending them."[288] Teachers, ministers, government officials, etc., would fall into this category. Dr.

Laura Schlesinger wrote in her book *The Ten Commandments: The Significance of God's Laws in Everyday Life*:

> Parents are teachers of faith and morality. What God is to the world, parents are to their children. Unfortunately, some parents become so focused on the element of friendship or their own convenience, comfort, self-fulfillment, happiness, or love life that they forget their job is to help mold moral character so their children will have the strength to do what is right in a world that sometimes encourages them to do otherwise.[289]

So when God tells us to respect our parents, by implication he's also telling us to respect government authority, church authority, and even those in authority over us at work.

How should we honor our parents? Here are four "Parental Proverbs."

1. Live righteously (Proverbs 23:24-25): "The father of a righteous child has great joy; a man who fathers a wise son rejoices in him. May your father and mother rejoice; may she who gave you birth be joyful!"[290] This is a picture of proud parents—proud of their children who live a wise and righteous (moral) life. Righteous living comes only from living a life in tune with God.

2. Love graciously (Proverbs 19:26): "Only a shameful, disgraceful person would ill-treat his father or turn his mother away from his home."[291] In that day, children would work the farm of their parents until the parents died, and then the farm would become theirs. This passage is referring to occasions when the children would kick their parents off their farm and take it for themselves. It is wrong to exploit our parents. It is estimated that every year senior adults are scammed out of $40 million dollars.[292] We need to do everything in our power to prevent our parents from becoming victims of these unscrupulous practices.

3. Speak lovingly (Proverbs 20:20): "The lamp of the person who curses his father and mother will be snuffed out in total darkness."[293] The picture of a lamp going out throughout Proverbs is a picture of a person's life being cut short. We can speak curses or blessings. If you embrace a lifestyle of hatred and contempt for your parents, your own life

is at risk. Words can hurt; speak blessings, not curses. For some people, it will take the grace of God to speak to their parents this lovingly and with blessings in mind, but this is what pleases God.

4. Listen attentively (Proverbs 23:22): "Listen to your father; without him you would not exist. When your mother is old, show her your appreciation."[294] The word *listen* in this context means "to pay attention." More than our financial assistance, more than our advice, they want our attention. As they age, stay in touch with them. Listen to them, even when they repeat the same stories over and over. The opposite of listening to parents in this verse is despising them; it means having disdain for them. The way to honor our parents is to live righteously, love graciously, speak lovingly, and listen attentively to them.

The Practical Application of the Fifth Commandment

How does this command apply to us? As children, we accept their authority. God wants us to obey our parents. He wants us to speak respectfully to them. He wants us to tell them the truth. He wants us to listen to what they have to say. Your parents may not always do everything right, but most often they know what's best for you. And if we honor them, our lives will be happier. Review Ephesians 6:1, and remember that, as a child, you have one job, to honor through obedience. You get the benefits with one caveat: honor your parents. That is exactly what Jesus did with Mary and Joseph (Luke 2:51): "Then he returned to Nazareth with them and was obedient to them; and his mother stored away all these things in her heart."[295] He was not obedient because they were always right, not because they were morally superior to Him, not because they knew more than He did. He did it because "it was right." It was what His Father in heaven wanted Him to do as a son honoring his parents correctly.

Children need to know that disobedience brings discipline. Proverbs 13:24 tells us that our love for our children is seen in our disciplining them: "If you don't punish your son, you don't love him. If you do love him, you will correct him."[296] Hebrews 12:7-11 explains that we should discipline our children as God shows His love for us by disciplining us:

> Endure hardship as discipline; God is treating you as his children. For what children are not disciplined by their father? If you are not disciplined—and everyone undergoes discipline—then you are not legitimate, not true sons and daughters at all. Moreover, we have all had human fathers who disciplined us and we respected them for it. How much more should we submit to the Father of spirits and live! They disciplined us for a little while as they thought best; but God disciplines us for our good, in order that we may share in his holiness. No discipline seems pleasant at the time, but painful. Later on, however, it produces a harvest of righteousness and peace for those who have been trained by it.[297]

With that thought in mind, I know my daddy loved me a tremendous amount, for he regularly applied the rod of correction to the seat of my understanding! Remember, though, when a child's behavior forces you to punish him, you must do it in love and with the understanding that this will bring about the greatest potential for his future success in life.[298]

Too many parents have turned to giving children what they want instead of what they need. A lack of discipline is ruining the fabric of our society.[299] As a young child, our primary way of honoring our parents will be through our obedience. As teenagers, we should appreciate their wisdom. Proverbs 15:5 tells us, "It is foolish to ignore what your father taught you; it is wise to accept his correction."[300] If you think you're smarter than your parents, then you're just demonstrating your ignorance. At this point, your parents have wisdom you just can't have yet and experience that is beyond the years of any young person. Teenagers, you have the biggest challenge, your middle-school or high-school culture tells you that your parents are out of it, that they just don't get the world you live in. You may think your job is just to keep them happy enough to stay out of your business and let you live the way you want. But I encourage you to rethink that mentality. God gave you the parents you have; they were His choice for you. And almost without exception, they're what you need and no one knows you better than they do.

So honor them by accepting them and thanking God for them; honor them by speaking well of them to your friends; honor them by listening to their perspective. Some of their warnings about who you spend your time with and the choices you make actually might save you from a lot of pain. Honor them by talking to them. A grunt here, a nod there is probably not enough. Dr. D. James Kennedy says that to honor parents means children should hold their parents in the highest esteem, both in their tone of voice and the attitude of their heart with respect to their communication to their parents.[301] Honor them by telling them the truth. Here is the answer to the $100,000 question: "Does this apply to me after I leave the home?" Yes it does; from birth to earth you are to honor your parents. As long as they are alive, you are to honor them.

How can we honor our parents when our parents are elderly? This is really the primary focus of this commandment. Honor your father and mother means more than simply to obey your parents. This commandment was addressed primarily to adults.[302] As adults, you should, with an attitude of responsibility, honor your parents. Though you may be on your own, this still applies. You honor your parents by attending to their needs. This commandment focuses not on children being obedient to their parents but rather on care for aged parents who are beyond their productive years and cannot work.[303] Most people think this is a commandment for children and teens. It is that too, but the weight of it falls to those who are adults. It's for people in their thirties, forties, fifties, and even sixties. Many scholars believe the fifth commandment was primarily meant for adults with older parents.[304] Remember, in those days there was no Social Security system, and several generations would live together under one roof. If their kids didn't care for them, they were sunk! Honoring our parents means we take responsibility for their care. J.I. Packer said, "Children do in fact owe their parents a huge debt of gratitude for years of care and provision."[305] When Jesus saw Pharisees refusing to care for their parents because of money they said was devoted to God, He accused them of breaking the fifth commandment (Matthew 15:3-9):

> And why do your traditions violate the direct commandments of God? For instance, God's law is "Honor your father and mother; anyone who reviles his parents must die." But you say, "Even if your parents are in need, you may give their support money to the church instead." And so, by your man-made rule, you nullify the

direct command of God to honor and care for your parents. You hypocrites! Well did Isaiah prophesy of you, "These people say they honor me, but their hearts are far away." Their worship is worthless, for they teach their man-made laws instead of those from God.[306]

Jesus took issue with this tradition by teaching that the honoring of parents was one of the weightier commandments.[307] Honoring your parents means you make sure they're taken care of. It also means you continue to give them weight and value in your life, continue to spend time with them, talk to them, and listen to them. Too many are just waiting around for an inheritance.

When we honor our parents in this way, we honor God. Leviticus 19:32 says: "You shall rise up before the gray headed and honor the aged, and you shall revere your God; I am the LORD."[308] In our society today, we have Medicare, Medicaid, Social Security, and so on. While these are good in their place, no government program can honor your parents for you. The shame in America today is how we treat our parents, the aged, of our society. We put them on a shelf, out of the way. The Bible has not placed your parents in the government's hands, but yours; it's your job to care for your parents and grandparents. "We should honor our parents today by making sure they are taken care of when they can no longer take care of themselves."[309] In Dr. D. James Kennedy's book, *Why the Ten Commandments Matter*, he directs the understanding that as the family goes, so goes the nation. He gives the understanding that as children treat their parents, they will treat and act accordingly as citizens of the nation.[310]

Here is the family cycle: As children, our parents care for us, not leaving us to the government or society. When we become adults, we are to take care of our parents when they can no longer take care of themselves. Aristotle said, "Our parents have the first claim on us for maintenance, since we owe it to them as a debt, and to support the authors of our being stands before self-preservation in moral nobility."[311] Here is what the apostle Paul said concerning caring for the needs of the elderly among us (1 Timothy 5:3-4, 8):

Give proper recognition to those widows who are really in need. But if a widow has children or grandchildren, these should learn first of all to put their religion into practice by caring for their own family and so repaying their parents and grandparents, for this is pleasing to God.... If anyone does not provide for his relatives, and especially for his immediate family, he has denied the faith and is worse than an unbeliever.[312]

As Jesus was dying on the cross, He looked down and spoke to one of His disciples, John, and in the middle of saving the world and redeeming all of mankind, He paused to care for His mother (John 19:26-27): "Jesus saw his mother and the disciple he loved standing there; so he said to his mother, 'He is your son.' Then he said to the disciple, 'She is your mother.' From that time the disciple took her to live in his home."[313] His complete obedience to the fifth commandment demonstrates that it includes caring for our parents in their later years.[314]

We need to keep in mind that as we honor our parents, we honor God. As we honor our parents, we model how we ourselves are to be honored as parents. And, depending on our stage of life and theirs, the honor we give our parents will take different forms. Some may have this attitude about caring for their father: "My father doesn't deserve to be respected! He was never there for our family; he's a loser; he's a drunk! And the way he treated my mother was inexcusable. How could I ever honor and respect a man like that?" But "this commandment does not say to honor parents only if they are good parents. Even bad parents deserve to be honored if only at a minimal level."[315] Here is what this commandment means for you. Remember that the Bible is full of dysfunctional parents, and their life lessons still speak to us today.

It started with Adam and Eve, who had a son who murdered his brother. And then we have Abraham and Sarah; he passed his wife off as his sister and handed her over to another man to save his own skin. How about Isaac and Rebecca? She manipulated and deceived her husband to secure her favorite son's future. It goes on and on. Dishonorable parents are nothing new.

Maybe the best example in Scripture of how to handle dysfunctional parents comes from the story of two best friends, David and Jonathan. Consider their story: David and Jonathan were spiritual brothers, bound together early in life on the battlefield against the Philistines. But they had bigger problems than the Philistines. Jonathan's father, King Saul, was an angry, insecure, and unpredictable man. During one battle, Saul swore to curse any soldier who ate anything before he avenged his enemies. Jonathan didn't hear his father's oath, and he ate some honey. When Saul heard of it, he said to his son, "You shall surely die!" The other soldiers intervened to save Jonathan's life, but that shows the kind of man Saul was; he'd kill his own son over a mouthful of food.

Saul treated David even worse. At first he loved him, but then he became jealous of him. David was becoming more and more popular, more so than Saul, and so one day Saul tried to nail David to the wall with a spear. When he failed, he then tried to get him killed on the battlefield. He even ordered his son Jonathan to kill him, which clearly put Jonathan in a bind. He knew he was supposed to honor his father, but he also knew murder was wrong. So he did the right thing; he honored God by disobeying his father. He warned David of what his father was up to, and then he confronted his father and said, "Why would you shed innocent blood by killing David without cause?" In doing this, Jonathan wasn't dishonoring his father, but he was honoring him by trying to get him to do the right thing.

As adults, the command to honor parents doesn't mean that we do everything they tell us to do. We have to honor God first. Sometimes we honor our parents the most by trying to preserve their honor and keep them from doing something that will dishonor God.

David faced a similar dilemma. Although Saul wasn't his father, as king he was an authority in David's life. On one occasion, after Saul had been on a manhunt for David, David had a perfect opportunity to kill his pursuer. David's men saw this as a God-thing. They said, "'David, didn't God promise to deliver you from your enemy and make you king? Here's your opportunity. Take advantage of this moment.' But David refused and said, 'The Lord forbid that I should put my hand against the Lord's anointed.'" David was honoring Saul, not because Saul was honorable but because he was in an honorable position by the Lord's choice. When Saul found out that David passed up a chance to kill him, he repented and invited David to make peace with him and return with him. But David refused. He honored Saul as king, but he had learned by repeated experience that he couldn't trust him.

The command to honor our parents doesn't mean that we never set up boundaries in our relationships with them. Submitting to authority never means subjecting ourselves to violence or abuse. There are times to say to a parent, "Because of how you've broken my trust over and over again, at least for now I can't be in a close relationship with you." You honor your parents more by doing that than by allowing them to continue in their destructive ways. Even when boundaries are established and complete obedience is not possible, the parents should still be treated with respect because of God's undergirding principle in His command to honor.[316]

The first thing you need to do is to release your anger by praying for them (Ephesians 4:26-27): "If you are angry, don't sin by nursing your grudge. Don't let the sun go down with you still angry—get over it quickly;"[317] The reason so many people have crummy marriages today is because they've never resolved the anger that they feel toward their parents. And they bring all of that bitterness and dysfunction from childhood with them into the marriage relationship. Deuteronomy 5:16 tells us, "Respect your father and your mother, as I, the LORD your God, command you, so that all may go well with you and so that you may live a long time in the land that I am giving you."[318] The bottom line is that if you honor your parents, the rest of your life will go well. If you don't honor your parents, then it won't go well. This is what the Bible says, and this is what the Bible means. Do we want the rest of our lives to go well? Rhetorically asked, the answer is obviously yes. Then, according to the Word of God, we should honor our parents all of their life as God's Word commands, and in so doing we will experience the key to a long and healthy life.

CHAPTER SEVEN
The Sixth Commandment

PRO-LIFE

Exodus 20:13

"Do not commit murder."[319] What does the sixth Commandment mean; how does it affect us? I'm not a murderer . . . well . . . maybe? Let's come back to that thought later. What we need to understand is that in a world of death and murderous destruction, where people have lost their respect for human life and where we've descended into a baser level in society, God is pro-life. Everything about God is life; in Him is life; He is life. Jesus died so that we could have life and have it more abundantly. And what God is, is what we should be, for according to Genesis 1:27, "God created man in His *own* image; in the image of God He created him; male and female He created them."[320] We were created in His image. John Calvin wrote, "Our neighbor bears the image of God; to use him, abuse, or misuse him is to do violence to the person of God, who images himself in every human soul."[321]

The sixth commandment speaks about murder, the taking of life. In order to be pro-life, we must be anti-murder. So, with that in mind, we discover what God is saying to us about murder in the sixth commandment.

The Abomination of Murder

Murder is an abomination before God, because God values human life. Life is sacred, and murder is detestable before God. Dr. D. James Kennedy states in his book *Why the Ten Commandments Matter*, "Murder is a grievous sin to God because it is an attack upon those who are made in His image. It is an indirect attack on God Himself."[322] Why is it wrong to kill people, but it's okay to kill animals? Value! God has placed the greatest value on human life, above all life. God is pro-life; He believes in life; He gave life; He gives life; He sustains life. He is "the way, the truth, and the life." Life is God's gift by creation and redemption, Jesus gives life and Satan destroys life (John 10:10): "The thief comes only in order to steal, kill, and destroy. I have come in order that you might have life—life in all its fullness."[323] God chose life for us to live, and He wants us to choose life for all. Why is murder an abomination before God? Because of the value God has placed on life.[324]

Our life has value because God created it. Picasso's paintings are ugly in my opinion, yet in 2010 one sold for $106 million.[325] Why? Because it was a Picasso—he painted it, so it had great value just for being a Picasso. In John 1:3 the Word says, "Through him all things were made; without him nothing was made that has been made."[326] And in Genesis 1:1 is stated, "In the beginning God created the heavens and the earth."[327] Notice that "God used the Hebrew word *'elohim*, the most commonly used of the general words for God in the Old Testament. It is the only word for God found in this creation story. The Hebrew word is plural in form but functions grammatically as a singular noun . . . *'elohim* should be translated by a general term . . . descriptive expression meaning 'Creator' or 'Creator God' that may be used in the creation story."[328] It speaks of the triune Godhead being involved in the whole Creation process, especially when it came to human beings. God created and gives life.

Look at Genesis 2:7 for a record of the creation of *physical life*: "Then the LORD God formed a man from the dust of the ground and breathed into his nostrils the breath of life, and the man became a living being."[329] Breath of life . . . not evolution, but the breath of God! "He breathed into his nostrils the breath of life—not that the creator literally performed this act, but respiration being the medium and sign of life, this phrase is used to show that man's life originated in a different way from his body—being implanted directly by God (Ecclesiastes 12:7), and hence in the new creation of the soul Christ breathed on His disciples (John 20:22)."[330] The only thing that can give life value is God. Human life began with one statement in Genesis 1:27: "Let us make man in our image." At that point, because we are made "in His image," human life took on value. We are the only ones created in the image of God. Not random chance but by sovereign choice. You are living because God created you, breathed life into you, and chose you. He put life in you; *God is pro-life*.

God also created *spiritual life* (John 14:6): "Jesus said to him, 'I am the way, and the truth, and the life. No one comes to the Father except through me.'"[331] Supernatural, spiritual life is given by God through Jesus Christ. Christians are not just nice people trying to do better by some creed or code; they are new creatures who have been regenerated supernaturally by Jesus who comes into them with His Spirit and gives them Life—supernatural life.

God created *social life* (John 10:10): "My purpose is to give them a rich and satisfying life."[332]

God created *eternal life* (John 10:27-28): "My sheep listen to my voice; I know them, and they follow me. I give them eternal life, and they shall never perish."[333]

If Jesus gives life, then the life takers are thieves, as stated in John 8:44: "You are of your father the devil, and the desires of your father you want to do. He was a murderer from the beginning."[334] "Thou shalt not kill" is another way of saying we must reject Satan and his lies. He wants to take life and kill it, destroy it, and ruin it. He is *evil*, which is *live* spelled backward, and *lived* is the *devil* turned around. He turns everything all backward. Satan is antithetically against life; he hates man. Why? Man is made in the image of God, and Satan hates God. He vicariously attacks God by attacking us. Satan is a murderer who wants to deceive, destroy, and kill. Murder is an assassination of life; it is an abomination before God. Why? Because it is an attack on God's image. Pro-life is anti-murder; to love life, you must hate murder.

Our life has virtue because God controls it. The same God that created us controls our life functions. He's in charge. Murder denies the sovereignty of God. Only one has the right to take life, and that is God, who gave it. The Bible affirms this for the Christian's life. God never gives the individual the power to execute justice; instead, He commands us to show mercy and put our trust in Him to avenge us in His own time and in His own way.

Murder commits three sins: Murder is transgression against God's law. Murder is stealing, as a thief takes what is not his; and to take a life is to take from God. Murder is also blasphemy, as the murderer takes God's place. Murder is unlawful and unbiblical, and such an action is prohibited.

The Analogy of Murder

To properly analyze murder, we must examine three areas of murder. First we must look at its inception. Murder has always been around as a part of humanity's fall. Satan was a murderer from the beginning. The Old Testament and the New Testament begin with murderers: Cain murdered Abel; Herod murdered the boys of Bethlehem. Remember the context of this commandment. For over four hundred years, life had been marginalized for the Israelites. The Israelites had been treated as less than human. They were treated as slaves and brick makers for four hundred years. The Israelites had seen their people—friends and family members—murdered by Pharaoh and the Egyptians. And now, having been rescued by God and preparing to enter the Promised Land, in this sixth commandment God was calling his people to live differently than what they had experienced themselves—*not to murder but to honor life.*

Second, we need to see the zero intolerance God has for murder (Exodus 20:13): "You shall not murder." Four words, and in Hebrew it's even less. "The commandment is expressed in just two words in the Hebrew, equivalent to 'never murder.'"[335] The King James Version fails to adequately convey God's original command. In it, the words are translated. "Thou shalt not kill." But that's not what the Hebrew text says. Rather, it says, "You shall not murder." This commandment deals with private morality, with an individual unjustly taking the life of another person. The Hebrew language has eight different words for killing, some of which are translated as kill, slaughter, sacrifice, and slay. "The verb חָצַר (*ratsakh*) refers to the unpremeditated or accidental taking of the life of another human being; it includes any unauthorized killing (it is used for the punishment of a murderer, but that would not be included in the prohibition). This commandment teaches the sanctity of all human life."[336] In Genesis 9:6, after the Flood, God re-established His covenant with Noah. He commanded that no one take the life of another, for man is made in His image: "Whoever sheds human blood, by humans shall their blood be shed; for in the image of God has God made mankind."[337] If one took a life, that one's life was to be taken—blood for blood.

Finally, we need to examine the inclusion. What is murder? All murder is killing, but not all killing is murder. There are some allowances for killing given in the Bible, and here are four of them: *Animals* (Exodus 20:24): "Build for me an altar made of earth, and offer your sacrifices to me—your burnt offerings and peace offerings, your sheep and goats, and your cattle."[338] God had animals killed for sacrifices in the Old Testament. Also in Matthew 6:26, we discover that our value is greater than any animal's life: "Look at the birds of the air: they neither sow nor reap nor gather into barns, and yet your heavenly Father feeds them. Are you not of more value than they?"[339] And in Acts 10:13, while Peter was in a vision, the Lord spoke these words to him concerning the animals he had seen: "Get up, Peter, kill and eat!"[340]

Capital punishment is another accepted type of killing (Exodus 21:12): "Whoever hits someone and kills him is to be put to death."[341] Just think of the 9/11 terrorist and those who have wrongfully taken innocent lives. God's Word says they are to be put to death. Remember what Genesis 9:6 states—for those who shed human blood, so also shall their blood be shed. Dr. Mark F. Rooker shares Martin Luther's view: "The sixth commandment prohibits killing by private individuals but does not abrogate that right for governments."[342]

Self-defense is acceptable as well (Exodus 22:2): "If anyone catches a thief breaking in and hits him so that he dies, he is not guilty of murder."[343]

Death by *war* is allowed by God. You may not believe in war, but marriage and becoming a parent just might change your mind. Sometimes war is necessary for the defense of the innocent and the protection of a nation from evildoers. God allowed and even instigated war on countless occasions in the Old Testament. There were times that He instructed Israel to kill everyone they encountered in battle. In Joshua

6:17, when the Israelites were attacking Jericho, God said they were not to spare any accept for Rahab the harlot and her household. It's right to fight when you fight for right. Ecclesiastes 3:8 says there is "a time for war and a time for peace."[344]

The Anatomy of a Murderer

What is murder and how do we define it? The Word is speaking of three areas when it talks about not murdering someone: intentional or direct, indirect, and inward.

The first one is *intentional* murder, those who deliberately take another's life. Remember that the sixth commandment prohibits the intentional killing of another person, the taking of an innocent person's life. Homicide is a big problem in the United States. Every twenty-two minutes in America, a murder occurs. America has the highest homicide rate in the world.

Today's young people have grown up watching terrible scenes of murder: the Columbine shooting, the Virginia Tech shooting, 9/11, and the terrorist mass murders. We have moved from a culture of life to a culture of death. From the many faces of death in the '90s to death all around us in our ... TV, video games, news, actions ... people have become callous to death. The American Psychological Association reports that by the time the average child finishes elementary school, he or she will have watched eight thousand televised murders and a hundred thousand acts of on-screen violence.

Our children are being raised with an anti-life bias. When you teach people they came from animals, they'll act like animals; they'll treat others like animals; they'll view and value others like animals. The spirit of murder is upon America, and murder is an attack on God, for it devalues life. Murder, homicide, is evil and the sixth commandment commands us not to do it.

The sixth commandment prohibits *suicide*: Suicide is self-murder. Suicide is claiming lordship over one's own life. It is the number-two killer of college students. Suicide is the number-three killer of teenagers. More die from suicide than automobile accidents. Suicide is murder; it takes a life that doesn't belong to you. Suicide doesn't end misery; it only multiplies it. Suicide doesn't pay bills or right a wrong, it never healed a hurt or disease, and it brings extreme heartache to those left behind. There are many today who have thought it, attempted it, or are even contemplating it now. When life is difficult, when we despair, when suicide tempts us, we're presented with the challenge to trust in a caring God, a God who loves us.

The unholy cousin of suicide is *euthanasia*—murder by remote control. Euthanasia is commissioning someone else to take your life for you. In April 2001, Holland became the first country to legalize doctor-assisted suicide when the Dutch Senate legalized euthanasia. But only a generation earlier, during the Nazi occupation of the Netherlands, Dutch doctors refused to obey orders to let elderly or terminally ill patients die without further treatment. It took only one generation, in the words of Malcolm Muggeridge, "to transform a war crime into an act of compassion."[345] Today in the Netherlands, thousands of medical patients are killed every year. Actually, voluntary euthanasia has become involuntary as an increasing number of requests for death are coming not from patients but from their family members who want to get rid of them.[346] Even in America, with the likes of Dr. Kevorkian and others, we attempt or border the edges of euthanasia every day. Euthanasia is murder that blinds itself to the preciousness of human life.

The sixth commandment prohibits *feticide*, murder by abortion. This is murder of the most helpless members of our society. Since the Roe v. Wade court case, over forty-three million babies have been aborted in America.[347] J.I. Packer addresses this form of murder quite well:

> As genetic science shows, the fetus is from the moment of conception a human being in process of arriving. The fact that for several months it cannot survive outside the womb does not affect its right to the same protection that other human beings merit, and that it will itself merit after birth. Abortion can only ever be justified (and then only as a necessary evil) when the pregnancy genuinely endangers the mother's life, and as doctors know, there are few such

cases today. Legalizing abortion on other grounds is a social evil, whatever arguments of convenience are invoked.[348]

Abortion isn't new; abortion was popular and common in the ancient world. It was the Jewish people and the early Christians who took a strong stand against the practice of abortion because of their understanding of the sixth commandment and their understanding of the God who gave the commandment. The Supreme Court of the United States ruled in February 1973: "A women has the right to abortion in the first six months of pregnancy as she does with any other minor surgery."[349]

We protect the spotted owls, whales, eagles, gopher turtles, etc., but act as if unborn babies are disposable. Dr. Adrian Rogers said, "The most dangerous place for a child today is in the womb of the mother."[350]

There are many who have thought of abortion, some are facing it, and others have done it. God can forgive those who've failed, and God will help those who are struggling, but you must first see that *abortion* is *murder,* and *murder* is *sin*. We must understand there can be only one reason why abortion is wrong; it takes human life, and that is murder. If you don't believe that, then you can't believe it's wrong. The number of babies murdered is 1.3 million a year, 3,700 a day, equaling forty-three million to date. Proverbs 6:16-17 states: "There are six things which the Lord hates . . . [including] hands that shed innocent blood."[351] Politicians take a stand, but taking a stand is not enough. A stand can open the door for debate for those who have an opposing view. A conviction is not enough. "I was raised . . ." doesn't work. The taking of a life is murder, no matter how it's done. It has been argued, "A fetus is not a person," but God said it is in Jeremiah 1:5: "I chose you before I gave you life, and before you were born I selected you to be a prophet to the nations."[352] Notice what Isaiah said in Isaiah 5:20: "How horrible it will be for those who call evil good and good evil."[353]

"It's my body!" someone says, but is it? God created us and redeemed us. Look at Colossians 1:16: "For through him God created everything in the heavenly realms and on earth. He made the things we can see and the things we can't see."[354] Look as well at 1 Corinthians 6:19-20:

"Don't you know that your body is the temple of the Holy Spirit, who lives in you and who was given to you by God? You do not belong to yourselves but to God; he bought you for a price. So use your bodies for God's glory."[355] "You shall not murder!" Doesn't every child deserve a birthday?

Second, we need to understand *indirect* murders. We must recognize the culpability of our actions . . . the way we live, the way we treat others, and how those actions affect others. Habakkuk 2:12, 15 states: "Woe to him who builds a city with bloodshed and founds a town with violence! Woe to you who make your neighbors drink, who mix in your venom even to make them drunk so as to look on their nakedness!"[356] This speaks of those who contribute to others delinquency. PETA doesn't buy animal skins because they do not want to contribute to a business that kills innocent animals for their fur. Union leaders who support NAFTA buy only products made with the union label. At least that's their story in theory. The liquor industry has killed and destroyed untold millions of lives, and God says the industry is guilty for the deaths that occur every twenty-two minutes, for those maimed every sixty seconds, for the murderous effects alcohol has caused through the people who drink. *Alcohol has many defenders and no defense.*

The tobacco and other related industries have their indirect causes as well. The food and beverage industries are not without their own culpability. The drug industry, legal and illegal, has also been the reason many have lost their lives. The gun and ammunitions industry, though their motto is "Guns don't kill; people kill" must accept its part in this indirect murderous industry. The entertainment industry that develops violence in our young people and the sex industry, which propagates the sale of women and children around the world, have to take responsibility for their actions. These and others like them will probably never answer in a human court of law, but one day they will give an answer to God for their part in the murder of innocent life.

When we don't stand up for what is right, when we don't speak up for right policies and against unjust policies that cost lives, are we too indirectly responsible for murder? Psalm 82:2-5 addresses this situation:

Enough! You've corrupted justice long enough, you've let the wicked get away with murder. You're here to defend the defenseless, to make sure that underdogs get a fair break; your job is to stand up for the powerless, and prosecute all those who exploit them. Ignorant judges! Head-in-the-sand judges! They haven't a clue to what's going on. And now everything's falling apart, the world's coming unglued.[357]

When it's in our power to do good and we don't, will we answer as well? James 4:17 says, "Therefore to him that knoweth to do good, and doeth it not, to him it is sin."[358]

I often wonder how God views our lack of care for those who are dying without care around the world—widows, orphans, and the poor. James 1:27 addresses this: "What God the Father considers to be pure and genuine religion is this: to take care of orphans and widows in their suffering and to keep oneself from being corrupted by the world."[359] World hunger and the tyranny of oppressive nations must not be ignored as though it's not our problem when it's in our power to do something. In 1 John 3:17-18 the Bible says it is our concern and questions the Christianity of those who see it differently: "Now, suppose a person has enough to live on and notices another believer in need. How can God's love be in that person if he doesn't bother to help the other believer? Dear children, we must show love through actions that are sincere, not through empty words."[360] Sounds like pacifism of the heart and hand. . . . You know the old saying "It's not my problem." Dr. Edmund P. Clowney, in his book *How Jesus Transforms the Ten Commandments*, states: "We who are new creatures are all to be ambassadors and administrators of life."[361]

The German Protestant minister Martin Niemoeller wrote:

> They came for the communist, but I wasn't a communist so I didn't object. They came for the socialist but I was not a socialist, so I did not object; they came for the trade leaders; but I was not a trade leader, so I did not object; they came for the union leaders, but I was not a union leader, so I did not object; they came for the Jews, but I

was not a Jew, so I did not object. They came for me, and there was no one left to object.[362]

Finally, there is *inward* murder—New Testament murderers. These are the life destroyers in their hearts. Murder is beyond an action; it's an attitude as well. Here are five kinds of inward murderers. There are those who murder by conscience. Have you ever harbored unjust anger toward another human being? Have you hurled insults, gossip, or name calling at another person? Is there anyone in your life right now with whom you are un-reconciled because you've refused to move through your anger to repentance and forgiveness? Jesus said you can be a murderer by the emotions of your heart (Matthew 5:21-22).

> You have heard that people were told in the past, "Do not commit murder; anyone who does will be brought to trial." But now I tell you: whoever is angry with his brother will be brought to trial, whoever calls his brother "You good-for-nothing!" will be brought before the Council, and whoever calls his brother a worthless fool will be in danger of going to the fire of hell.[363]

C.S. Lewis said, "If you look upon ham and eggs with lust, you have already committed breakfast in your heart."[364] And Jesus said; "If you look upon another person with anger or insult, you have already committed murder in your heart." The apostle John said the same thing in 1 John 3:15, "Anyone who hates a brother or sister is a murderer, and you know that no murderer has eternal life residing in him."[365] Clarence Darrow said, "I've never killed anyone, yet I've read many obituaries with great joy."[366] The words you speak or the way you feel may reveal that you have the heart of a murderer.

There is murder by condemnation: Romans 14:10-11 asks: "Why do you criticize or despise other Christians? Everyone will stand in front of God to be judged. Scripture says, 'As certainly as I live, says the Lord, everyone will worship me, and everyone will praise God.'"[367] We can kill with our tongues according to Proverbs 13:2-3: "From the fruit of their lips people enjoy good things, but the unfaithful have an appetite for violence. Those who guard their lips preserve their lives, but those who speak rashly will come to ruin."[368] Proverbs 18:20-21 teaches us that there are consequences for what we say: "You will have to live with the consequences of everything you say. What you say can preserve life or destroy it; so you must accept the consequences of your words."[369] Jewish Rabbinical Law forbids slander, embarrassing a person, humiliation, etc.[370]

There is murder by corruption. Seducing others to sin, by enticing them to do wrong, by setting evil examples and practicing bad principles, by hindering men and women from serving God, by destroying your own life, can be considered murder by corruption. Consider Mark 7:20-23: "It's what comes out of a person that pollutes: obscenities, lusts, thefts, murders, adulteries, greed, depravity, deceptive dealings, carousing, mean looks, slander, arrogance, foolishness—all these are vomit from the heart. There is the source of your pollution."[371]

There is murder by consent. If we could in some way stem the violence when another is making a murderous attack on someone but instead we stand idly by and do nothing, as Paul did (Acts 8:1), we would be guilty of murder by consent. Such a murder could be religiously, racially, or vengefully inspired, but in any case, it is a violation of the sixth command forbidding murder. The Bible says, "Now Saul was consenting to his death."[372] That made him a partaker in the murderous actions of a crazed religious crowd, seeking to destroy the early Christians *and* Christianity.

There is murder by contentment (Ezekiel 3:17-21):

> "Mortal man," he said, "I am making you a watchman for the nation of Israel. You will pass on to them the warnings I give you. If I announce that an evil person is going to die but you do not warn him to change his ways so that he can save his life, he will die, still a sinner, and I will hold you responsible for his death. If you do warn an evil man and he doesn't stop sinning, he will die, still a sinner, but your life will be spared. If a truly good person starts doing evil and I put him in a dangerous situation, he will die if you do not warn him. He will die because of his sins—I will not remember the good he did—and I will hold you responsible for his death. If you

do warn a good man not to sin and he listens to you and doesn't sin, he will stay alive, and your life will also be spared.[373]

Think of the souls of those whom we have never told about Jesus because we were content in our lives, and because of our lethargy we let them die the eternal death of not knowing Jesus Christ as their Savior.

The Antithesis of Murder

To be pro-life is the antithesis of murder. Jesus is pro-life; He came to give life and not to take life. Satan still comes to take life as well as the joy and peace of the life that Jesus gives to His own. John said Jesus is life and His life is our light (John 1:4-5): "In Him was life, and the life was the light of men. And the light shines in the darkness, and the darkness did not comprehend it."[374] Following are some ways we can be actively pro-life.

Live God's love. This is the true fulfillment of all of the law. James 2:8 calls this the royal law: "You do well if you really fulfill the royal law according to the scripture, You shall love your neighbor as yourself."[375] We can do this by living life from the heart and not from the head up (Romans 5:5), "because God has poured out his love to fill our hearts."[376] Therefore, we have been given the power to love our neighbor and thus fulfill all of God's commands. The passage in 1 John 2:5 states: "But whoever obeys what Christ says is the kind of person in whom God's love is perfected. That's how we know we are in Christ."[377] And we should never forget what is said in 1 Peter 4:8: "Most important of all, continue to show deep love for each other, for love makes up for many of your faults."[378]

Breathe God's life. God breathed into Adam the breath of life (Genesis 2:7). Adam was made in God's image. If we have Christ living in us, we are called to breathe His life into this world, to be life givers, especially among those we share our lives with. How's your breath? Do you breathe life or decay? When you walk into a room, are you a life giver or a life taker? Every day, keep the sixth commandment by doing breath checks and forging forward with new life-giving habits.

Finally, become a life giver, not a life taker. Be a Good Samaritan (Luke 10:30-36):

> There was once a man who was going down from Jerusalem to Jericho when robbers attacked him, stripped him, and beat him up, leaving him half dead. It so happened that a priest was going down that road; but when he saw the man, he walked on by, on the other side. In the same way a Levite also came along, went over and looked at the man, and then walked on by, on the other side. But a Samaritan who was travelling that way came upon the man, and when he saw him, his heart was filled with pity. He went over to him, poured oil and wine on his wounds and bandaged them; then he put the man on his own animal and took him to an inn, where he took care of him. The next day he took out two silver coins and gave them to the innkeeper. "Take care of him," he told the innkeeper, "and when I come back this way, I will pay you whatever else you spend on him."[379]

The robbers broke the commandment by harming the man and putting his life in jeopardy; they were takers. The religious people broke the commandment by not doing anything; they were fakers. They were too busy or too self-absorbed and disinterested to save a life. Sometimes all it takes to murder is to do nothing at all—to just allow someone to die without doing anything to prevent death. The Samaritan kept the commandment. He got involved even though it was an inconvenience. He didn't let the idea of getting messy stop him from binding up the man's wounds, and he didn't let the fact that this wounded stranger was someone outside his people group stop him from saving his life, at great cost to himself. He was a maker—a life giver.

Jesus is the ultimate Good Samaritan who got messy and laid down His life to give you life. It cost Him everything to rescue you. Who are you going to rescue? Our city is a Jericho full of people half-dead on the side of the road. What do you have a burden for—foster care, the unemployed, pro-life causes, unwed mothers, the homeless, the poor, the lonely? Get involved; get messy. "Do not commit murder." Murder is an action by a person to a person, but so is the giving of life. Be a life giver, not a taker.

CHAPTER SEVEN:
The Sixth Commandment
Pro-Life

The ultimate act of murder is *deicide*—the killing of God. Maybe you're not guilty of murder as stated, yet we're all guilty of this one. "Jesus died for our sins." My sins murdered Jesus.[380]

You're as guilty as anyone who ever murdered another. Remember that three of the most recognizable personalities in the Bible were all murderers—Moses, David, and Paul. The good news is that by the killing of one man—the Son of man—God can forgive the sin of murder. That's the good news of Jesus Christ, who is so pro-life that He was willing to die to give us life eternal, and I am so grateful to Him for it.

CHAPTER EIGHT

The Seventh Commandment

SEX OFFENDERS

Exodus 20:14

"You shall not commit adultery"[381] is not merely a suggestion, nor is it arbitrary, but it is commanded without equivocation. It's not just a good way to a better life, although it is that too. But more particularly, it is God's law to liberate and protect. Protect what? The family and life! This is the paradox of human nature, the flesh wanting what is spiritually forbidden by God. Adultery is a violation of the sanctity of the family, as murder is a violation of the sanctity of life. The family is the foundation of human society, and marriage is the highest earthly form of relationship. Adultery is a crime against God, the family, and society in general. God demands fidelity in marriage and life and sexual purity from all of His children.

To commit adultery is, as God sees it, a sex crime, a sexual offense. In today's society you can Google sex offenders and find a registry on the Internet. Many have tried it and found things they didn't want to know about those who are living in their community. What if everyone who commits adultery was on that list of sex offenders for their offense against God, the family and society; and what if we were to see adultery as God sees it, all sexual misconduct? We would act quite differently in life and our approach to sexual misconduct.

The sexual revolution of the '60s was an all-out assault on the seventh commandment.[382] The seventh commandment is scorned, ridiculed, and belittled. It's considered outdated and archaic, old-fashioned and irrelevant. We hear so much about consenting adults that if we're not careful we will begin to consent to it and accept it. This so-called revolution stood against the rules of morality. It's my body . . . I'm free . . . yet it has enslaved us and ruined more homes, hearts, and lives than any other revolution. Dr. J. Vernon McGee stated, "We are living today in the middle of a sex revolution. Sex is certainly not new, but it is still adultery when it is committed outside of wedlock. God makes this very clear. Man may think he has changed this commandment but he has not. This commandment still stands."[383] The church no longer speaks out against it as it should, and the family and society has suffered because of the church's silence. I have seen people die with sexual diseases, marriages destroyed, families devastated, churches divided, leaders fall, and untold damage and devastation.

Though the seventh commandment deals primarily with the act of physical adultery (extramarital affairs), I believe we'll learn it ultimately addresses all sex offenders, those who commit fornication, those who engage in behavior deviant to the Word, and those who look at and lust in a sexual way. Here are five biblical truths concerning the seventh commandment and sex offenders as the Bible enlightens us. Remember that God's laws serve not to bind us but to liberate us and bring us life. Psalm 119:130 states, "The entrance of thy words giveth light; it giveth understanding unto the simple."[384]

God's Plan Concerning Sex

God has given you a drive called sex; it's necessary and natural. Properly controlled and expressed within marriage, it is beautiful and fantastic. But outside of marriage, it is destructive and detrimental to your health—emotionally, physically, and spiritually. Following are three scripturally outlined areas concerning God's plan for sex.

The *boundaries* of His plan are simple—marriage only! In Hebrews 13:4, we discover this truth: "Let marriage be held in honor among all, and let the marriage bed be undefiled."[385] In marriage God wants us to use sex as a tool for building a marriage and family, not to destroy it. God thought up sex. It's His idea. Marriage can be most exciting when each person seeks to meet the needs of the spouse. God has established the rules. We win when we follow them. Notice what is said in Genesis 2:18-24:

> Then the LORD God said, "It is not good for the man to live alone. I will make a suitable companion to help him." So he took some

soil from the ground and formed all the animals and all the birds. Then he brought them to the man to see what he would name them; and that is how they all got their names. So the man named all the birds and all the animals; but not one of them was a suitable companion to help him. Then the LORD God made the man fall into a deep sleep, and while he was sleeping, he took out one of the man's ribs and closed up the flesh. He formed a woman out of the rib and brought her to him. Then the man said, "At last, here is one of my own kind—Bone taken from my bone, and flesh from my flesh. 'Woman' is her name because she was taken out of man." That is why a man leaves his father and mother and is united with his wife, and they become one.[386]

This is God's earthly plan for a heavenly marriage. The plan of God for a man and a woman is that a man shall *leave* father and mother, *cleave* to his wife, and they become one (see v. 24 KJV).

That tells us three things: First of all, the *priority of marriage*. Marriage is the highest priority of all relationships, and we should leave behind all others and place our marriage as our priority. Second, the *permanence of marriage* is to cleave, as to weld or permanently adhere to. Look into the New Testament words of Christ in Mark 10:9: "What therefore God has joined together, let no man separate."[387] God put together marriage—"until death do us part." If divorce is an option, then it's a probability. Notice the order: leave and cleave. Adultery is when you cleave before you leave.

Third is the *purpose of marriage,* to become "one flesh." That's more than a sexual union; it's holistic to the trichotomy of a person. It speaks of when the two are joined spiritually and emotionally as well as physically, and the first two mentioned should come first. It takes two now to make one, as a violin and bow must accompany each other to make music, so it is with a man and woman in marriage. Marriage is not a contract but a covenant whereby, according to Mark 10:8, "'the two will become one flesh.' So they are no longer two, but one flesh,"[388] forming a holy union in Christ. To simplify it, God's plan for sex, marriage, and the family is one man, one wife, one life, just one time. It's much like what is supposed Adam answered when Eve asked him, "Do you love me only?" and Adam reaffirmed, "As far as I'm concerned, you're the only girl in the world."

What are the *benefits* of God's plan for sex? Go back to the beginning and look at Genesis 1:28: "Then God blessed them and said, Be fruitful and multiply. Fill the earth and govern it. Reign over the fish in the sea, the birds in the sky, and all the animals that scurry along the ground."[389] This tells us three things about the benefits of sex according to God's Word. They are threefold: *Pleasure*: "Be fruitful." *Procreation*: "Multiply and replenish the earth." *Protection*: Sex according to God's plan keeps people from sinning against God. The apostle Paul said in 1 Corinthians 7:2, "But because of the temptation to sexual immorality, each man should have his own wife and each woman her own husband."[390]

Last, let's look at the *barriers* of God's plan concerning sex. What are the barriers outside of the seventh commandment? All sex outside of marriage is wrong; "shall not commit adultery"—there can be no exceptions at any time in any way. God's Sex Education 101 class is simple: Don't do it. *Do what?* is the question for many. Help me to know what *it* is. What does adultery include? *Harpers Bible Dictionary* says:

> Pre-Marital Sex—Fornication, (Gk. porneía "unchastity")—any type of illicit sexual activity. Included in the realm of sexual misconduct in the OT are seduction, rape, sodomy, bestiality, certain forms of incest, prostitution (male or female), and homosexual relations (Lev. 18; 19:20-22, 29; 20:10-21). The specific sin of adultery, related to marriage, was considered more serious than the others, however, so that a special set of laws governed it. In the NEW TESTAMENT, almost any form of sexual misconduct (that is, sexual activity outside the marriage relationship) could be designated as fornication or "immorality"[391]

Eerdmans Dictionary of the Bible states:

> In general, illicit sexual intercourse (Heb. zānâ), a sin violating the spirit of the Seventh Commandment (Exod. 20:14), which was meant to protect the integrity of the family. Fornication (Gk. porneía) can be linked with adultery (Matt. 5:32; 19:9) or distinguished from it (15:19 = Mark 7:21). Committing fornication is noted and rebuked

(1 Cor. 6:18; 10:8; Jude 7). Paul advised monogamous marriage "because of cases of sexual immorality" (1 Cor. 7:2). Metaphorically, fornication can describe the corruption of God's people with pagan idolatry (e.g., Jer. 2:20-36; Ezek. 16:15-43; Rev. 2:14, 20-22; 17:1-18; 18:2-9). Abstaining from fornication (unchastity) was one of the four conditions demanded of the Gentiles for their admission into the Church by the Jerusalem conference (Acts 15:20, 29).[392]

Some commentaries state that all forms of foreplay and mental involvement that lead to illicit sex are fornication. Upon careful examination of *The Pulpit Commentary* we discover similar findings, "Here again we have the inestimable advantage of our Lord's comment on the commandment, to help us to understand what it ought to mean *to us*. Not only adultery, but fornication—not only fornication, but impurity of any and every kind—in act, in word, in thought—is forbidden to the Christian."[393]

Finally, in Matthew Henry's Commentary these words confirm our earlier findings of what adultery is:

> The seventh commandment concerns our own and our neighbor's chastity: Thou shalt not commit adultery, v. 14. This is put before the sixth by our Saviour (Mk. 10:19): Do not commit adultery, do not kill; for our chastity should be as dear to us as our lives, and we should be as much afraid of that which defiles the body as of that which destroys it. This commandment forbids all acts of uncleanness, with all those fleshly lusts which produce those acts and war against the soul, and all those practices which cherish and excite those fleshly lusts, as looking, in order to lust, which, Christ tells us, is forbidden in this commandment, Mt. 5:28.[394]

Don't look, lust, touch, or take; in fact, Jesus said in Matthew 5:28, "But I say to you that everyone who looks at a woman with lust for her has already committed adultery with her in his heart."[395] Go back to Hebrews 13:4 and read the rest of the scripture, "God will judge those who are immoral and those who commit adultery."[396] Paul mentions fornication first in list of sins in 1 Corinthians 5:11: "But now I have written unto you not to keep company, if any man that is called a brother be a fornicator, or covetous, or an idolater, or a railer, or a drunkard, or an extortioner; with such an one no not to eat."[397] And in Colossians 3:5: "Therefore put to death your members which are on the earth: fornication, uncleanness, passion, evil desire, and covetousness, which is idolatry."[398]

Adultery includes extra-marital sex, willful sexual intercourse with someone other than one's husband or wife. This is both physical and emotional according to Jesus in Matthew 5:28: "But I say to you that whoever looks at a woman to lust for her has already committed adultery with her in his heart."[399]

Un-marital sex, such as homosexuality is included in this list; any sex at any time of any kind with the same sex is sinful sex before God. The seventh commandment forbids all violations of God's boundaries for sexuality of any kind of illegal sex. Of course, homosexuality has been a huge issue in our culture the last few years. Many TV shows now have characters that are gay or lesbian, along with characters that are involved in pre-marital sex and adultery. According to Princeton University's National Opinion Research Counsel only about one percent of the population is actively homosexual.[400] According to that same study, seventy-four percent of male homosexuals have more than one hundred partners in their lifetime; forty-one percent have more than five hundred; and twenty-eight percent had more than one thousand.[401] He goes on to say, "Promiscuity among homosexual men is not a mere stereotype, and it is not merely the majority experience—it is virtually the only experience.[402] But, of course, this is nothing new. Homosexuality permeated ancient Greek society."[403] The study continues by saying, "Fourteen out of the first fifteen Roman Emperors were actively homosexual, with the Emperor Nero himself publicly marrying his male lover Sporus with an imperial wedding in Rome."[404] The Bible consistently calls same-sex activity a violation of God's boundaries for our sexuality.

Two things we should never do concerning the barriers of sex: *Don't downplay it.* Many in today's generation not only commit sexual sins, but they also won't admit it. Look at Proverbs 30:20: "This is how an unfaithful wife acts: she commits adultery, has a bath, and says, 'But I haven't done anything wrong!'"[405] We play word games; instead of calling it adultery, it's a fling, or we're just fooling around. How about this one, it's only an affair; and thus we dignify the wrong of adultery as though it is some small thing. *Don't disguise it either*. Too often people hide it as if no one sees it, as is described in Job 24:15: "The eye of the adulterer watches for dusk; he thinks, 'No eye will see me,' and he keeps his face concealed."[406] God said you can keep it from everyone and call it anything else, but He sees it and knows all about it. Call it what God calls it, *sin*. And we need to remember what Ezekiel 18:20 says: "The soul that sinneth, it shall die."[407]

Man's Problem With Sex

Sex is the strongest desire known to man, but God said to control it, put it under submission to His will for our lives according to His Word. Robert Wright's book *The Moral Animal* suggests that "men are genetically predisposed to sleep around." According to Wright, "It's in a man's best interest from an evolutionary perspective to impregnate as many women as possible to ensure that he passes his genes to the next generation."[408] Jane Weaver of MSNBC reported, "About one in five adults in monogamous relationships, or twenty-two percent, have cheated on their current partner. The rate is even higher among married men. And nearly half of people admit to being unfaithful at some point in their lives, according to the results of the MSNBC.com/iVillage Lust, Love & Loyalty survey."[409] *Readers Digest* said that fifty percent of all husbands and thirty-five percent of all wives have committed adultery. And Dr. Annette Lawson, a sociologist affiliated with the Institute for Research on Women and Gender at Stanford University, said, "Various studies suggest adultery has been increasing, with twenty-five to fifty percent of married women and fifty to sixty-five percent of married men now having at least one liaison at some time in a marriage."[410] Why? The influence of the physical and emotional desire is usually greater than the spiritual control we have in our lives.

Where do these influences come from? Society's influences are very strong on our decision-making process of our approach concerning sex. When you consider our society—the things that entertain us, the things we read about, and the loose and relaxed attitudes toward sex, it is a wonder than anyone can resist the temptation! We see it in ads, television, movies, music, pornography, clothing styles, and dancing; we talk about it at work, among friends, and on talk shows. Sex is everywhere, and sex sells. All of these things arouse sexual interest and desire in a person. I believe that it's not only the influence of society that causes mankind such great problems concerning sexual offenses against God, but also the Church's lack of influence. Dr. Laura Schlessinger wrote, "We have become a society that is increasingly reluctant to make any judgments about sexual behavior."[411] In Matthew 5:14-16 Jesus said, "You are the light of the world. A city that is set on a hill cannot be hidden. Nor do they light a lamp and put it under a basket, but on a lampstand, and it gives light to all who are in the house. Let your light so shine before men, that they may see your good works and glorify your Father in heaven."[412]

Illegal sex is three things to man: First of all it is *divisive*. Jesus addressed the seventh commandment in Matthew 5:27-28, "You have heard that it was said, 'You shall not commit adultery.' But I say to you that everyone who looks at a woman with lust has already committed adultery with her in his heart." Can't I look and not lust? Yes, but be careful; sexual sin happens in the mind long before it ever happens in the flesh. In verse 28, the word *looks* is a progressive present tense verb, meaning an ongoing situation. The literal sense is this: "If any man continues to lust after a woman . . . " Adultery doesn't begin in the bed but in the mind. Guard your mind . . . heart . . . body in purity, in the home. Keep the conscience free from the consequences of sexual sin. I've heard it all, and it's all bad. It's divisive. The R. Fausset Jamieson commentary states:

> We are not to suppose, from the word here used—"adultery"—that our Lord means to restrict the breach of this commandment to married persons, or to criminal intercourse with such. The expressions, "whosoever looketh," and "looketh upon a woman," seem clearly to extend the range of this commandment to all forms of impurity, and the counsels which follow—as they most certainly were intended for all, whether married or unmarried—seem to confirm this. As in dealing with the sixth commandment our Lord first expounds it,

and then in the four following verses applies His exposition (5:21-25), so here He first expounds the seventh commandment, and then in the four following verses applies His exposition (Mt 5:28-32).[413]

The standard that Jesus sets for us is not an easy one because there is a steady stream of sexual immorality in everything from books, to magazines, to TV shows and commercials, to movies, to music, to the Internet that are constantly calling for us to "look lustfully," as Jesus put it. We've all heard it said, "Looking never hurt anyone, does it?" Yes it does, and it's destroying the mind of this nation. Pornography in the United States is a $12 to $13 billion a year industry[414]—greater than the combined revenues of the NHL, NBA, NFL, MLB.[415]

Following are four divisive steps that lead to sexual sin that comes out of the Old Testament story of David and his sin with Bathsheba in 2 Samuel 11:2-4:

> Late one afternoon, David got up from a nap and was walking around on the flat roof of his palace. A beautiful young woman was down below in her courtyard, bathing as her religion required. David happened to see her, and he sent one of his servants to find out who she was. The servant came back and told David, "Her name is Bathsheba. She is the daughter of Eliam, and she is the wife of Uriah the Hittite." David sent some messengers to bring her to his palace. She came to him, and he slept with her. Then she returned home.[416]

Distraction: First you notice. It gets your attention. *Attraction*: Next you are drawn to it; it has appeal, and you give it your attentiveness. *Interaction*: You pursue and plan out your sin because it is attractive and has your allowance, at least in your mind. *Transaction*: Now comes the real problem; you're participating, and the sin has your allocation. You began with "just looking," and today you're in the trap of sexual sin. Most of us say, "Not me, I would never; it couldn't happen with me." But it does, much too frequently, and we are not immune. Remember the words of the apostle Paul in 1 Corinthians 10:12, "Wherefore let him that thinketh he standeth take heed lest he fall."[417] To preserve purity, we must guard what we look at as taught in Psalm 101:3: "I will set nothing wicked before my eyes."[418] Eyes are windows to the mind, and the mind is the door to the soul, and it all starts with a look.

Second, illegal sex is *deceptive:* In a society that glamorizes adultery and whose role models plaster the front pages of the tabloids with news of all their illicit lovers, we become conditioned to think that such is both normal and desirable. It hides many of its consequences. It offers pleasure without responsibility, and gratification without commitment. Young people are persuaded to "prove their love" with sex. Fornication promises that no one will know. Don't be deceived by its lies; God will know. Look closely at 1 Peter 3:12: "For the eyes of the Lord are on the righteous, and his ears are open to their prayer."[419] The Bible paints the true picture of adultery. Look at the wisdom of Solomon in these passages. Proverbs 5:3: "For the lips of the adulterous woman drip honey, and her speech is smoother than oil."[420] Proverbs 7:21: "With much seductive speech she persuades him; with her smooth talk she compels him."[421] Look at Proverbs 6:25-26: "Don't be tempted by their beauty; don't be trapped by their flirting eyes. A man can hire a prostitute for the price of a loaf of bread, but adultery will cost him all he has."[422] Examine Proverbs 7:26-27 as well: "Many are the victims she has brought down; her slain are a mighty throng. Her house is a highway to the grave, leading down to the chambers of death."[423]

The price of free love is not so free, as one stated some years ago: "Sin will take you further than you wanted to go; it will cost you more than you wanted to pay; and it will keep you longer than you wanted to stay."[424] This is echoed in Proverbs 2:16-19: "To deliver you from the immoral woman, from the seductress who flatters with her words, who forsakes the companion of her youth, and forgets the covenant of her God. For her house leads down to death, and her paths to the dead; none who go to her return, nor do they regain the paths of life."[425] Adultery is full of empty promises. It promises pleasure, love, and fulfillment, but in the end it gives pain, suffering, and destruction.

Third, illegal sex (sexual sin) is *destructive. Adulterate* means "to make impure." Adultery corrupts, adultery is sin, and sin destroys. Here are four ways sexual sin is destructive: *It is physical sin*—a sin against one's *self.* Look at 1 Corinthians 6:18: "Flee sexual immorality. Every sin that a man does is outside the body, but he who commits sexual immorality sins against his own body."[426] No sin is more damaging to yourself than adultery, fornication, homosexuality, lesbianism, pornography. You are sinning against your body, but you are also sinning against your soul and mind, as well as your heart. Notice verses 19-20: "Do you not know that your body is the temple of the Holy Spirit who is in you, whom you have from God, and you are not your own? For you were bought at a price; therefore glorify God in your body and in your spirit, which are God's."

Your body is not yours; it is the temple of the Holy Spirit. It's not your body to do as you please, but God has the right, the ownership of who you are, and you are obligated to allow Him to direct your life in obedience to Him. If our bodies are His temple, and they are, we must align ourselves with His will for our bodies, and that includes no illegal sex.

It is a marital sin—a sin against the home (Proverbs 27:8): "A person who strays from home is like a bird that strays from its nest."[427] Dr. Kent Hughes said, "The man who commits adultery says this to his children, your mother is not worth much, and your father is a liar and a cheater. Honor is not as important as pleasure; in fact, my own satisfaction is more important than you are."[428] Sexual sins destroy the very foundation of the family. Homes are being torn apart because of the pervasive problem with pornography and free sex, which is ultimately not so free, for the price is the family and its well-being.

It is a social sin—a sin against Church and society. Examine Romans 14:7: "For not one of us lives for himself, and not one dies for himself"[429] and 1 Corinthians 6:15 as well: "You know that your bodies are parts of the body of Christ. Shall I take a part of Christ's body and make it part of the body of a prostitute?"[430] Further, according to William Barclay in his writing on the Ten Commandments, "The fall of nearly every great empire was the sin of sexual immorality. Greece, Rome, Egypt, Babylon . . ."[431] and now America. The sexual offenses of this nation will one day destroy it if we don't change as a nation and turn away from our sexual sins. The weight of our sin is pressing against the dam of God's grace.

Judgment is coming one day as stated in Proverbs 14:34: "Righteousness makes a nation great; sin is a disgrace to any nation." Going back to the Old Testament, a careful look at Deuteronomy 22:22 discloses God's warnings to the nation of Israel concerning the impending destruction for their previous and ongoing sins. God was saying to the nation, "You must purge the evil from Israel. Put away this evil so your land can survive." And that is what must be done in America today. We must put away this evil if we are to survive as a nation.

It is a spiritual sin—a sin against God. In Genesis 37—50 we read the story of Joseph. His boss's wife continually attempted to seduce him. Notice his words in answer to her advancements, "I would be sinning against you, me, my family, my people . . . but most of all against God!" (39:8-9). Proverbs 6:32 states: "Adultery is a brainless act, soul-destroying, self-destructive."[432] King David of the Old Testament, after he sinned with Bathsheba, wrote Psalm 51:4. Notice that he said, "Against You, You only, have I sinned, and done this evil in Your sight."[433]

The Ten Commandments are not advice but laws of God, and a law without penalty is only advice! A pure life is not optional; if you're not sexually pure, then you have no right to call yourself a Christian. Look at what 1 Corinthians 6:9-10 says: "Do you not know that wrongdoers will not inherit the kingdom of God? Do not be deceived! Fornicators, idolaters, adulterers, male prostitutes, sodomites, thieves, the greedy, drunkards, revilers, robbers—none of these will inherit the kingdom of God."[434] Also, examine Ephesians 5:5: "For this ye know of a surety, that no fornicator, nor unclean person, nor covetous man, who is an idolater, hath any inheritance in the kingdom of Christ and God."[435] The apostle Paul, who wrote these passages, knew that sexual sin would separate us from God and ultimately lead to one's own destruction, while blocking the path to heaven. This is underscored in Numbers 32:23: "Be sure your sin will find you out."[436] God's Word says you cannot get away with it. In Revelations 21:8 we see with great clarity the final destination for those who do such things without repentance. "But cowardly, unfaithful, and detestable people, murderers, sexual sinners, sorcerers, idolaters, and all liars will find themselves in the fiery lake of burning sulfur. This is the second death."[437] God said its sin and He will punish all offenders. I have heard many people make this statement in my twenty-five years of pastoring: "I don't feel any conviction." My response is as the Word states, "You're not one of His then." Look at what Hebrews 12:5-6 says:

> My dear child, don't shrug off God's discipline, but don't be crushed by it either. It's the child he loves that he disciplines; the child he embraces, he also corrects. God is educating you; that's why you must never drop out. He's treating you as dear children. This trouble you're in isn't punishment; it's training, the normal experience of children.[438]

He disciplines and chastises His; those He doesn't are illegitimate.

A Biblical Prevention Plan for Man

The prevention to adultery and sexual offenses is to first of all *make a commitment* to God's standards. God's Word is the rule of law for living. The Bible says that sex is for marriage only, not before marriage, not outside of marriage, not extramarital, not any other way but God's way. Notice Psalm 119:9, 11: "How can young people keep their lives pure? By obeying your commands. . . . I keep your law in my heart, so that I will not sin against you."[439] The key to a pure and holy life before God is to first make a commitment to living by God's laws in our life.

Adultery should never be an option for our life. There is no justification for it. Joseph could have given in when tempted by Potiphar's wife. He could have reasoned "I'm young, attractive, single, I'm in a foreign country, it's acceptable in this society, she wants it, I desire it, it might help me in my career, I am emotionally scarred, my brothers hate me, sold me into slavery, my mother died when I was young, I've had a terrible life, and I've been deprived of love." Simply put, he could have said "I *deserve* it!" But instead, Joseph turned and ran. He said, "I will not sin against my God." Look at Proverbs 5:15: "You should be faithful to your wife, just as you take water from your own well."[440] God tells us to not allow adultery to ever be an option *and* to stay with the wife we have. As someone once said, "I'm dancing with the one I brought to the dance."

Not only should we make a commitment, but we also need to *magnify the consequences* of sexual sin. Be conscious of the consequences; remind yourself of the devastation that is caused by sexual sin. The shame never goes away. The sense of loss to everyone is enormous. Proverbs 6:26 says, "A man can hire a prostitute for the price of a loaf of bread, but adultery will cost him all he has."[441] Adultery is basically selfishness, because the adulterer says, "Forget how it hurts others, I want sexual gratification." Instead of working to improve your sexual relationship with your spouse, you seek after the image of sex given by Hollywood or the Internet. One counselor said that pornography has become so prevalent in the lives of men that it is tearing marriages apart. It creates a sexual addiction, an alternate or skewed version of reality.

America is in a mess. Think about our schools; if they taught drug education today like they teach sex education, they would be passing out needles and showing our kids how to shoot up. School leaders think that kids are going to be doing sex anyway so we should show them how to do it safely. God's plans for Sex Ed 101 are marital fidelity, sexual chastity, and complete abstinence outside of marriage.

Third, we need to *maintain our marriage*. A growing relationship with your spouse will reduce the pull and attraction of adultery. Too often we miss the meaning of 1 Corinthians 7:3: "Husbands and wives should satisfy each other's sexual needs."[442] In *His Needs, Her Needs*, Dr. Willard Harley gives the five top needs of most men and the five top needs of most women, which are as listed below.[443]

MEN
1. Sexual Fulfillment
2. Recreational Companionship
3. An Attractive Spouse
4. Domestic Support
5. Admiration

WOMEN
1. Affection
2. Conversation
3. Honesty and Openness
4. Financial Support
5. Family Commitment

Are there any similarities? NO! So what is the solution? Find out what your spouse needs, and set out to meet those needs. When you said, "I do," you thought your spouse would meet these important needs in your life. Unfortunately, many men and women feel cheated and begin to look outside marriage to satisfy these needs. We need to stop pleasing ourselves and start pleasing our spouses according to their needs.

One of the biggest problems in marriages today is the physical relationship. Money, sex, and communication are the top three problems in the marriage today, and of these, sex seems to surface the most. What does God's Word say about this in 1 Corinthians 7:5? "Do not refuse to give your bodies to each other, unless you both agree to stay away from sexual relations for a time so you can give your time to prayer. Then come together again so Satan cannot tempt you because of a lack of self-control."[444] One "scientific" study was done to discover what days men want sex. They discovered that they like days that begin with the letter *T*: Tuesday, Thursday, Today, Tomorrow, Taturday, and Tunday. I know this is but amusing to most, but it is probably true for most men. Here's a decision we should make: "If my mate is going to have a good lover in his/her life, I'm going to be it."

Another thing to note, a great goal in marriage is to become best friends. Mary Alda (wife of actor, Alan Alda) said, "It's real easy to leave your spouse. It's not easy to leave your best friend."[445] Talk together, walk together, and be together. Number one: make a commitment to God's standards. Number two: magnify the consequences of the sin. And number three: maintain your marriage in a biblically healthy way.

The fourth area of prevention is to *manage your mind*. Immorality is a process; there is no such thing as a "one night stand." You are not a moral, upright person one day and the next day an adulterer and fornicator.

Read again Matthew 5:27-28: "You have heard that it was said to those of old, 'You shall not commit adultery.' But I say to you that whoever looks at a woman to lust for her has already committed adultery with her in his heart." Here is the way that I understand what Jesus is saying to us: Thoughts lead to feelings, feeling lead to actions, and actions lead to adultery. It is a degenerative process of destruction. Look at the way James lays it out in James 1:14-15: "But each person is tempted when he is lured and enticed by his own desire. Then desire [*lust*] when it has conceived gives birth to sin, and sin when it is fully grown brings forth death."[446] It's a process; it's how we run the race, either for good or for bad.

Here's how it goes according to James as I outline his four steps to failure:

Step 1: Accepting sinful thoughts in your mind

Step 2: Emotional, non-physical involvement (talking about needs with him/her)

Step 3: Physical involvement. Once this happens, it's really hard to break away. It takes everything you have and the grace of God to manage the breakaway because the passion and power involved in adultery is very strong.

Step 4: Rationalizing the affair. Justification of the sin: "My spouse doesn't pay enough attention to me/understand me."

In agreement with James and Jesus, Jeremiah 17:9 tells us where the problem lies: "The heart is deceitful above all things, and desperately wicked; who can know it?"[447] It's a heart issue, and it's always been the heart that has led us astray from God's perfect plan for our lives. Just look at what the apostle Paul says in 2 Corinthians 10:3-5:

> For though we live in the world, we do not wage war as the world does. The weapons we fight with are not the weapons of the world. On the contrary, they have divine power to demolish strongholds. We demolish arguments and every pretension that sets itself up

against the knowledge of God, and we take captive every thought to make it obedient to Christ.[448]

Our thoughts are developed from the seat of our mind and our emotions. We must manage our mind if we are to live a sexually pure life through prevention.

The fifth area that we need to learn to apply in preventing sexual sin in our lives is *to maintain proper relationships.* Most affairs occur between close personal friends, coworkers, or relatives. How should we maintain proper relationships?

- Never pay compliments that are out of line.
- Never put yourself in a private situation.
- Never chat online/ Facebook/ phone/ text or sexting. To keep from hiding things or the temptation to cover up something that seems innocent or casual, give your spouse your passwords to all electronics. This may not stop bad behavior, but it will certainly cause one to think twice before engaging in it.
- Never touch inappropriately. Be careful of a gentle hug or a soft touch, it could be the beginning of an open door to more.
- Never discuss inappropriate subjects with the opposite sex, it's an open door to the mind to think and communicate bad things.
- Never listen to a member of the opposite sex tell you about his/her marriage problems.
- Women, don't go fishing for compliments. Your husband may not notice if you die your hair green, but that doesn't mean you should look outside marriage for those deep emotional needs. Husbands, watch out what you say to women. If you are not sure what to say, better to say nothing than risk being misunderstood in giving a compliment.
- Avoid a prolonged stare. It's okay for singles to flirt but not married people.

Ephesians 5:3 says, "Since you are God's people, it is not right that any matters of sexual immorality or indecency or greed should even be mentioned among you."[449] As Christians, you and I have an obligation to avoid at all costs those things that will destroy us in the end. If we can start straight, we can stay straight, but if we allow a path that could cause us to veer off the path, it can become the ruination of our lives and families.

Last, when it comes to a biblical prevention plan for man, we need to *minimize the opportunity*. If you don't want to get stung, stay away from the bees. Avoidance is one of the best ways to stay out of trouble. Here are three key areas to practice avoidance.

Number one: We need to *avoid walking near fire*. Solomon surely understood this as he indicated in Proverbs 7:6-27. He realized the danger of sexual sin and tried to warn his son. Solomon tells about a young man he observed as he looked out his window one evening around twilight, as the sun was going down. This young man was walking near the corner of the street where a seductive woman lived. He then took a turn down the street she lived on, walking near her house. Of course, the woman came out to greet him, kissed him, and seduced him by telling him things like, "I came out to meet you; I was looking just for you." She even used religious language to make it sound respectable: "I have my fellowship offering." The fellowship offering was an animal sacrifice offered to God at the Temple, it was cooked there, and part of the meal the person brought back home to eat. In other words, she was saying, "I have this meal with no one to eat it with me." She went on to say she had prepared her bed with the finest perfumes, and her husband was gone away for a long time. In other words, her words were like honey, smooth as oil (5:3). And sure enough, like an "ox going to slaughter" or "like a deer stepping into a noose," as Solomon noted, the man fell for it, hook, line, and sinker.

Whose fault was it that this young man found himself in the arms of this woman? People who fall into sexual sin always start with the same step. They walk near the fire. They pretend that the casual stroll by temptation is innocent. The little office flirtation didn't mean anything. Flipping by the provocative channel on TV is no big deal. Looking at the inappropriate magazines or clicking on the graphic website doesn't hurt anybody. This passage asks us a rhetorical question (6:27): "Can a man scoop fire into his lap without his clothes being burned?"[450] The answer, of course, is no; and what we don't avoid, we may end up regretting.

The second area of avoidance is to *avoid wrong relationships*: One of the most common places people walk near the fire is at the office. The coworker begins paying more attention to you, and you begin to think that person cares more about you than your spouse does. A comment you might hear is "He actually listens to me," or "She treats me better than my wife." Perhaps it becomes a little office flirtation, which you suppose is harmless. If you begin to rationalize your need to spend more time with this person, you are walking too close to the fire, and no good can come from it. Work is one of the easiest places to fall because that is where you have the greatest opportunity. You might be spending large amounts of time with the opposite gender, and generally people are at their best. They look good, they are dressed nice, makeup is on, as well as their kind and friendly mask. I have personally witnessed too many who thought of it as nothing less than office frivolity or friendly laughter; yet they ended up in adultery. For some of them their homes were destroyed, and others were fortunate to find grace in the heart of their spouse. Avoid wrong relationships!

Finally, *avoid pornography*. It usually starts off with glimpses in magazines as a teenager, accidentally clicking on an X-rated website on the Internet, or watching videos in college. As John Holbert stated: "It is astonishing how much network TV is based on flagrant adultery between consenting hot-blooded adults."[451] Pretty soon it increases with the rationale "What will it hurt if I just look?" The Internet is making pornography even more accessible than ever before. "The Nua Internet Survey reports that seventy-five percent of hits on the Web are looking for a porno site."[452] Also, "In 1991—before the birth of the Internet as we know it—there were fewer than ninety porn magazines published in the U.S. Today, more than 2.5 million porn sites are blocked by CYBERsitter. In 2008, approximately one hundred million men in North America logged on to porn."[453]

Doug Stringer, author of *Living Life Well*, wrote, "Pornography is man's greatest seduction and temptation; it will consume every part of one's life and destroy their family and everything they have worked for."[454] It's becoming a major problem. What's wrong with just looking? It's not like it's committing adultery or anything, right? Wrong. Let's go back to Matthew 5:27. When Jesus taught on the commandment "Do not commit adultery," he explained that adultery wasn't just about committing the act, it begins long before that with what we think, what we allow to enter into our mind and, inadvertently, into our heart. Jesus taught, "I tell you that anyone who looks at a woman lustfully has already committed adultery with her in his heart" (Matthew 5:28). It doesn't matter if that woman is in person, on a magazine, a website, a video, or cable, according to Jesus, if the view causes lust within you, you have already committed adultery in your heart.

The images make a permanent mark on the brain, particularly for men. Once you see the image, it is ingrained there for a very long time. For many men, it even becomes addictive and escalates. Pretty soon it goes from looking at magazines to watching videos, then from watching videos to watching more graphic videos. Ted Bundy, the serial killer, who brutally killed more than twenty-four women, told Dr. James Dobson that it all began when he was a teen with pornographic magazines.[455] That was where it started, but it escalated from there. What begins seemingly innocently can and often does escalate. The reason Jesus taught that even thinking lustful thoughts is sin is because those images in our mind will eventually affect our behavior. We compare our spouse to the unrealistic image we have in our brain. Our spouse isn't attractive enough, sexy enough, romantic enough (you fill in the blank), and when they don't meet our unrealistic expectations, we draw farther away from them, and the wedge begins. We get closer to the fire.

Here are three ways to help all of us in avoiding pornography. *Protect your mind.* The eye-gate and the ear-gate are so important. They are the pathways to the mind. The apostle Peter states in 2 Peter 2:14: "With eyes full of adultery, they never stop sinning; they seduce the unstable; they are experts in greed—an accursed brood!"[456] Men, protect your eyes. The Bible says in Psalm 101:3 that we should be careful what we look at: "I will set no wicked thing before my eyes."[457] Job said, "I have made a covenant with my eyes, why then should I think upon a maid?" Get away from music whose theme is predominantly lust and sex.

Don't accommodate sin. If you can't browse the internet and stay pure, then you souldn't look at all! If you can't flip around the channels without looking for something dirty to look at, then cut it off. HBO/Cinemax/Showtime—get them out of your house for fear of what they will bring into your home and heart. If you can't be alone together in that car, then be sure to take along a friend. Romans 13:14 is a powerful passage on how to not accommodate sin: "Make not provision for the flesh, to fulfil the lusts thereof."[458] Peter has a good word for all of us in 1 Peter 2:11 as well: "Abstain from fleshly lusts which wage war against the soul."[459] My favorite may very well be from 1 Thessalonians 5:22: "Abstain from every form of evil."[460] It is here we discover that if it even has the appearance of bad, we should avoid it. That ought to change our thinking completely.

Decide in advance. Make a predetermined decision to stay pure, and that you won't date anyone who hasn't made the same commitment. Remember the words of a fool that have crossed the lips of many a hopeful spouse-to-be: "He'll change after we're married." Make one good decision now that will save you from many bad decisions later. Decide in advance to avoid those who will take you toward things that are contrary to God's Word and will for your life.

God's Power to Restore Sex Offenders

There's still hope for a pathway back from adultery, if you are willing. Adultery (sexual sin) does not have to kill a marriage or ruin a life. Here are five steps that anyone, everyone, who has failed in this area can and should take to make their way back from sexual failure.

Acknowledge the sin. David's prayer in Psalm 51, after he committed adultery, was to first of all acknowledge before God that he had sinned: "I recognize my faults; I am always conscious of my sins."[461]

End the relationship or sinful activity immediately (Psalm 95:7-8): "For he is our God. We are the people he watches over, the flock under his care. If only you would listen to his voice today! The LORD says,

'Don't harden your hearts as Israel did at Meribah, as they did at Massah in the wilderness.'"[462]

Avoid contact with that person or situation from now on. You can't be friends after you've become lovers. No letters, cards, calls, visits. Defriend them and avoid them at all cost. You cannot casually look at what you once lusted for: it will consume you again.

Be converted to the lordship of Jesus Christ. Some of you may feel trapped as a sex offender. Take a close look at the church at Corinth. Every kind of sexual offender was in the church (1 Corinthians 6:9-13):

> Do not be deceived. Neither fornicators, nor idolaters, nor adulterers, nor homosexuals, nor sodomites, nor thieves, nor covetous, nor drunkards, nor revilers, nor extortioners will inherit the kingdom of God. And such were some of you. But you were washed, but you were sanctified, but you were justified in the name of the Lord Jesus and by the Spirit of our God.[463]

Adultery and fornication will keep you out of the Church and heaven. "I was born this way" is too often the excuse of many today. But if God can deliver us from every other area of addiction that once controlled our life, and He can, then He can and will most certainly deliver you from sexual addiction as well. There is nothing God can't deliver you from, and here are six steps to maintaining freedom from sexual addiction. *First of all,* surrender your life to the Lordship of Christ; it's a daily decision; as Paul said in 1 Corinthians 15:31, "I die daily."[464]

Second, we need to put our trust in God, which speaks of our dependence on Him. Let His life empower you. He not only forgives you, but He now also lives in you to enable you. We cannot do it without Him. Jesus said in John 15:5, "Without me ye can do nothing."[465]

Third, we should pour out our love to Christ and our family. This means our complete devotion. Love is a decision that we make every day. The scripture says in Ephesians 5:25: "Husbands, love your wives, just as Christ also loved the church and gave Himself for her," [466] Love them like Christ loved us, in every way to meet every need in our life.

Fourth, grow every day; this addresses our need for ongoing development in our life.

Love is not a diamond we find, but a flower we grow and cultivate. Our honeymoon should last a lifetime, his and hers.

Fifth, guard your company; we need to operate with personal discipline at all times. Look at Proverbs 13:20: "Keep company with the wise and you will become wise. If you make friends with stupid people, you will be ruined."[467] Friends who urge us to do wrong are not friends we need. Watch your eyes; you won't eat garbage, so don't watch it either, and don't live around it. Watch what you watch and flee fornication!

And finally, make up your mind; be determined to living victoriously free from sexual sins in your life. Don't let every situation be circumstantial. Decide to follow Jesus. Have the attitude of Psalms 112:7: "Their hearts are steadfast, trusting in the LORD."[468] Make one big decision, and all the rest will follow: "I have decided!" Remember the decisive words of Joshua in Joshua 24:15: "But as for me and my house, we will serve the LORD." [469]

Be cleansed from your past sexual sins. John 8, describing the story of a woman caught in the act of adultery, may very well describe some of you today and your situation. It may be that you're a sex offender or were one. Remember that it is not the unpardonable sin. God never runs out of mercy and grace. A careful interpretation of 1 John 1:9 helps us to see this: "If we confess our sins, He is faithful and just to forgive us *our* sins and to cleanse us from all unrighteousness,"[470]

> The word *confess* is homologeō (it means, therefore, to say the same thing that God does about that sin, to agree with God as to ὁμολογεω), from *homos* (ὁμος), "the same," and *legō* (λεγω), "to say," thus, "to say the same thing as another," or, "to agree with another." "Confession of sin on the part of the saint means, therefore, to say the same thing God does about that sin, to agree with God

as to all the implication of that sin as it relates to the Christian who commits it and to a holy God against whom it is committed.[471]

Confess—say what God says. If you'll come clean with God, you'll leave cleansed by God. God's plan is purity; but if you fail, God is a God of grace and mercy. You need to change some things that can only come by the power of His unchanging hand, and we should all reach for it. One third-century writer, Origen, took resisting the temptation of sexual sin to the extreme of personal castration.[472] A little over the top perhaps, but it accomplished his goal. I say trust God and serve Him completely.

CHAPTER NINE
The Eighth Commandment
THE POSSESSION PARADOX

Exodus 20:15
"Thou shalt not steal."[473]

Somebody once said the Hebrew slang for this command, "Do not steal," is "Don't jack your neighbor's stuff." If I were to get into a man's pocket and take his billfold with all his money, what would I be? The somewhat humorous answer is "You'd be his wife!" In any other circumstance, however, to take or keep from someone anything or everything, even just one thing, is stealing. To defraud someone is stealing, to take advantage of someone or to do anything that wrongfully benefits you in any situation can be considered stealing. Do not steal is not just number eight on the top ten list, but it is number one on the first sin list. Go back to when Adam and Eve were in the Garden of Eden and took what was not theirs. They took from a tree that was forbidden for them to touch. Adam transgressed in eating the forbidden fruit, and this was the sin whereby he and all his posterity were ruined.[474] It was stealing. J.I. Packer said, "It is not God's will for us to have anything that we cannot obtain by honorable means, and the only right attitude to others' property is scrupulous concern that ownership be fully respected."[475]

Here's the paradox, God's will says that wrong is never right; stealing is wrong even if you are Robin Hood, who took from the rich and gave to the poor. Man's will says, "But I have certain desires in my life that want to be satisfied." The problem is people do steal and in no small way. One little boy was hanging around a fruit stand when the owner asked, "Are you looking to steal an apple?" to which the boy replied, "I'm trying not to steal it, sir." According to Ephesians 4:28, "Those who used to rob must stop robbing and start working, in order to earn an honest living for themselves and to be able to help the poor."[476] There are only three ways to acquire anything: work for it, receive it as a gift, or steal it. The Scripture states that one should stop stealing, start working, and start giving to help others. The problem is, "I want" can only be satisfied by "I have." Now I have a choice to follow the right path of God's plan or to bypass it by breaking the eighth commandment and taking what doesn't belong to me. This is the paradoxical position of life—I want vs. God's will. Dr. D. James Kennedy says: "Stealing is the great American pastime."[477] Stealing is at epidemic levels, the temptation to take and, thus, to break this eighth command. In New York City, there are eight million cats and eleven million dogs. New York City is basically just concrete and steel, so when your pet dies, you can't just go out in the back yard and bury it. The city would dispose of your dead pet, but charges $50. So one lady had this great thought: I can get rid of dead pets for less than that! I'd be providing a service to people in the city and saving them money. She placed an ad in the newspaper saying that she would provide this service for just $25, half what the city charged. Her plan for disposal was brilliant. She would go to the Salvation Army and pay two bucks for an old suitcase. Then she'd pick up the dearly departed pet and put it in the suitcase. She'd hop on the subway, put the suitcase down, and act as if she wasn't watching it. Invariably, a thief would come by and steal her suitcase. Not only did she save money for grieving pet owners, but also she may have rehabilitated a thief or two! This woman was able to use the prevalence of theft to her advantage; she trusted in American greed.[478]

We live every day with the challenges of the paradox of possession, and here are four ways to understand and overcome it.

I Want What I Want and Will Take What I Want
When human desire transcends divine truth, it often creates the problem of stealing. Some may question, "What is stealing?" or "What is the danger in stealing?" First of all, it is a violation of God's law: "Do not

steal." God's laws are for living a righteous life, and when we violate any of them, we will pay both individual and corporate consequences (Romans 6:23): "For the wages of sin is death, but the free gift of God is eternal life in Christ Jesus our Lord."[479] Also notice what Solomon said in Proverbs 14:34: "Righteousness exalts a nation, but sin condemns any people."[480] Look what it did to the human race when Adam and Eve plunged us into sin. We, as the human race, have been paying the price for their sin ever since (Romans 5:12): "Therefore, just as sin came into the world through one man, and death came through sin, and so death spread to all because all have sinned."[481] We can read Achan's explanation of his sin, as recorded in Joshua 7:21: "When I saw among the spoils a beautiful Babylonian garment, two hundred shekels of silver, and a wedge of gold weighing fifty shekels, I coveted them and took them."[482] In this story, we discover what the sin of stealing can do to a nation when just one man engages in such behavior. Achan took what was not his; it was the Lord's, and it cost the nation of Israel greatly.

> Achan's actions, besides violating (1) the Eighth Commandment (about stealing: Exod 20:15), (2) God's instructions in Deut 20:10-20 (see on v. 11), (3) the injunction against lying (Lev 19:11), and (4) the First Commandment (about not having any other gods before the Lord: Exod 20:3; see on v. 1), also directly violated the Ninth Commandment (about coveting: Exod 20:17) ... Achan "saw" (r'h) and "desired" (or "coveted") (ḥmd) and "took" (lqḥ) what was forbidden to them.[483] Because Achan and his family refused to live for the honour of God and the good of God's people, they paid a terrible price (vv. 24-26). They were stoned.[484]

It cost Achan, his family, and Israel as well, and it will cost us. It has cost us already. *US News and World Report* said the following in 1977:

> Merchants this yuletide are bracing for a wave of shoplifting and employee theft that could easily exceed 1 billion dollars. About 500 million dollars will be lost to light-fingered shoppers and another 600 million to pilfering employees this year, according to Gordon Williams of the National Retail Merchants Association. The total will be swollen by another 400 million spent by merchants on loss prevention.[485]

Billions of dollars are lost every year in this country over the theft of goods and services. One estimate says that one out of every fifty-two shoppers carries something out of the supermarket for which they haven't paid. According to the U.S. Department of Commerce, four million people are caught shoplifting every year. But for every one caught, thirty-five others get away with it. This means that there are over 140 million incidents of shoplifting every year in America! What's shocking is that only ten percent of all shoplifters come from low incomes households. Seventy percent are middle class, and twenty percent are classified as wealthy.[486] America is a country of thieves. One new hotel reported that in their first ten months of operation they lost thirty-eight thousand spoons, eighteen thousand towels, 355 silver coffee pots, fifteen hundred finger bowls, and one hundred Bibles.[487] Regardless of the reason, stealing is wrong! God declares it to be a sin; it is a violation of God's law.

Second, it is a violation of loyalty. When we steal, we are breaking the trust of right relationships and care. Now people's trust has been broken, and they are afraid. It used to be that we could go to bed at night and not worry about locking the door. Today we lock the doors, put bars on the windows, install a security system, and train the dog to kill! It's the same with our cars; we not only lock them everywhere now, but we put "The Club" on the wheel, take the face off the stereo, and lock the hubcaps. In some neighborhoods, folks will take your paint job at a stoplight if you're not watching!

Stealing has an impact on our relationship with God, because it says, "I don't really trust You to give me what I need, God," or "My desire for material possessions is greater than my desire to obey You."

Third, it is a violation of love—our love for God and our love for our fellowman. On breaking the Great Commandment, Paul wrote in Romans 13:8-10:

> Be under obligation to no one—the only obligation you have is to love one another. Whoever does this has obeyed the Law. The commandments, "Do not commit adultery; do not commit murder; do not steal; do not desire what belongs to someone else"—all these,

CHAPTER NINE:
The Eighth Commandment
THE POSSESSION PARADOX

and any others besides, are summed up in the one command, "Love your neighbor as you love yourself." If you love someone, you will never do them wrong; to love, then, is to obey the whole Law.[488]

Stealing is a self-centered act, not caring what this costs somebody else. Stealing violates Jesus' command to "love your neighbor." You wouldn't steal from someone you love. And saying, "Well, I'm not stealing from a person; I'm stealing from a corporation" just means you are one part of stealing people's jobs. Stealing disregards the needs and well-being of others, considering oneself more important than the person or persons who is the victim of the theft.

What drives us to steal? It's when desire overtakes discipline; it's when selfishness and possessive greed—yearning for what we are not earning—overcomes personal integrity. It's the easy way out . . . lust without labor. It's when wronging someone is more important than doing right. It can also be the "They-owe-me" mentality—the boss doesn't pay me enough, the government should do better, and big business is ripping us off. It's how some people feel about life; they have a sense of entitlement, with the attitude "I have a right," but the truth is, they are still doing wrong. Speaking of such, Dr. Laura uses the phrase "I deserve it because I don't have it."[489] Proverbs 14:12 says, "Some people think they are doing right, but in the end it leads to death."[490] And in Isaiah 5:20 we read, "Woe to those who call evil good, and good evil; who put darkness for light, and light for darkness; who put bitter for sweet, and sweet for bitter!"[491] We hear such quips as, "They charge too much anyway," . . . "I had no choice; I had to in order to survive," and "Everyone does it." But does that change God's opinion about it? No, not according to Matthew 7:13-14: "Go in through the narrow gate, because the gate to hell is wide and the road that leads to it is easy, and there are many who travel it. But the gate to life is narrow and the way that leads to it is hard, and there are few people who find it."[492]

Some people feel that stealing is okay because no one sees it, but Jesus is watching you!

> A burglar broke into a house and began to steal all of the valuables. At that moment he heard a voice that said "Jesus is watching you."

He was so scared he froze for a second. He regained his composure and started stealing again, when the voice came louder, "Jesus is watching you." He just about lost it right there. After regaining his composure he began to steal again this time watching very intent around him when he heard the voice again, this time he recognized a shape in the corner. As he approached he realized it was a birdcage. He removed the cover to find a parrot. He almost laughed. "What is your name?" The parrot replied "Moses." The thief then said what kind of person would name a parrot Moses? The parrot replied, "The same kind of person that named a Rottweiler 'Jesus.'"[493]

Proverbs 15:3 states, "The eyes of the LORD are in every place, watching the evil and the good."[494] Most thieves look left and right, before and behind, to see if someone is watching, but they need to look up!

Justification is another reason people feel it's okay to steal, that it's not really stealing. They offer many palpable synonyms such as, extortion, burglary, fraud, misappropriation, cheating, embezzling, robbing, swindling, or balancing the scales. Yet we notice in 1 Corinthians 6:10 that God views it differently: ". . . nor thieves, nor the greedy, nor drunkards, nor revilers, nor swindlers will inherit the kingdom of God."[495]

How about this one? "No one will miss it." It costs the American economy hundreds of billions each year. In the most comprehensive study of its type, an article in the October issue of the *Journal of Law and Economics* says that crime costs $4,100 or $17 per day per person, or $1.7 trillion in 1997 dollars per year. The report, researched and written by David Anderson, an economist at Davidson College in North Carolina, covered such details as police and private security expenses, corrections costs, expenses of crime-related injuries, amount of theft. Anderson says that criminals annually steal $603 billion in assets while also creating an additional $1.1 trillion worth of lost productivity.[496] I once read that if you stopped all theft in America we would balance the national budget in three years. Now that ought to be a part of any politician's agenda!

What determines a thief? Anyone who takes anything that doesn't belong to him. Anyone who in any way takes what's not his own is a thief:

CHAPTER NINE:
The Eighth Commandment
THE POSSESSION PARADOX

> A thief decided to siphon gas from Dennis Quiggley's motor home in Seattle. When Dennis, inside the motor home, heard the noises outside he investigated [and] discovered the thief curled up on the ground violently vomiting. Intending to suck up the contents of the gas tank the thief had put his hose into the wrong hole—and had sucked up the contents of the sewage tank instead. The thief, a boy 14, will not be prosecuted; Dennis and the police agree that he has suffered enough.[497]

God's Word says, "Do not steal." Whether it's by force, stealth, deceit, at gunpoint, in daylight or through a window at night, it's all stealing. It doesn't matter if it's candy or jewelry, a dime or a dollar, or if it's big or little; to take what doesn't belong to you is stealing!

There is no such thing as private stealing—dark of night, masked, or at your desk filling out your taxes; God sees through dark masks and into your office. God sees it all, and we will never get away with it with Him. Just look at Job 34:31-32: "Why don't people exclaim to their God, 'We have sinned, but we will stop,' or 'We know not what evil we have done; only tell us, and we will cease at once'?"[498] Whether it's a school test, or at the store when one changes the price tags, or any attempt to manipulate the system, God sees it, it's stealing, and it's wrong.

There are many types of stealing to take note of. There is simple stealing: This is the common, ordinary thief who takes anything, from CDs, cigarettes and batteries to bicycles, cars, and the like. "Why buy when you can just take?" seems to be the attitude. I once heard the story of a man who told his wife to fire the maid because he caught her stealing their bath towels. His wife asked, "Which towels did she take?" "The ones we got on vacation from the Holiday Inn," exclaimed the man.

Simple stealing includes shoplifting. Stores are being robbed blind—they have spent billions trying to prevent stealing. They use anything from mirrors, alarms, ink, and cameras to locks and monitors. Theft from stores, including employee and vendor theft, costs retailers many billions of dollars per year. Independent retail studies have estimated theft from retail stores costs the American public $33.21 billion per year. Depending on the type of retail store, retail inventory loss ranges from .7 percent to 2.2 percent of gross sales with the average falling around 1.7 percent. Whole retail store chains have gone out of business due to their inability to control retail theft losses, and the cost of these losses is passed on to us the consumer, as well. Shoplifting losses vary by store type, but they can account for about one-third of the total inventory shrinkage. It is estimated that shoplifting occurs 330 million to 440 million times per year at a loss of $10 billion to $13 billion. Nationwide, that equates from one million to 1.2 million shoplifting incidents every day at a loss rate of $19,000 to $25,300 stolen per minute. When you factor in employee and vendor theft, this sum skyrockets to an estimate of over $33 billion stolen per year.[499]

The U.S. Department of Commerce estimates that thirty-five million Americans engage in this activity every year. That's one in every fifty shoppers. About five million get caught. Next time you go to Wal-Mart, look around at the other five hundred people there, and realize that ten of them are there to steal something! Who pays for that? We all do! Some take candy from a jar at the store or something from their own parents or at home. Or maybe you stole a glance at your neighbor's paper in school and then stole her answers. Some people are like the man who was standing before the judge two days before Christmas. The judge asked, "What are you charged with?" "Early Christmas shopping is all I was doing, Your Honor." "How early?" asked the judge. "Two hours before the store opened," answered the man.

There is sophisticated stealing. Even Christians fall prey to this and may not even realize they are stealing. It's seen in such activity as employee theft. *The Day America Told the Truth* is a very revealing book on ethics. When it comes to work ethics, the average employee said they spent twenty percent of their time goofing off. Over one-half surveyed said they called in sick on occasion when all they were sick of was working. You are a liar and a thief when you do so. Other employees told of coming in late and leaving early, taking extended breaks, falsifying their time card, making personal calls when not allowed, surfing the Internet, and lying on expense accounts.[500] It is stealing when you don't give honest work for honest pay. Colossians 3:22 says: "Servants, do what you're told by your earthly masters. And don't just do the minimum that will get you by."[501] A national retail security survey states that retailers lost $13 billion from employee thefts. Of the $34.5 billion in 2011 lost by retailers, forty-four percent was from employee theft, and shoplifting was thirty-two percent—together at seventy-six percent, they are the largest source of property crime in America.[502] In 1996, Adrian Rogers claimed that the American economy loses forty billion dollars annually from theft on the job.[503] In Ephesians 4:28 the Word says: "Anyone who has been stealing must steal no longer, but must work, doing something useful with their own hands, that they may have something to share with those in need."[504]

There is employer theft that is done by business owners and bosses, as well. But listen to what James 5:4 has to say: "All the workers you've exploited and cheated cry out for judgment. The groans of the workers you used and abused are a roar in the ears of the Master Avenger."[505] God is your best labor union who vindicates you when cheated. It is a form of stealing to take advantage of people in dire straits, to accept work but not give a fair wage. Just because you can doesn't mean that you should. I'm reminded of Hurricane Andrew that hit Homestead, Florida, in the mid 1990s. It was a time when many company's sought to gouge the needy consumer because of the desperate shortages the hurricane created. Prices went out the roof; a sheet of plywood that had sold for $20 was then selling for $60. Later, the state of Florida stepped in and created strict guidelines for these awful situations. So much more has God already stepped in for those of us who live in everyday life (Colossians 4:1): "Masters, be fair and just in the way you treat your slaves. Remember that you too have a Master in heaven."[506] Jesus warned and even rebuked the Pharisees who took advantage of widows (Luke 20:47): "They devour widows' houses and for a show make lengthy prayers. These men will be punished most severely."[507]

We must realize there is the theft of not paying our taxes: Jesus said in Luke 20:25: "So Jesus said, 'Well, then, pay the Emperor what belongs to the Emperor, and pay God what belongs to God."[508] The apostle Paul wrote in Romans 13:7: "Give to everyone what you owe them: Pay your taxes and government fees to those who collect them, and give respect and honor to those who are in authority."[509] No normal human enjoys paying taxes, but in a civilized society it is a necessary evil. Tax evasion is a form of stealing. Tax avoidance is perfectly legal. Trying to pay as little as possible is fine, and normal. But God wants His children to be honest.

Unpaid debt is a type of stealing as well: Christians should pay their bills, and on time. And if unable to do so, you should call your creditors and make arrangements, rather than try to dodge them (Romans 13:8): "Owe nothing to anyone."[510] God is not against borrowing and lending within certain guidelines. But after the due date, you become a thief. Again, just because you may be able get away with it doesn't mean you should! Too many have been known to just make providers eat their losses by putting their electricity or their cell phone, or whatever in someone else's name instead of paying their previous debt. You are not only stealing from that company when you do that, but you are also stealing from me and others who use that company, and we have to pay their increased prices to cover all their write-offs. It's more about your character than your credit rating. It's about being right with God and man. Just try to do the right thing, and God will reward you. Maybe your creditor won't give you grace or be reasonable. That's no excuse to not do what's right, trusting God with the end result.

Stealing happens when we cheat in school:

> 73% of all test takers, including prospective graduate students and teachers agree that most students do cheat at some point. 86% of high school students agreed. Cheating no longer carries the stigma that it used to. Less social disapproval coupled with increased competition for admission into universities and graduate schools has made students more willing to do whatever it takes to get the A. Grades, rather than education, have become the major focus of many students. Fewer college officials (35%) believe that cheating is a problem in this country than do members of the public (41%). High school students are less likely than younger test takers to report cheaters, because it would be "tattling" or "ratting out a friend." Many students feel that their individual honesty in

CHAPTER NINE:
The Eighth Commandment
THE POSSESSION PARADOX

academic endeavors will not affect anyone else. While about 20% of college students admitted to cheating in high school during the 1940s, today between 75 and 98 percent of college students surveyed each year report having cheated in high school.[511]

The gambling industry is a stealing business. It is stealing from those who can least afford it. Morally it's wrong; you can't win without someone losing. Truely legitimate business is a win-win. Gambling is profit and pleasure at someone else's pain and loss. It's an attempt to get without giving. One person said it's like a duel; a duel is murder by mutual consent. Habakkuk 2:6 states: "Woe to him who increases what is not his—for how long—and makes himself rich with loans."[512]

Swindling is stealing. In Amos 8:5 we read, "You say to yourselves, 'We can hardly wait for the holy days to be over so that we can sell our corn. When will the Sabbath end, so that we can start selling again? Then we can overcharge, use false measures, and tamper with the scales to cheat our customers.'"[513] The repairman who sells a fix that didn't need fixing or the doctor who suggests a surgery that is not needed is swindling. So it is when the car salesman sells a bad car or tells us we didn't read the fine print—you know, the print that is too fine to read.

Electronic theft has become a huge form of stealing in America. Pirating copies of programs—CDs, DVDs, computer software, etc.—is also a form of electronic theft. The cover of the July 14 issue of *U.S. News & World Report* a few years ago has a picture of an All-American teenage boy wearing a pair of headphones, looking pretty much like millions of teenage boys in any city and town in America. The caption says, "Wanted." And in smaller letters, it asks, "Got a digital pirate in your house? Get a lawyer."[514] "File sharing" looks more like this: I get a music CD, put the songs on my computer's hard drive, and with the right software—which I got for free on the Internet—I can "share" them over the Internet with anyone who might want them. And, of course, I also have access to the files of millions of others who are doing the same thing. Why buy CDs at fifteen to twenty bucks a pop when I can get all the music on them for free? Some folks reason, "Even if it is illegal, most really don't care." DVDs are stolen with over six hundred thousand copies of films being traded digitally every day. Many movies are available on the Internet before they hit the theaters, thanks to illegally copied pre-release versions that are offered to the press. The essence of stealing is found in one word: *taking*—taking what is not yours. Martin Luther said, "If we look at mankind in all its conditions, it is nothing but a vast, wide stable of great thieves."[515]

There is spiritual stealing, which is stealing from God. Arthur Pink states, "We rob God by unfaithful discharge of our stewardship in which God has trusted us."[516] How do we steal from God? The earth is the Lord's, we are His servants, and our life is not ours (1 Corinthians 6:19-20): "You should know that your body is a temple for the Holy Spirit who is in you. You have received the Holy Spirit from God. So you do not belong to yourselves, because you were bought by God for a price. So honor God with your bodies."[517] God owns us by both creation and redemption. Look at Isaiah 43:1: "Do not fear, for I have redeemed you; I have called you by name; you are Mine!"[518] When you live your life for yourself alone as if Christ never died, you're a thief; you've stolen from God in three ways. In the use of your time (Ephesians 5:16): "So be careful how you act; these are difficult days. Don't be fools; be wise: make the most of every opportunity you have for doing good."[519] In the use of your talent (Ephesians 2:10): "For we are His workmanship, created in Christ Jesus for good works, which God prepared beforehand that we should walk in them:" [520] And in the use or misuse of tithes, the emblem and symbol that all belongs to God (Malachi 3:8-12):

> I ask you, is it right for a person to cheat God? Of course not, yet you are cheating me. "How?" you ask. In the matter of tithes and offerings. A curse is on all of you because the whole nation is cheating me. Bring the full amount of your tithes to the Temple, so that there will be plenty of food there. Put me to the test and you will see that I will open the windows of heaven and pour out on you in abundance all kinds of good things. I will not let insects destroy your crops, and your grapevines will be loaded with grapes. Then

the people of all nations will call you happy, because your land will be a good place to live in.[521]

The tithe is ten percent of your increase (income or other blessings you receive) that is to go into the local spiritual storehouse where you are fed spiritually. God blesses His people when they obey in this area, and a financial curse is upon those who do not. The tithe: Abraham commenced it (long before the law), Moses commanded it, Jacob continued it, and Jesus commended it. Who are you to cancel it? A tithe is a trust fund, because you are saying, "God, I trust you with my finances." God's plan is that the ninety percent with His blessing will go further than one hundred percent that is cursed. Shoes last longer, and the roof is stronger! If our faith isn't strong enough to tithe, we should worry about whether it's truly strong enough to get us to heaven. If you can trust God with your soul, then you can trust Him with your savings. God owns it all anyway. He doesn't need our money. He wants our heart. Tithing is not His way of raising money; it's His way of raising Christians! Without faith it's impossible to please Him. Don't rob from God, and don't rob yourself of the blessing.

Some Christians live in stolen houses, drive stolen cars, and wear stolen jewelry all paid for with tithe money. Spiritual stealing, sophisticated stealing, simple stealing—it's all displeasing to God. We need to strive to please Him who is all about giving, by not being takers. The possession paradox of wanting what we want until we are willing to take what we want is wrong.

I Want What I Want and Will Work for What I Want

Ephesians 4:28 is a powerful verse of overcoming the possession paradox: "Anyone who has been stealing must steal no longer, but must work, doing something useful with their own hands, that they may have something to share with those in need."[522] There are three clear areas that this passage gives us in overcoming the possession paradox.

The first is integrity, doing the right thing. "Let him that stole steal no more." Stop doing what you're doing . . . go and sin no more is the answer. How do we do this? Repent and have a change of mind. "This is wrong" is what we need to say. Recognize and remove bad behavior as David prayed in Psalm 51:2-4: "Wash away all my evil and make me clean from my sin! I recognize my faults; I am always conscious of my sins. I have sinned against you—only against you— and done what you consider evil. So you are right in judging me."[523]

The second area in Ephesians 4:28 that shows us the path to overcoming the possession paradox is industry, hard work. And it's all wrapped up in the eighth commandment. Working is good for us, but the problem today is many don't know it very well. Its importance is well-established in 2 Thessalonians 3:10-13: "Don't you remember the rule we had when we lived with you? If you don't work, you don't eat. And now we're getting reports that a bunch of lazy good-for-nothings are taking advantage of you. This must not be tolerated. We command them to get to work immediately—no excuses, no arguments—and earn their own keep. Friends, don't slack off in doing your duty."[524] Ancient Jews understood this—work followed by the Sabbath as God's plan for a healthy life. Here is a corresponding rabbinical saying: "He who doesn't teach his son a trade teaches him to steal."[525] The rabbis saw work as a blessing from God.

The Preacher also saw work as a blessing from God (Ecclesiastes 5:18-19): "This is what I have found out: the best thing anyone can do is to eat and drink and enjoy what he has worked for during the short life that God has given him; this is man's fate. If God gives a man wealth and property and lets him enjoy them, he should be grateful and enjoy what he has worked for. It is a gift from God."[526] Labor is a gift from God as seen in the fourth commandment (Exodus 20:8-9): "Remember the sabbath day, to keep it holy. Six days shalt thou labour, and do all thy work:"[527] People want to win the Powerball to be able to not work, when it's work that keeps them healthy. We've lost vision of the value of an honest day's work. Our fathers taught us a work ethic that is generally lost today. We're called workaholics if we work long hours today; back then we were called industrious. Ephesians 4:28 says, "Let him work with his hands." It's God's plan.

Socialism says pool the wealth, but it has failed around the world. Communism says the government should control the wealth, and it has failed. Today we've created a society where people have figured out how to not work: aid, food, welfare, SSI, etc. There is an old aphorism that states this well: "Why, America doesn't work!" Look at our prisons: ten percent of prisoners work, yet in 1829 ninety percent worked. Chuck Colson commented, "We are destroying all hope for over a million men by not demanding and teaching them to work."[528] Today, we have too many lazy people; you cannot legislate the poor into freedom by legislating the rich out of freedom. When we give to those who don't work, we take from those who do. When a man receives without working, someone works without receiving. Wealth is not multiplied by dividing. Lamentations 3:27 states, "It is good for someone to work hard while he is young."[529] Work won't hurt them; in fact, it will help them. Many of us grew up working and have worked all our lives and still work. Work is good for all of us. Not everyone is capable of manual labor, but almost everyone can do some kind of work, and we should all find some form of work if we are able to work at all, even if we don't get paid for it—for example, volunteering at a food distribution center, sewing or knitting, or working with wood in your workshop. The sense of accomplishment we enjoy from the work we do is good for our health.

The third area to note in Ephesians 4:28 is generosity: ". . . that they may have to give to those in need." The opposite of stealing is not refraining from stealing; it's giving. Everything God controls *gives*. For God so loved the world that He *gave*; the sun gives light; plant seed in the earth, and that ground will give it life; rivers give water, so do clouds. Our world produces petroleum, more than we could use. The more we use, the more the world produces to fill the void we create. The cycle of life is found and formed through giving. Squeeze your fist then release it: it feels better to give than to hold tight. Notice Acts 20:33-35:

> I've never, as you so well know, had any taste for wealth or fashion. With these bare hands I took care of my own basic needs and those who worked with me. In everything I've done, I have demonstrated to you how necessary it is to work on behalf of the weak and not exploit them. You'll not likely go wrong here if you keep

remembering that our Master said, "You're far happier giving than getting."[530]

Laboring to have and to give, it's not the government's job to care for poor. Stealing is taking what's not yours to satisfy your wants; the opposite is to give to others what you've earned to meet their needs.

Life is made up of takers and givers; the greatest key to breaking the possession paradox is generosity. The philosophy of the world is "Get all you can, can all you get, and then sit on the can!" John Wesley put a Christian twist on that philosophy, and it set him free. He taught, "Earn all you can, save all you can, and give all you can."[531] That is the Christian's faith (Psalm 24:1): "The earth is the Lord's and the fullness thereof, the world and those who dwell therein."[532] All you own is from God; everything you are and have is His. He has given you a management responsibility; you are a steward, or a caretaker, of God's gifts. Look at 1 Corinthians 4:2: "In this case, moreover, it is required of stewards that one be found trustworthy."[533]

Generosity is seen in helping others and serving others, remember that what we hold can hinder our walk with God (1 Timothy 6:17-19):

> Tell those rich in this world's wealth to quit being so full of themselves and so obsessed with money, which is here today and gone tomorrow. Tell them to go after God, who piles on all the riches we could ever manage—to do good, to be rich in helping others, to be extravagantly generous. If they do that, they'll build a treasury that will last, gaining life that is truly life.[534]

It was A.W. Tozer who said:

> Money often comes between men and God. Someone has said that you can take two ten-cent pieces, just two dimes, and shut out the view of a panoramic landscape. Go to the mountain and hold just two coins closely in front of your eyes—the mountains are still there, but you cannot see them at all because there is a dime shutting off the vision in each eye.[535]

Such a small amount of money can come between us and the Lord; the commitment is far more important than the amount.

CHAPTER NINE:
The Eighth Commandment
THE POSSESSION PARADOX

The eighth commandment is a statute of liberty; as we serve others instead of stealing from them, we are released from greed and selfishness. God did not establish the tithe just to raise money for the Temple or the church. Its purpose is to teach dependence upon God and to share with others what God abundantly gives. Giving is a means of grace, and we all need the liberating experience of giving.

I Want What I Want and Will Trust God for What I Want

Rely on God's property, on what God has given to you. A very real problem associated with the sin of breaking this commandment is a lack of trust in God's ability to provide for your needs. When we break the eighth commandment what we may be saying is that we can't trust God. Whenever we take something that doesn't belong to us, we're saying that God isn't able to give us everything we truly need. As a matter of fact, when we steal in any of the ways previously mentioned, including withholding money that should be given, we're robbing God of the opportunity to supply our needs. The apostle Paul gives us this confidence in Philippians 4:19: "But my God shall supply all your need according to his riches in glory by Christ Jesus."[536] We should pray Matthew 6:13-15 every day of our lives. If we pray this prayer with sincerity, it means we submit ourselves completely for Him to supply our needs by His hands, ". . .Give us the food we need for each day. . ."[537]

He is your source, He is the church's source, He is the source for all who will trust Him. If this is true, and it is, why would we ever steal; if this is true, why wouldn't we tithe; if it is true, why wouldn't we give what's not really ours in the first place? Look again at the story of God's deliverance for the people of Israel in the Book of Exodus. The names of God—Jehovah Jireh, "my provider," El Shaddai, "He is sufficient," etc., indicate the many ways He has supplied our needs and come to our rescue, time and time again. For the Israelites, He parted the Red Sea, He gave them light at night, He led them by the cloud by day, and He gave them food each day by providing them with manna. He supplied water from a rock, and He clothed them. God had every reason to ask them, "Did I not take care of you in every situation?" Yes, He did; so what reason would they ever have to steal, not tithe, not serve, not obey, when He had proved to them He was their provider? By His provisions, God plainly spoke: "I am responsible for you, and I will take care of you." Jesus said in Matthew 6:28-33:

> And why worry about clothes? Look how the wild flowers grow: they do not work or make clothes for themselves. But I tell you that not even King Solomon with all his wealth had clothes as beautiful as one of these flowers. It is God who clothes the wild grass—grass that is here today and gone tomorrow, burnt up in the oven. Won't he be all the more sure to clothe you? How little faith you have! So do not start worrying: "Where will my food come from? or my drink? or my clothes?" (These are the things the pagans are always concerned about.) Your Father in heaven knows that you need all these things. Instead, be concerned above everything else with the Kingdom of God and with what he requires of you, and he will provide you with all these other things. So do not worry about tomorrow; it will have enough worries of its own. There is no need to add to the troubles each day brings.[538]

Why steal at all? Trust God and serve Him: He'll see to it that everything will be taken care of. Stealing and cheating is telling God, "I don't believe you can meet my needs."

Stealing is a sin against God in two ways: A failure to believe He will provide for your needs and a failure to respect what He has already given to others. If someone else has what you don't, that means God doesn't want you to have that right now. When you steal, you're saying, "God you're not doing things the way I want." You're saying, "I know better than God how to take care of my wants."

All of us stand before God guilty in some way of breaking the eighth commandment.

Luther said, "It is the smallest part of the thieves that are hung. If we were to hang them all, where shall we get enough rope? We must make all our belts and straps into halters."[539] Jesus died on the cross between two thieves. The Bible says that when Jesus was crucified, "two robbers were crucified with him; one on the right and one on the left" (Matthew 27:38). This was a fulfillment of the ancient prophecy of Isaiah, who wrote, "He was numbered with the transgressors" (Isaiah 53:12). Jesus was numbered among thieves so that he might suffer and die for our thievery. He died as a thief for thieves, so that every thief who trusts in Him could be forgiven and saved. The first thief to be saved was hanging right next to him. He said, "Jesus, remember me when you come into your kingdom." And Jesus said to him what he says to all who trust in him: "Today you will be with me in paradise."

The single greatest sin against God is to steal what belongs to Him—not the tithes, His glory, our respect, or the honor that's due Him. No, as terrible as it would be to steal any one of those, that's not what God wants most from you. What He wants first and foremost from all of us is our heart. When He has our heart, He has all of us, and then the other things mentioned will automatically be His as well. Two thieves died with Christ that day; one kept his heart, the other gave his heart to Him. Today many people are stealing from God by keeping their heart when it all belongs to Him.

CHAPTER TEN
The Ninth Commandment
THE LYING TRUTH
Exodus 20:16

"You must not lie."[540] Not everyone tells the truth; in fact, we are all liars in some way. We lie by nature; we're born liars. Psalm 58:3 says, "Evildoers go wrong all their lives; they tell lies from the day they are born."[541] If you've had a child, you know kids know how to lie. Some of you grew up figuring out ways to lie so you wouldn't get into trouble. It never does work; we always ended up getting found out. "Oh what a tangled web we weave when first we practice to deceive."[542] That's what Sir Walter Scott said almost two hundred years ago, and it's just as true today as it was then. Yet that doesn't stop most of us from lying, does it? The 1992 book *The Day America Told the Truth* says, that ninety-one percent of those surveyed lie routinely about matters they consider trivial, and thirty-six percent lie about important matters; eighty-six percent lie regularly to parents, seventy-five percent to friends, seventy-three percent to siblings, and sixty-nine percent to spouses.[543] We lie about our weight, our income, our grade point average, our work experience, our age, even how many fish we caught during our last vacation. We hate it when people are dishonest to us, but most of us can't resist being dishonest to other people. A former staff member told me he would lie if it meant protecting his family from a jail sentence or if it would keep them from major legal trouble. It is terribly sad to excuse one's lack of truthfulness and consider it legitimate in order to keep one's family from life's troubles. One man said that a lie is summed up in three former U.S. Presidents—Washington couldn't tell a lie, Nixon couldn't tell the truth, and Reagan could't tell the difference.[544] God says, "Don't do it!" (Exodus 20:16). When you deal with other people, tell the truth and let the veracity of your life line up with the truthfulness of God and His Word.

What does a little white lie hurt? Maybe you agree with the little boy who was asked what a lie was and replied, "A lie is an abomination to the Lord, but a very present help in time of trouble!" But the truth is, there is a cost to lying. Those who lie discover that it causes a loss of trust, and they often find it hard to win their way back to being trusted again. The lying truth in our character is seen by the veracity of our words. Who we are is to a large extent determined by what we say. Friedrich Nietzsche said: "What upsets me is not that you lied to me, but that from now on, I can no longer believe you."[545] It's very interesting that in our culture of lying, it's still one of the worst things you can say of someone that he or she is a liar. We want complete honesty, while practicing partial truth; we want an honest salesman, unless we are doing the selling.

As people who follow Jesus, who said, "I am the way, and the truth,"[546] the hallmark of our character, a mark of our integrity, should be that we are truth-tellers. Have you ever thought about what the world would be like if there wasn't at least a general agreement that we should relate to one another on some level of truthfulness? Would you want a surgeon who cheated on the final examine or a pilot that didn't put in enough hours? Would it be okay if your children's teacher had a fake degree or the police department lied concerning evidence in a case against you? What if the government was full of liars? Oh, wait . . . maybe you already know that answer by present-day experiences. Sissela Bok wrote:

> In such a world, you could never trust anything you were told or anything you read. You would have to find out everything for yourself, first-hand. You would have to invest enormous amounts of your time to find out the simplest matters. In fact, you probably couldn't even find out the simplest matters: in a world without trust, you could never acquire the education you need to find out anything for yourself, since such an education depends upon your taking the word of what you read in your lesson books. A moment's reflection of this sort makes it crystal clear that you benefit enormously by living in a world in which a great deal of trust exists—a world in which the practice of truth-telling is widespread. All the important things you want to do in life are made possible by widespread trust.[547]

CHAPTER TEN:
The Ninth Commandment
THE LYING TRUTH

Lying, however, has reached epidemic proportions in our society; being truthful is becoming a lost art. In our nation we've come to expect our leaders to be liars, we expect sales people to lie to us, and honesty is not something that comes easy for many people. Many find truth as fluid and situational, that honesty is based on outcome and lies are relevant. Robert Feldman said: "We found that convincing lying is actually associated with good social skills. It takes social skills to be able to control your words as well as what you say non-verbally."[548] Study after study shows that lying seems to be a way of life for many. Of course, that's if you believe the study. A national survey by Rutgers' Management Education Center found that of forty-five hundred high school students that seventy-five percent of them engage in serious cheating. More than half have plagiarized work they found on the Internet. Perhaps most disturbing, many of them don't see anything wrong with cheating: some fifty percent of those responding to the survey said they don't think copying answers to questions on a test is even cheating. Notice three areas concerning the lying truth and how it affects all of us.[549]

Lying Dishonors God

In Proverbs 12:22 we discover this truth: "The LORD hates liars, but is pleased with those who keep their word."[550] What's a lie? Any distortion or violation of the truth; an inaccurate reflection of the true reality is a lie; the circus mirrors of life whereby we see things out of proportion to what they really are, are all lies. Nora B. Kathrins stated it this way: "Mirror, mirror, on the wall; you're not pleasing me at all; I know you cannot lie forsooth, but can't you slightly bend the truth?"[551] What kind of lies do people tell? There are many different kinds of lies—whoppers, white lies, half-truths, fibs, gossip lies, exaggerations, misleading silences, lying on paper, lying at home, lying at work, lies that make you look better, lies that make others look bad. Are you a self-focused liar (you tell lies to make yourself look better) or an others-focused liar (you tell lies to avoid hurting others)? To say I'll do something, anything, and don't do it or to say what one doesn't mean, simply put, is to lie. Maybe you fall under this list of "Famous Fibs":

The check is in the mail; I'll start my diet tomorrow; We service what we sell; Give me your number, and the doctor will call you right back; Money cheerfully refunded; One size fits all; This offer limited to the first 100 people who call in; this hurts me more than it hurts you; I just need five minutes of your time; Your table will be ready in a few minutes; Open wide, it won't hurt a bit; Let's have lunch sometime; It's not the money, it's the principle.[552]

A man and woman are going out to eat. He looks in the mirror and sees the age of his body. "Honey," he ponders, "what happened to my head of beautiful brown hair? Where did my chiseled abs go? What happened to my athletic figure? Please tell me something good about myself." With that, his adoring wife says, "Well, at least you have 20/20 eyesight." This is truly rare honesty in its best form.

God hates lying (Proverbs 6:16-19): "There are six things the LORD hates, seven that are detestable to him: haughty eyes, a lying tongue, hands that shed innocent blood, a heart that devises wicked schemes, feet that are quick to rush into evil, a false witness who pours out lies and a person who stirs up conflict in the community."[553] Notice that two out of seven are about lying. Why does this bother God? First of all, it treats God as though He's not God. He knows everything we do, and we act as if He doesn't. Lying insults not only those whom you manage to fool, but also God, whom you can never fool.[554] You can fool some of the people all of the time and all of the people some of the time, but God none of the time. So why lie? There are always two who know the truth about it, you and God. Second, lying discredits His deity. When we look at the story in Acts 5:1-11, we see two main characters, Ananias and Sapphira. They held back a portion of what they promised to the church. Both fell dead for their lies unto God. The punishment was not over their personal property but their disregard for truth and the righteousness of God. They lied not to man but to God. We need not forget what the apostle Paul said in Galatians 6:7: "Do not be deceived, God is not mocked; for whatever a man sows, this he will also reap."[555]

Go back to the text: Exodus 20:16. The primary context of this commandment is the courtroom. This commandment is also reinforced in

CHAPTER TEN:
The Ninth Commandment
THE LYING TRUTH

Leviticus 5:1, where false testimony appears to include refusing to divulge pertinent information at a trial, thus creating a false impression of what the facts really are, and in Deuteronomy 19:18-19. A decent society requires a reliable court system and court process. Because crimes and disputes do occur, it must be the case that they can be adjudicated and the criminal behavior or unfairness thereby stopped. If witnesses in a trial, whether civil or criminal, do not tell the truth, it is extremely difficult for judges to render proper decisions. In other words, the court system of a nation depends on the honesty of its people.[556]

Courtrooms in the ancient world were different from today. Before forensic evidence, everything hinged on the witness's testimony, and usually there was only one witness. The primary context of this commandment is the courtroom because the courtroom is the place where the truth counts the most; it's the place where lying can cost the most. Lack of truth and justice in the courtroom leads to lack of truth and justice in the wider community. So it was in the early church. Technically, this commandment deals with testimony in a court of law and the impact on the judicial system, but there are clearly vast implications for not telling the truth in our everyday lives as well. While many of us do not worry about false testimony in a court of law, we should worry about what ramifications there are to our daily lies.[557]

Lying is completely antithetical to the nature of God. He is the truth-telling God (1 John1:5): "This is the message we have heard from him and declare to you: God is light; in him there is no darkness at all."[558] No darkness at all—"strong negation; Greek, 'No, not even one speck of darkness'; no ignorance, error, untruthfulness, sin, or death."[559] Hebrews 6:18 speaks of the immutability (unchangeableness) of the impossibility for God to lie. A careful examination of the Bible confirms this. Of the Father, Romans 3:4 says, "God is Truth and every man a liar"; of the Son, John 14:6 says, "I am the Truth"; of the Holy Spirit, 1 John 4:6 says, "He is the Spirit of Truth"; of the Word, John 17:17 says, "Thy word is truth." People don't like the Word, for it is truth, and truth is the light that exposes their deeds.

This commandment extends beyond the courtroom of evidence to the boardroom, the schoolroom, the bedroom, the living room of life. Augustine stated, "In the Decalogue itself it is written, 'You shall not bear false witness, in which classification every lie is embraced.'"[560] It calls us to be true witnesses in all of life. Before God we are always under oath. God commands us to not lie, not in any context. In every day of ordinary life, our hand is figuratively on the Bible, and we're commanded to tell "the truth, the whole truth, and nothing but the truth."

Lying Deceives Others

Proverbs 10:10 states, "Someone who holds back the truth causes trouble."[561] This commandment is pretty specific. It is concerned with how we should deal with other people's names and reputations. You might recall the third commandment dealt with respecting the name of God, this commandment deals with respecting the name of others. And, specifically, it is concerned with not lying about them. The sixth deals with murder, and yet lying is character assassination. The eighth is stealing, and lying takes from everyone: "You shall not give false testimony against your neighbor."[562] This is the first time that neighbor is used in the Ten Commandments. Back in Old Testament Israel, virtually every legal decision was based on the truthfulness of the witnesses. They didn't have DNA testing or fingerprinting back then, so a false witness could ruin a person's reputation. However, even though this was originally talking about just perjury, by implication this commandment is also talking about truth telling in all areas of life. Lying causes an inordinate amount of trouble and hurt for others, and often for yourself as well.

Notice two important things here: First, the origin of lying. Jesus was speaking to the Pharisees in John 8:44 when He said, "You are of your father the devil, and you want to do the desires of your father. He was a murderer from the beginning, and does not stand in the truth because there is no truth in him. Whenever he speaks a lie, he speaks from his own nature, for he is a liar and the father of lies."[563] We're never more like Satan than when we lie. Every time we see the devil in Scripture, he's lying. The first time we see him in the Bible, he lied about God to

CHAPTER TEN:
The Ninth Commandment
THE LYING TRUTH

man. Devil means slanderer, and he slanders to corrupt a good man by lying about God to man. Notice what Genesis 3:1 says: "Now the serpent was more crafty than any beast of the field which the LORD God had made. And he said to the woman, 'Indeed, has God said, "You shall not eat from any tree of the garden"'?" [564] *Crafty* means "cunning or deceitful."[565]

He lied about the truthfulness of God. "Hath God said?" Questioning God's Word is skating on thin ice. Yet many question God's Word all the time today. We are not to stand in judgment with whether it makes sense or is practical or not. The Word is to stand in judgment of us, not the other way around. Satan lied about the righteousness of God: "Ye shall not surely die." In other words, God won't judge you if you sin. He lied about the goodness of God, saying in essence: "God is trying to keep back from you good things!"

Satan slandered to criticize a godly man by lying about man to God. Job 1:9-12 is summed up in this statement: "The only reason Job obeys you is because you're so good to him." What a liar. To Adam and Eve he said that God isn't good enough, and now he's saying that God is too good!

He slanders to crucify the God-man by lying to man about Jesus. False witnesses were summoned to lie about Jesus (Matthew 26:59-60). Satan put it in their hearts to bear false witness against Jesus in the kangaroo court they put together. In Genesis he used a lie to corrupt a godly man. In Job he used a lie to criticize a good man. In the New Testament he used a lie to crucify the God-man. In Revelation it is told that he will embody the Antichrist, who will tell a lie so big and believable that it brings about the end of the world. So, from beginning to end, Satan is a liar! And when we lie, we align ourselves with everything that brings death, destruction, doom, and damnation to this world. Sin is what leads to death, and that sin was brought about by a lie!

Notice also the operation of lying. Lying has many faces. Lying has many children in its family—sons of Satan, so to speak ("your father the devil"). In Bible times, truth was all you had, no forensic science, only someone's word. Your word was everything. Your word joined with another could sentence anyone to a crime they did or did not commit and get them killed. The deception of a lie could destroy innocent lives. We don't always see a lie for what it is, so here are the *seven lying sons of Satan*:

Perjury. Exodus 23:1 states: "You must not tell lies. If you are a witness in court, don't help a wicked person by telling lies."[566] Those who accuse the innocent and set free the guilty will answer to God. Today perjury is a huge offense. Look at recent events in MLB where Roger Clemens almost went to jail for perjury concerning enhancement drugs.[567] Your word is your richest asset or greatest liability. Proverbs 25:18 informs us, "A false accusation is as deadly as a sword, a club, or a sharp arrow."[568] Go back to Genesis 39, where we read about how Potiphar's wife perjured herself with a story of rape with false evidence; that lie sent Joseph to prison for two years.[569] One lie can ruin a life.

Insinuation. You don't actually say the falsehood; you just suggest it. What if I told you, "Today was a good day because my wife is sober"? Is it true? Yes, but I've suggested something else. I can make the same wrong implication by the tone of my voice. Both of these leave questions to the question "Is my wife a drunk?" No, but the insinuation says otherwise.

Slander. Psalm 101:5 says, "Whoever secretly slanders his neighbor, him I will destroy."[570] This is lying with the intention of doing harm to another's reputation. Some sins are worse than others in terms of damage done. Steal my car but not my character. Exodus 23:1 tells us, "Never spread false rumors."[571] Leviticus 19:16 declares, "Do not go about spreading slander among your people."[572] There is a legend of a peasant with a troubled conscience who went to the village priest for advice. The peasant had repeated some slander about a friend and later had found that his words were untrue. He asked the priest what he could do to make amends. The priest told the man, "If you want to make peace with your conscience, you must fill a bag with goose feathers and drop a feather at every door in the village." The peasant did as he was told, and then returned to the priest. "Is this all that I need to do?" he asked.

"No, that is not all," was the reply. "There is one thing more. Take up your bag and gather up every feather." The peasant left. After a long time, he returned, saying, "I could not find all the feathers, for the wind had blown them away." The priest said, "So it is with gossip. Unkind words are so easily dropped, but we can never take them back again."[573] And so it is with what we do with our words; you can repent, but you can't repair. When we slander someone's reputation, we do irreparable damage. And we'll answer to God for it!

Gossip. This person loves to tell things; they don't care if their facts are correct or not. The two biggest liars in the world are "They said" and "I heard." First Timothy 5:13 informs us, "At the same time they also learn to be idle, as they go around from house to house; and not merely idle, but also gossips and busybodies, talking about things not proper to mention."[574] Proverbs 16:28 states, "A perverse person stirs up conflict, and a gossip separates close friends."[575] There is the story of a new pastor who came to the church. The ladies meeting started a rumor and said the pastor rudely treated his wife in taking her from a meeting they had. The gossip spread to the pulpit until on Sunday he chose to address it: "I never tell my wife what to do . . . my wife was not at the meeting . . . I was not at the meeting . . . furthermore, I'm not married!" Truth only needs to exchange hands a few times before it becomes fiction. Second Corinthians 12:20 says, "For I am afraid that when I come I may not find you as I want you to be, and you may not find me as you want me to be. I fear that there may be discord, jealousy, fits of rage, selfish ambition, slander, gossip, arrogance and disorder."[576] A listener to gossip is also guilty. It's a small compliment indeed that people would choose your ears for garbage bins, is it not? Give Proverbs 15:14 a close look: "A wise man is hungry for truth, while the mocker feeds on trash."[577] Next time you're enjoying listening to someone gossip, remember this fact; anyone who will gossip *to* you, will gossip *about* you! Don't allow your ears to become someone's personal trashcans.

The Bible says for us to direct people to the source. Matthew 18:15-17 gives us the answer: "If you have a problem with someone, go to them, and only them." A.B. Simpson, Christian missionary, once said,

"I'd rather play with forked lighting or take in my hands living wires of fiery currents than to speak a reckless word against any servant of Christ or idly repeat the slanderous darts which thousands of Christians are hurling on others."[578]

Flattery, insincere praise (Psalm 55:21): "His talk is smooth as butter, yet war is in his heart; his words are more soothing than oil, yet they are drawn swords."[579] This is not speaking of the sincere words of an encourager or one who is giving honor to bless someone. Flattery uses people and manipulates them for selfish purposes. Proverbs 26:28 declares, "A flattering mouth works ruin."[580] The flatterer and a hypocrite are alike. The flatterer will say to your face what he will not say behind your back. The hypocrite will speak to your back what he won't speak to your face. Both are heads and tails of the same coin. When someone starts buttering you up, remember it's possible they are about to have you for lunch! Gossip is backstabbing, and flattery is front-stabbing; either way it's lying. Don't say what you don't mean. If you praise someone to their face then say it to their back as well. Mean it, but don't go beyond what is needed to convey your sincere appreciation; just treat people with dignity and honesty. If they ask for an honest opinion, give them an honest answer. The doctor said to his patient, "You're deathly ill." The patient convincingly replied, "I want a second opinion." "You're ugly too," retorted the doctor. At least he was honest, although I don't recommend that kind of brutal honesty. It is usually not necessary. *US News and World Report* published this question and answer: "What is the most important attribute or quality in a person or friend? And 94 percent said the one above all is honesty?"[581] We all need someone who will be honest with us. Proverbs 27:5-6 informs us: "Better to correct someone openly than to let him think you don't care for him at all. Friends mean well, even when they hurt you. But when an enemy puts an arm round your shoulder—watch out!"[582] The truth is not popular, but it's always right. Lee Iacocca stated: "I have found that being honest is the best technique I can use. Right up front, tell people what you're trying to accomplish and what you're willing to sacrifice to accomplish it."[583]

Half-truths. This is not telling the whole story. You break the spirit of the law when you do this. This is why in court you swear to not just tell the truth, but "the whole truth." Half the truth equals a whole lie. By holding our peace when something injurious is said of another we tacitly give our assent.[584]

Exaggeration. Preachers have a reputation for this failure. The story is told of one pastor who was brought before the deacons for exaggerating so much. When they confronted him, he acknowledged they were right: "I've cried a barrel of tears over it, and I've tried to quit a million times!" A person can also break this commandment by silence, for the negative always implies the positive. Bear true witness. "It's none of my business" is how many people feel, but that's not what God's Word says (Leviticus 5:1): "If anyone sins because they do not speak up when they hear a public charge to testify regarding something they have seen or learned about, they will be held responsible."[585] When you fail to speak up, it is hurtful to people and hellish before God. Dr. Martin Luther King Jr. once said, "The words of mine enemies have not hurt as much as the silence of my friends."[586] The devil is a slanderer, who lies and spreads lies. Jesus is the Truth and spreads truth.

Lying Destroys Character

Some people are chronic liars; they just can't seem to tell the truth. It's in their DNA and part of their personality. How can you tell if a liar is lying? Their lips are moving! Some people can't be trusted and can't trust those around them. If you are lying, you are ruining your character, life, and relationships. Lying is character assassination. This is the one time when words are more important than our actions. We are marked by our words—Honest Abe, lying politician, crooked preacher, etc.

You can't separate the lie from the liar. Lying is not a problem of the mouth, but of the heart. It's a heart defect, a character flaw. Look at Matthew 12:34: "For out of the abundance of the heart the mouth speaks."[587] People are not liars because they lie; they lie because they are liars, as Jesus declared in Matthew 15:19: "What comes out of the mouth gets its start in the heart. It's from the heart that we vomit up evil arguments, murders, adulteries, fornications, thefts, lies, and cussing. That's what pollutes."[588] Lying will make a coward out of a person when they do wrong and lie about it, because they are afraid of the consequences. It takes courage to tell truth, and it's cowardice to lie. We too often lie for fear of the consequences of our actions. What do you say when the police officer says, "Were you wearing your seatbelt?"

Here is the root reason for lying. When we lie, we are saying, "I don't trust God to help me own up to the consequences of the truth, so I lie." A lie says to God, "I don't trust You; I'd rather tell a lie alone than the truth with You." Isaiah 57:11 states, "Of whom were you worried and fearful when you lied, and did not remember Me nor give Me a thought? Was I not silent even for a long time so you do not fear Me?"[589] Why are we so concerned about others and not God? God says I stand with truth tellers. A lie is only deferred adjudication; sooner or later we will answer for our deeds. Notice what God says will happen when this world winds down (Revelation 21:8): ". . . and all liars, their part will be in the lake that burns with fire and brimstone, which is the second death."[590] A real problem with lying is, it's never just one lie; it's like Lay's potato chips—always one more. Austin O'Malley states: "A lie has no legs. It requires other lies to support it. Tell one lie, and you are forced to tell others to back it up. Stretching the truth won't make it last any longer. Those who think it's permissible to tell white lies soon grow color-blind."[591] Abraham Lincoln said, "No man has a good enough memory to make a successful liar."[592]

Every family needs two things, love and trust. Trust and love are the superglue of life in all relationships, personal and business. Trust is integrity, and integrity is wholeness of truth; to be whole and honest is what God wants for His people. There are those who grew up with this understanding: "Your word is your bond," and a handshake was a contract. If we want what's good for our families—to live a long and prosperous life, then tell the truth. Psalm 34:11-13 speaks of this: "Come, my young friends, and listen to me, and I will teach you to honor the LORD. Would you like to enjoy life? Do you want long life and happiness? Then hold back from speaking evil and from telling lies."[593]

CHAPTER TEN:
The Ninth Commandment
THE LYING TRUTH

Jesus said, in John 8:44, the mess we are in is because of a lie—the devil's lie. Now he sells us on the three biggest lies of all: *First, you can get away with it.* Steal, lie, cheat, adultery, etc.—it's all okay. You can get away with it. But that is not what the Bible says in Numbers 32:23: "Make no mistake about it; you will be punished for your sin."[594] Hell was prepared for the devil and his angels (messengers). Liars are Satan's witnesses. Romans 6:23 agrees with this thought: "For the wages of sin is death."[595]

Second, Satan tells you that you can't get away from it. You're bound for the rest of your life to lie. This leaves us with the question, "How can we overcome lying?

Every negative command could be reworded positively. For instance, "Thou shalt not commit adultery" could be rephrased as "Thou shalt be sexually pure." The positive side of the Ten Commandments calls for a commitment to truth in all our dealings.[596] We could say today, "Thou shalt tell the truth." And truth is the very character and nature of our God. Jesus said, "I am the way, the truth, and the life." He called the Holy Spirit "the Spirit of truth." The truth sets us free! John 8:31-36 says: "The truth shall make you free. . . . If the Son makes you free, you shall be free indeed." *Love the truth.* This is a heart change. David spoke of "truth in the inward parts." We need an inward change as described in Philippians 2:5: "Let this mind be in you, which was also in Christ Jesus."[597] *Learn the truth* (Philippians 4:8): "Finally, brethren, whatsoever things are true, whatsoever things are honest, whatsoever things are just, whatsoever things are pure, whatsoever things are lovely, whatsoever things are of good report; if there be any virtue, and if there be any praise, think on these things."[598] *Live the truth.* Ephesians 4:25 is the perfect example: "No more lying, then! Each of you must tell the truth to one another, because we are all members together in the body of Christ."[599] Be accountable to others; be open to others who will stop you when you gossip or slander. Immediately confess, immediately correct, and immediately commit yourself to the truth.

Satan tells you that you can get to God without Jesus. Why do liars go to hell? People in hell bought the biggest lie of all: "You can get to God any way you want." Don't believe it; believe only God's Word (John 14:6): "Jesus answered him, 'I am the way, the truth, and the life; no one goes to the Father except by me.'"[600] Some say it's your choice; that's a lie that is not congruent with God's Word. The truth is to spend eternity with God requires one thing, that we have Jesus (Acts 4:12): "And there is salvation in no one else, for there is no other name under heaven given among men by which we must be saved."[601] Do you trust God enough to be open and honest with Him concerning your life that He may save you from the lies of this world?

CHAPTER ELEVEN
The Tenth Commandment
ENOUGH ALREADY
Exodus 20:17

"You shall not covet your neighbor's house; you shall not covet your neighbor's wife, or his male servant, or his female servant, or his ox, or his donkey, or anything that is your neighbor's."[602] God has provided each one of us with "enough already." In every facet of life, there will always be enough (Philippians 4:19): "And with all his abundant wealth through Christ Jesus, my God will supply all your needs."[603] Yet the problem for most is that enough is never enough, and we covet and contrive to have more than enough. "Thou shalt not covet" is the commandment, yet as Americans we do covet while living in the top ninety-eight percent of income in the world. In Hank Ketcham's comic strip "Dennis the Menace," Dennis is looking through a catalog, saying, "This catalog's got a lot of toys I didn't even know I wanted."[604]

What does it mean to covet? It is an inordinate desire to possess what belongs to another, usually tangible things.[605] Coveting does not just want something, but it wants something at the expense of another. Covet means to have inordinate desire for what belongs to someone else.[606] While the Hebrew word for "covet" can also be translated "to desire," in the tenth commandment it means an ungoverned and selfish desire that threatens the basic rights of others. Coveting was sinful because it focused greedily on the property of a neighbor that was his share in the land God had promised His people.[607] Webster defines *covet* as "to want ardently something that another person has; to long for with envy."[608] Our inner desires exercise enormous influence over our behavior because what lives in the human heart never stays hidden for long. When we read the tenth commandment, it is as if we have moved away from the externals of life and into the dark regions of the human heart, that territory where Jesus claimed that most of the really bad things in this world are hatched. We covet when we set our hearts on something God has not given to us.

Is it wrong to simply want nice things? No, God wants good things in our lives (Psalm 37:4): "Seek your happiness in the LORD, and he will give you your heart's desire."[609] Psalm 84:11 is great reassurance that God wants to give us good things: "No good thing does he withhold from those who walk uprightly."[610] Coveting wants the wrong things by any method, and coveting wants the right things but for the wrong reason, which demonstrates one's selfishness. Coveting also wants the right things at the wrong time. We may want to enter into a marriage relationship and before the marriage takes place, we start living together outside of God's laws for physical intimacy. Coveting wants the right things but the wrong amount, as seen in those who have an inordinate desire for money.

This commandment is from God and can only be from God, but it is sometimes thought of as the unenforceable command. Who would know if you are breaking it? God would and He alone! Understand ambition, desire, and wanting to have nice things is okay. Our desire to provide for the family, make money, and have a good living is okay. The problem is when you become dissatisfied with your hoard and want someone else's. It's when you become envious, jealous, and covetous, when you let things and the desire for them control you to such an extent that your intentions are turned into actions. "I want what they have, and I'll sacrifice everything to have it. No matter that it costs my marriage, my kids, my sleep, my peace, my joy, and my Christianity, I want what I want!

Notice the Ten Commandments begin with worshipping *God* and end with the intolerance of worshipping *things*. The tenth command is the final capstone on how to live for God. No commandment is more quickly viewed through the lens of the New Testament than the tenth. The Sermon on the Mount, which begins in Matthew chapter 5, teaches us that what we do inwardly has the same consequences as what we do outwardly. Hence, to wrongly desire what is not in line with God's purpose for anyone is to break this tenth command. With that in mind, here are

CHAPTER ELEVEN:
The Tenth Commandment
ENOUGH ALREADY

three areas concerning covetousness and how we have enough already for acquiring all we need to sustain life.

The Price We Pay When Enough Is Not Enough Already

We pay a high price for covetousness; it's a disease that affects our finances and our families. Until *debt* do us part, and we find no contentment. What we can't afford we buy anyway, as once stated, "We buy now and pay maybe." How many people are truly content? Epicurus once said, "Nothing is enough to whom enough is too little"[611] The only true cure to covetousness is contentment. The Bible says, "Do not covet"—an unlawful desire for what is not yours: money, influence, home, popularity, power, appearance, anything. Why? Because we have enough already.

Coveting puts my focus in the wrong place. Our love for God is viewed through the lens of our approach toward possession as seen in 1 John 2:15-17:

> Do not love this world nor the things it offers you, for when you love the world, you do not have the love of the Father in you. For the world offers only a craving for physical pleasure, a craving for everything we see, and pride in our achievements and possessions. These are not from the Father, but are from this world. And this world is fading away, along with everything that people crave. But anyone who does what pleases God will live forever.[612]

Jesus said in Luke 12:15: "Watch out! Be on your guard against all kinds of greed; life does not consist in an abundance of possessions."[613] You can covet anything and everything, yet all the things we covet are temporary. They are a part of the world that we will leave behind when we die.

The Word teaches us that our focus is first to be on heavenly things (Colossians 3:2): "Keep your mind on things above, not on worldly things."[614] Further, we are also reminded to be Kingdom-minded in Matthew 6:33: "But strive first for the kingdom of God and his righteousness, and all these things will be given to you as well."[615]

Coveting puts a barrier between my neighbor and me by causing us to wrongfully desire instead of rightfully giving love, God's love. The apostle Paul stated in Romans 13:9: "The commandments, 'You shall not commit adultery,' 'You shall not murder,' 'You shall not steal,' 'You shall not covet,' and whatever other command there may be, are summed up in this one command: 'Love your neighbor as yourself.'"[616] Covetousness drives a wedge between people and destroys relationships. Your attitude toward your neighbor is supposed to be love. It's kind of hard to love someone who is standing in the way of your getting what you think you really need in order to be happy and satisfied in life. Love is characterized by self-sacrifice not by self-gratification. Love rejoices with those who rejoice and weeps with those who weep. A covetous spirit causes me to get envious when my neighbor gets a new car or new furniture or when he gets a raise at work. A covetous spirit causes me to laugh inside and secretly rejoice when that new car that he just bought gets banged up in a fender bender. It puts within us a spirit of competition and comparison instead of cooperation. Thomas Aquinas said, "Envy is sorrow for another man's good."[617] But a loving spirit allows us to be glad when someone else is able to purchase a BMW when we're still driving the same "hoopty" we've had for the last fifteen years.

Coveting leads to breaking all of God's commands. Forbidden desires lead to forbidden deeds. Desire always precedes destruction because our inward attitude will ultimately produce an outward action. Here's the worst example of this from the Bible as seen by King David's life:

- David broke the tenth commandment coveting his neighbor's wife.
- That led to adultery, which broke the seventh commandment.
- Then, in order to steal Bathsheba (breaking the eighth commandment),
- He committed murder and broke the sixth commandment.
- He broke the ninth commandment by lying about it.
- This brought dishonor to his parents, breaking the fifth commandment.

CHAPTER ELEVEN:
The Tenth Commandment
ENOUGH ALREADY

- He didn't put God first, breaking the first and second commandments.
- This dishonored God's name, breaking the third commandment.[618]
- Why does this happen? Because it's a heart problem as Jesus stated in Matthew 15:19-20: "For from his heart come the evil ideas which lead you to kill, commit adultery, and do other immoral things; to rob, lie, and slander others. These are the things that make a person unclean. But to eat without washing your hands as they say you should—this doesn't make a person unclean."[619]

Coveting will ruin your spiritual life (Mark 4:18-19): "The seed that fell among the thorns represents others who hear God's word, but all too quickly the message is crowded out by the worries of this life, the lure of wealth, and the desire for other things, so no fruit is produced."[620] Luke 12:16-19 is a powerful illustration of what covetousness will do:

> Then he told them a story: "A rich man had a fertile farm that produced fine crops. He said to himself, 'What should I do? I don't have room for all my crops.' Then he said, 'I know! I'll tear down my barns and build bigger ones. Then I'll have room enough to store all my wheat and other goods. And I'll sit back and say to myself, "My friend, you have enough stored away for years to come. Now take it easy! Eat, drink, and be merry!"'"[621]

He had plenty and could have assisted so many others, but he failed to see beyond his own consumptive greed. "I'll tear down what I have and build bigger and better." How American he sounds—bigger, better, best! J.D. Rockefeller, once the richest man in the world, was asked, how much is enough money, and he replied, "A little bit more."[622] Listen to the Lord's evaluation in Luke 12:20: "But God said to him, 'You fool! This very night your life will be demanded from you. Then who will get what you have prepared for yourself?'" When God calls you a fool for the way you've approached things, you better give grave consideration, for you will answer for it in the end!

The Problems We Encounter When Enough Is Not Enough

Covetousness is a deceitful sin. The perplexing problem of covetousness offers many difficult challenges to the outcome it brings. Most people never realize this problem is their problem. It's one of the most deceptive sins. C.H. Spurgeon said, "I've seen thousands converted, yet I've never seen a covetous person converted."[623] Billy Graham said, "Only one man has ever expressed to me the fear that he might become covetous; and it is a suggestive fact that he was the most generous man I have ever known."[624] Francis Xavier, the famous Catholic priest who heard tens of thousands of confessions, said, "I have had many people resort to me for confession. The confession of every sin that I have ever known or heard of, and of sins so foul that I never dreamed of has been poured into my ear; but no one has ever confessed to me the sin of covetousness"[625] In twenty-five years of ministry, this writer has heard nearly every kind of confession imaginable and, no, not one concerning the sin of covetousness. Why? Because it's a stealth sin; it flies under the radar. It could be ruining you and your marriage and you don't even see it. The Bible speaks of the cloak of covetousness in 1 Thessalonians 2:5: "For neither at any time did we use flattering words, as you know, nor a cloak for covetousness—God is witness."[626]

Paul, a young Pharisee who had it all—birth, nobility, education, status, learning, respect—one day was taking a survey of himself and went over the Ten Commandments like a checklist (Romans 7:7-8): "Shall we say, then, that the Law itself is sinful? Of course not! But it was the Law that made me know what sin is. If the Law had not said, 'Do not desire what belongs to someone else,' I would not have known such a desire. But by means of that commandment sin found its chance to stir up all kinds of selfish desires in me. Apart from law, sin is a dead thing."[627] He was saying, "I've done well in every area and with every commandment until I came to the tenth. That was my conqueror, my weakness; that lust in my heart spoke to me that I was a sinner. Outwardly, I fooled them all, I kept them all, but inwardly it got me. It was that unlawful desire that reprehended the emotions of his heart."

It is the mother of all sins. Eve coveted the fruit, and it's still stuck in mankind's throat today! Lot coveted the best land, and mankind is still fighting over that land today. Judas coveted thirty pieces of silver, resulting not only in the Savior's death, but his own death as well. Covetousness sells a faulty product, a poison of passion that deceitfully destroys when we too strongly desire what we admire.

Covetousness is a debasing sin. Nothing shows our depravity more than covetousness; it will turn a person into someone else. Mark 7:21-22 says, "For from within, out of the heart of men, proceed the evil thoughts, fornications, thefts, murders, adulteries, deeds of coveting and wickedness, as well as deceit, sensuality, envy, slander, pride and foolishness."[628] It was an x-ray of the heart. A man is not a sinner because he sins; he sins because he's a sinner. Look again at verse 22, which demonstrates that deeds of coveting and wickedness, as well as deceit, sensuality, envy, slander, pride, and foolishness are all from the heart.

Covetousness is born in you; the sin nature you received from your father (John 8:44): "You come from your father, the devil, and you desire to do what your father wants you to do."[629] Satan coveted the throne of God (Ezekiel 28:15): "Your behavior was perfect from the time you were created, until evil was found in you."[630] It was covetousness; it's how the devil became the devil. He wrongfully desired what wasn't meant for him. We were born with it, this selfish desire to have what's not ours. Just look at children at play; they can be selfish with a "my" and a "mine" attitude. It's immature, and as an adult it's debasing. Charles Kingly wrote:

> If you wish to be miserable, think about yourself; about what you want, what you like, what respect people ought to pay you, what people think of you; and then to you nothing will be pure. You will spoil everything you touch; you will make sin and misery for yourself out of everything God sends you; you will be as wretched as you choose.[631]

Covetousness creates a self-centered perspective: Psychologist Erich Fromm stated, "If I am what I have and what I have is lost, then who am I?"[632] This is the reason that people who are depressed might commit suicide. They have linked their worth and value to what they have instead of who they are. To see what you really are, add up everything you have that money can't buy and that death can't take away.

Covetousness is destructive. First Timothy 6:9-10 states: "But those who want to be rich fall into temptation and are trapped by many senseless and harmful desires that plunge people into ruin and destruction. For the love of money is a root of all kinds of evil, and in their eagerness to be rich some have wandered away from the faith and pierced themselves with many pains."[633] Those who want to be rich or are determined to be rich will be destroyed. What they desired brought not what they wanted, but what they didn't want—more like a bankrupt spirit. It's not necessarily wrong to make all you can; just be sure you do it honestly and not at someone else's expense. For if gaining wealth is your highest goal, then you can't be rich in the nonmaterial things in life. No man can serve two masters. You must choose—God or the pursuit of riches. "I am determined to be rich" is setting up the idol of money, which causes you to break not only the tenth commandment but the first as well. Covetousness is idolatry (Colossians 3) whereby we place another god in our heart. Ephesians 5:5 speaks of this sin of covetousness: "For this you know, that no fornicator, unclean person, nor covetous man, who is an idolater, has any inheritance in the kingdom of Christ and God."[634]

Covetousness is dissatisfying. In 1965 Keith Richards of the Rolling Stones, at 3:00 a.m., woke up and wrote a number one hit "Can't Get No Satisfaction."[635] The reason he wrote it: he was fed up with the consumerism in the U.S. After forty years nothing is better, only worse. This could be our national anthem. Even though we in America have everything we could want, we just can't seem to get any satisfaction. *Newsweek* said people can be divided into three classes: "The haves, the have not's, and the have not paid for what they have."[636] Will Rogers stated: "We spend money we don't have to buy things we don't need, to please people we don't like."[637] Why do we do this? No matter what we have, we just can't get any satisfaction. People are too busy trying to fill a spiritual void with carnal things.

CHAPTER ELEVEN:
The Tenth Commandment
ENOUGH ALREADY

A covetous spirit comes from two things, a lack of satisfaction with what God has given us and dissatisfaction over the way God hands out His blessings. We figure that God is under obligation to hand out His blessings equally to those who follow Him. We judge fairness by our standards rather than by God's standards. We are not the judge of the way God thinks or acts. God gives us what we need and what we are ready for at each individual moment. Maybe we are too much like the spoiled dog that thought he deserved better.

> Once there lived a dog. He was very greedy. There were many times that he had to pay for his greed. Each time the dog promised himself, "I have learnt my lesson. Now I will never be greedy again." But he soon forgot his promises and was as greedy as ever. One afternoon, the dog was terribly hungry. He decided to go look for something to eat. Just outside his house, there was a bridge. "I will go and look for food on the other side of the bridge. The food there is definitely better," he thought to himself. He walked across the wooden bridge and started sniffing around for food. Suddenly, he spotted a bone lying at a distance. "Ah, I am in luck. This looks like a delicious bone," he said. Without wasting any time, the hungry dog picked up the bone and was just about to eat it, when he thought, "Somebody might see me here with this bone, and then I will have to share it with them. So, I had better go home and eat it." Holding the bone in his mouth, he ran toward his house. While crossing the wooden bridge, the dog looked down into the river. There he saw his own reflection. The foolish dog mistook it for another dog. "There is another dog in the water with a bone in its mouth," he thought. Greedy, as he was, he thought, "How nice it would be to snatch that piece of bone as well. Then, I will have two bones." So, the greedy dog looked at his reflection and growled. The reflection growled back. This made the dog angry. He looked down at his reflection and barked, "Woof! Woof!" As he opened his mouth, the bone in his mouth fell into the river. It was only when the water splashed that the greedy dog realized that what he had seen was nothing but his own reflections and not another dog. But it was too late. He had lost the piece of bone because of his greed. Now he had to go hungry.[638]

Covetousness is distracting. When we attempt to do too many things at once we often get rattled and accomplish even less. The story is told of young Charles Darwin that one day he was eagerly holding one rare beetle in his right fist, another in his left, and then suddenly he caught sight of a third beetle that he simply knew he must have for his collection. What to do? In a flash he put one of the beetles in his mouth for safekeeping and reached for the third beetle with his now free hand. But the mouth-imprisoned beetle squirted acid down Darwin's throat so that in a fit of coughing he lost all three beetles.[639] We end up losing those things that are closest to us when we chase after things that are not needed for us to enjoy the things we already have.

The Process We Engage in Practicing a Life of Enough Already

How can we practice a life of satisfaction? *Be glad for what others have.* Learn to be happy for other people when they are blessed. When you look at what others have, you'll always respond in one of two ways, with gladness or with jealousy for what they have. Why can't we be glad for others? Because a covetous person loves things over people, and they use people to get things! That's the real problem. You can love someone or covet their things, but not both; it's things or people. When you love people as God directs us to, you'll celebrate their increase and bless their wealth. To love someone is to want good for that person. Romans 12:15 declares: "Rejoice with those who rejoice, and weep with those who weep."[640] We need to understand that their blessing is not our loss. It's not losing; it's win, win. We need to realize that God is big enough to bless everyone in the way He chooses. Psalm 75:6-7 says: "The authority to reward someone does not come from the east, from the west, or even from the wilderness. God alone is the judge. He punishes one person and rewards another."[641] When a young preacher complained to Charles Spurgeon that his own congregation was too small, Spurgeon replied, "Well, maybe it is as large as you'd like to give account for in the Day of Judgment."[642] Other churches that teach the gospel are not our enemy, whether they are big or small. We are all in the fight together, the fight against Satan, not against one another. Look at James 4:1-2: "What causes fights and quarrels among you? Don't

CHAPTER ELEVEN:
The Tenth Commandment
ENOUGH ALREADY

they come from your desires that battle within you? You desire but do not have, so you kill. You covet but you cannot get what you want, so you quarrel and fight. You do not have because you do not ask God."[643]

If you see something on the other side of the fence that you want, you don't get mad at your neighbor for having it before you did. You pray, and ask God if He wants you to have something similar, and if you feel that He does, then you go out and work to make it happen. Bless them and thank God for it. When Jesus began His public ministry on earth, the crowds that had been following John the Baptist left him and began to follow Jesus. One of John's disciples came to him and basically said to him, "What are we going to do about this? Aren't you upset that this is happening?" John's response is found in John 3:30: "He must increase, but I must decrease."[644] We need to know that the timing of the Lord may be to bless them now, so be glad. God has a bigger purpose than satisfying our personal agendas of greed.

Be grateful for what we have. First Thessalonians 5:18 encourages us to be thankful for whatever we have: ". . .and give thanks whatever happens. That is what God wants for you in Christ Jesus."[645] Remember where you've been and what God has already done for and in your life. Israel's biggest problem when they came out of Egypt was their incessant complaining. They would time and time again forget where they had come from and what God had done for them. They murmured, and God judged them harshly for it. Mark Twain said: "What makes the good old days the good old days is a bad memory."[646] The children of Israel wanted their needs met back in Egypt; for us, we look to have our needs met by gathering things and possessions rather than seeking God. The root of covetousness is a rejection of God's sufficiency (Exodus 13:3): "Moses said to the people, 'Remember this day in which you went out from Egypt, from the house of slavery; for by a powerful hand the LORD brought you out from this place.'"[647] When we forget God's grace and goodness, we too often seek for something else to meet our needs.

Remind yourself where you're going. It helps us to realize this world is not our home; we're just passing through. Philippians 3:20 says this well: "We, however, are citizens of heaven, and we eagerly wait for our Savior, the Lord Jesus Christ, to come from heaven."[648] Instead of focusing on things we want, focus on the things we've sent ahead instead—the things we've already sent ahead of us into eternity. What have I been sending to my eternal home? Jesus tells us Matthew 6:19-21: "Don't store up treasures here on earth, where moths eat them and rust destroys them, and where thieves break in and steal. Store your treasures in heaven, where moths and rust cannot destroy, and thieves do not break in and steal. Wherever your treasure is, there the desires of your heart will also be."[649] The way to accomplish this is by sending treasures to heaven. Do good things for God and your fellowman. One man said, "I've never seen a U-Haul hitched to a hearse." So do good to others, and it will fill your account in heaven.

Rejoice in what you have. The quality of life is not determined by the quantity in our lives. We need to learn to be content and enjoy the rich life that God has already blessed us with. There is a story about a rich businessman who found a fisherman lying in a hammock on the beach. "Why aren't you out there fishing?" he asked. "Because I've caught enough fish for today," he replied. "Why don't you catch more fish than you need?" the rich man asked. "What would I do with them?" said the fisherman. "You could sell them for more money," came the impatient reply. "You could buy a bigger and better boat, go into deeper water, catch even more fish, and make lots of money. Soon you could have a fleet of fishing boats and be rich like me." The fisherman thought for a moment, then asked, "Then what would I do?" "You could sit down and enjoy life," said the businessman. The fisherman looked at him and said, "What do you think I'm doing right now?" The key is learning contentment for your present condition. The opposite of covetousness is contentment. People covet because they measure their success and worth by the things they possess. This attitude comes from a spirit of competition: "I want to be better than the Joneses." It comes from a spirit of comparison as well: "All my friends have this; how come I can't have it too?"

Acquire a right perspective. First Timothy 6:6-8 gives us one: "Yet true godliness with contentment is itself great wealth. After all, we

CHAPTER ELEVEN:
The Tenth Commandment
ENOUGH ALREADY

brought nothing with us when we came into the world, and we can't take anything with us when we leave it. So if we have enough food and clothing, let us be content."[650] The apostle Paul says in Philippians 4:11, "I have learned to be content in whatever circumstances I am."[651] Getting what you want may bring you temporary happiness, but it will soon evaporate, because stuff will never bring you satisfaction. Happiness doesn't come by getting what you want; happiness comes by wanting what you have.

Realize that only God can satisfy. You can't measure happiness, peace and joy by money. When you covet, you've missed two facts; one is that material things can never satisfy the physical. Solomon in Ecclesiastes 5:10 reminds all of us, "Whoever loves money never has enough; whoever loves wealth is never satisfied with their income. This too is meaningless."[652] He also advised in Proverbs 23: 4-5: "Be wise enough not to wear yourself out trying to get rich. Your money can be gone in a flash, as if it had grown wings and flown away like an eagle."[653]

The second fact that is missed is that material things can never satisfy the spiritual. We all have a void in our lives; money cannot fill what was left empty by the absence of a true presence, the presence of God. Things cannot do what only God was meant to do. The only person who can really quench your thirst in life is Jesus Christ. In John 4:13-14, Jesus said to a Samaritan woman who had come to draw water from Jacob's well: "All those who drink this water will be thirsty again, but whoever drinks the water that I will give him will never be thirsty again. The water that I will give him will become in him a spring which will provide him with life-giving water and give him eternal life."[654] Hebrews 13:5 says: "Don't love money. Be happy with what you have because God has said, 'I will never abandon you or leave you.'"[655] Jesus alone can satisfy you fully. Contentment is realizing what has true value in our lives. The grace of contentment is to know that you have God and that He is all you need. Look at this sad but true story of what a lack of contentment and a failure to trust God with what we already have will do in a person's life.

Danny Simpson of Ottawa, Canada, in 1990 was given six years imprisonment for robbing a bank of $6000 using an elderly Colt .45 pistol. He was arrested and the gun was impounded by the police, where it was recognized as an extremely rare collectors' item, worth up to $100,000. It was made under license by the Ross Rifle Company in Quebec City during WWI, one of only 100 Colt .45s ever made there. Simpson could have walked into any gun shop and sold the pistol for at least ten times the haul from his raid without breaking the law.[656]

Two things to note here: One, we covet the smallest of things when we have the greatest things of all. Two, Danny already had what he needed if he only looked at what he already had. He tried to take matters into his own hands, and by his hands he failed. Be content with what you already have. What do you have? God himself, family, children, friends, love, peace, joy, wisdom, the Word of God, and the satisfaction of knowing whose you are in Christ. Get a new perspective, look around, and know who and whose you are.

Be gracious with those who don't have, for this is the greatest antidote to covetousness. Proverbs 11:25 promises: "The generous will prosper; those who refresh others will themselves be refreshed."[657] Give, for God has blessed us all, but not all He's blessed us with is for ourselves. We are also to bless others. First Timothy 6:19 explains it this way: "In this way they will lay up treasure for themselves as a firm foundation for the coming age, so that they may take hold of the life that is truly life."[658] Covetousness wants to get; its opposite wants to give. When you give, whatever it is, you are breaking the grip of covetousness. You are saying to money, "You don't own or control me."

Consider the story of a congressman who took his son to McDonald's. Just to be nice, he supersized the meal. They sat down to eat. He had no fries, so he ate some of his son's fries. "Those are mine," stated the boy. This greatly upset the congressman. And he thought these things about his son: *He's a brat who forgot where the fries came from. He doesn't realize I could take all of them from him, and I have enough to buy all the fries at McDonald's today.* The story goes on to say that God spoke to

CHAPTER ELEVEN:
The Tenth Commandment
Enough Already

the congressman's heart at that moment and told him, "This is the same way you are with Me." The next time you go anywhere, remember this: God owns everything, and He could take it and leave us with nothing. The Lord owns it all, but He entrusts us as stewards to both use it and appreciate it according to His plan.

Bill Hybels writes of millionaire Howard Hughes:

> All he ever really wanted in life was more. He wanted more money, so he parlayed inherited wealth into a billion-dollar pile of assets. He wanted more fame, so he broke into the Hollywood scene and soon became a filmmaker and star. He wanted more sensual pleasures, so he paid handsome sums to indulge his every sexual urge. He wanted more thrills, so he designed, built, and piloted the fastest aircraft in the world. He wanted more power, so he secretly dealt political favors so skillfully that two U.S. presidents became his pawns. All he ever wanted was more. He was absolutely convinced that more would bring him true satisfaction. Unfortunately, history shows otherwise. He concluded his life . . . emaciated; colorless; sunken chest; fingernails in grotesque, inches-long corkscrews; rotting, black teeth; tumors, innumerable needle marks from drug addiction. Howard Hughes died . . . believing the myth of more. He died a billionaire junkie, insane by all reasonable standards.[659]

Epicurus said, "If you want to make a man happy, add not to his possessions, but take away from his desires."[660] Our desire should be, more than anything else, to experience God's peace and continual grace in our lives for He is *enough already*!

CHAPTER TWELVE

EPILOGUE

It's hard to believe when one looks at the moral decline in America that anyone would disregard this nation's need for the Ten Commandments. Life without law will always descend into chaos and social disorder. Millard Erickson so beautifully declared, "The law . . . should be seen as the expression of God's person and will."[661] We should be careful to remember the words of the apostle Paul in 2 Timothy 3:16: "All Scripture is God-breathed and is useful for teaching, rebuking, correcting and training in righteousness."[662] God gave us the entire Word for our benefit and guidance in life that we might live according to His perfect purpose and plan. If God approved of today's permissiveness He would have given us the "Ten Suggestions."

True, the ceremonial laws are fulfilled in Christ, for they were a foreshadowing of Christ, but the moral law (specifically the Ten Commandments) is a New Testament distinctive. Christ fulfilled the law, not by diminishing it, but by deepening and widening it. He put a larger demand upon us than the Ten Commandments of the Old Testament by the heart requirements of a proper attitude in fulfilling them. This is made possible because the Spirit that once was with man is now in every believer's life empowering all to do the works of Christ with a witness to the Christ living on the inside.

The Law and the gospel go hand in hand, working together to fulfill man's need for grace and his need of good behavior, or holiness, each working with the other, producing a right relationship with God the Father. God's moral laws are imperative and binding in this work, for they serve as the blueprints of God's expectations for us to live a complete and meaningful life in Christ. Even though there are many today who would dismiss the Ten Commandments as irrelevant to today's society, they have never been more contemporary and needed than they are today.

One thing we must always be careful to remember, though, is that the laws of God do not serve like rungs on a ladder to reach God. Rather, they are kept by a response from those who love God. Jesus said, "If you love Me, then you will keep My commandments." Love for God is most clearly seen by the way we approach and obey the Ten Commandments, not for salvation, but for the love we have as covenant believers that live under grace. Christ loved us enough to fulfill the law; we should love Him enough to keep the law, not just outwardly, but from the inside out.

D.T. Niles, a great theologian, once said that in all other religions good works are "in order to." But in Christianity they are "therefore."[663] We read over and over again in the New Testament epistles that Christ has given Himself as a propitiation for our sins. He has paid for our guilt and purchased for us eternal life; therefore, we should offer ourselves a living sacrifice unto Him.

ABOUT THE AUTHOR
God Spared My Life

The testimony of Dr. John Alexander, adapted from an article written by Hoyt E. Stone and published in the August, 1981 issue of *The Lighted Pathway*

The day dawned crisp. I left my wife, Lori, at the house and headed for work. It was just another Friday.

I was proud to be a part of my parents' business and our specialty was semitrailer and truck repair. On this particular morning I remember thinking of the welding jobs I wanted to complete before the week ended.

I started working on an aluminum tanker which carried highly flammable chemical called naphtha. Thirteen feet up, on top it, I found a crack in the outer hull and decided I would weld it. For some reason, the weld wouldn't take. It was a little awkward, working on top of the tanker, but I kept trying. I didn't consider the task dangerous because I wasn't welding on the tank itself, only on the outer shell.

I cleaned the metal and started again.

The tanker moved. It heaved ever so slightly, like something alive. For a moment I thought my co-worker had bumped into it, but he was outside. I applied more heat and again I felt the tanker vibrate. I shrugged and went on with the torch. I knew, of course, that naphtha was highly explosive but what I didn't know was that I was slowly heating up a bomb beneath me.

When the explosion came, it was like someone had clapped a metal tub down over my head and hit me at the same time with a giant club. Fire and darkness together! I felt weightless until slamming down on a table and cement floor. I learned later that I was blown thirty-five feet across the warehouse and that I landed on the table and then the floor. I smelled smoke. Saw flames. I had to get out of the building. Praying, I stumbled to the back door, vaguely conscious that most of my clothes had been shredded off.

Fresh air! How good to be able to breath!

Then ... Suddenly ... my body started yelling against the pain. I staggered around to the front, somewhat away from the burning building, and laid down. Darkness hovered mercifully over me and the whole scene began to fade in and out like bad movie film on the screen.

Flashes kept coming through to me. I remember scenes but I can't sequence them properly. Firemen came. The ambulance. I was rushed to the hospital, and then transferred to the burn center.

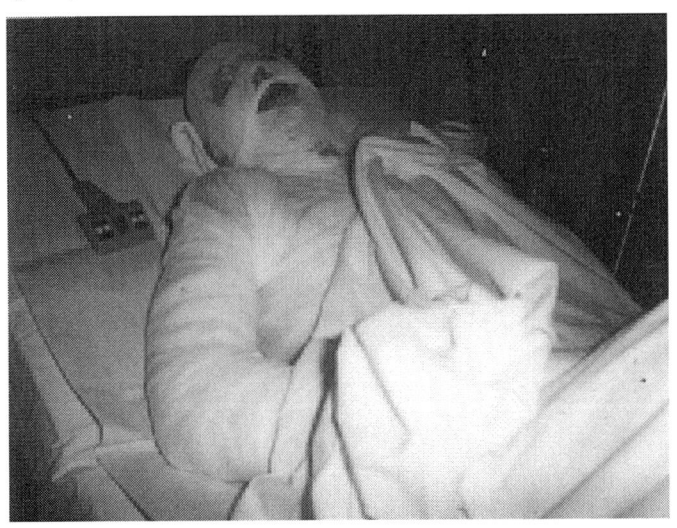

The physical damage to my body was assessed: Deep, second degree burns on face. Third degree on hands. Strained ligaments in knees and both ankles. Right forearm broken. Left arm chipped in the elbow, with triceps muscle and surrounding tendons completely ripped loose. At first the doctors said the muscles in my left arm were 90 percent destroyed—they later said 100 percent. They gave little encouragement that I would be able to use that arm again.

During this entire time, one big reality kept bouncing around in my mind—God had spared my life. That was a consciousness I never forgot; the beginning of a series of miracles for which I will be ever grateful.

Over the next twelve days in the hospital, my wife and church prayed constantly for my recovery. I knew there would be scars that I might not be as strong as previously, but I desperately prayed for God to restore the use of my arm.

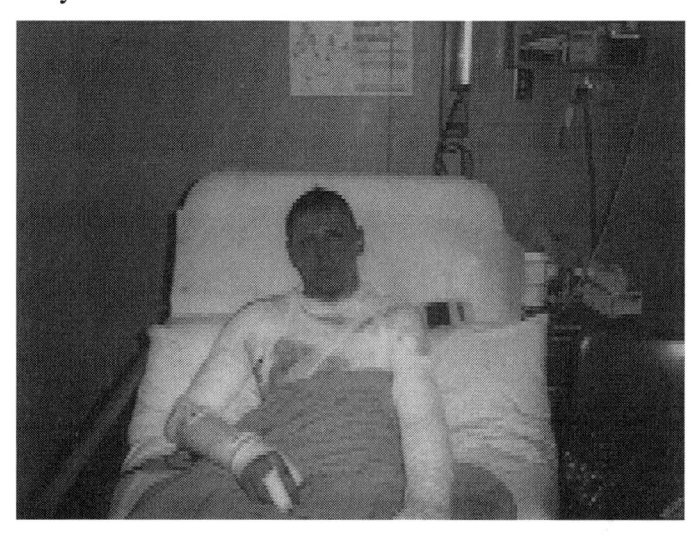

There were days when the pain was terrible, when every nerve in my body seemed to scream. Yet, God was always there. I felt His presence and I felt the effects of all those prayers.

Once out of the hospital, I began the long days of therapy. I fought mental and spiritual battles as doctors kept telling me there really wasn't much they could do for my left arm. They figured it would be useless.

Not long after I was home from the hospital. I slipped and fell tearing the muscles tendons in my arm loose all over again. Yet I prayed, knowing God was able. Faith was a struggle but somehow God gave me the strength to trust Him.

One week after my fall, when the doctors had determined I would never again be able to use my left arm, the Holy Spirit led me to the

Saturday night men's prayer service. Only three men were in attendance but God's miraculous power would be witnessed by those three and me. We gathered in prayer and God did what the doctors said could never be done. I felt God's healing touch on my arm. I took off the cast and bandages and for the first time in three months, and used my arm again. God had completely healed me!

The next week my doctors gave me a complete release, citing my arm as being normal and healthy. Today, thank God I am well with no scars or permanent damage to any part of my body. No skin grafts, contrary to the doctors' promises; nothing but a testimony of how God spared my life and healed my body.

God is wonderful!

END NOTES

1   *The New International Version*. 2011 (Mt 5:17). Grand Rapids, MI: Zondervan.
2   *The New International Version*. 2011 (Mt 5:18-19). Grand Rapids, MI: Zondervan.
3   http://www.truthusa.org/quotes/morality.htm
4   David Leininger, *God of Justice; A Look at the Ten Commandments for the Twenty-First Century*: (Lima, Ohio, CSS Publishing, 2007), p. 8
5   http://www.brainyquote.com/quotes/quotes/t/tedkoppel403196.html
6   http://www.sermonnotebook.org/old%20testament/exodus_20_1-17.htm
7   James Patterson, Peter Kim, *The Day America Told the Truth* (Prentice Hall, 1991). "To Verify," Leadership.
8   http://godstenlaws.com/ten-commandments-america.html
9   *The New International Version*. 2011 (Jdg 21:25-Ru). Grand Rapids, MI: Zondervan.
10 *New American Standard Bible: 1995 update*. 1995 (Ps 11:3). LaHabra, CA: The Lockman Foundation.
11 *The New International Version*. 2011 (Heb 12:14). Grand Rapids, MI: Zondervan.
12 *The Holy Bible: King James Version*. 2009 (Electronic Edition of the 1900 Authorized Version.) (2 Co 7). Bellingham, WA: Logos Research Systems, Inc.
13 *The New King James Version*. 1982 (Ro 7:14). Nashville: Thomas Nelson.
14 American Bible Society. (1992). *The Holy Bible: The Good News Translation* (2nd ed.) (Ex 20:1-3). New York: American Bible Society.
15 Anne Graham Lotz, God's Story: (Nashville, TN, Thomas Nelson, 1997), p. 232-233
16 American Bible Society. (1992). *The Holy Bible: The Good News Translation* (2nd ed.) (1 Pe 1:18-19). New York: American Bible Society.
17 *www.stewardshipcouncil.net/.../NIVStewardshipStudyBible_Sampler....*
18 Edmund P. Crowney, *How Jesus Transformed The Ten Commandments*: (Phillipsburg, NJ. P&R Publishing, 2007), p. 12
19 Tyndale House Publishers. (2007). *Holy Bible: New Living Translation* (3rd ed.) (Mt 22:37). Carol Stream, IL: Tyndale House Publishers.
20 *The New International Version*. 2011 (2 Ti 2:3-4). Grand Rapids, MI: Zondervan.
21 *The New International Version*. 2011 (Dt 28:1-14). Grand Rapids, MI: Zondervan.
22 Hoppe, L. J. (2000). Ten Commandments. In D. N. Freedman, A. C. Myers & A. B. Beck (Eds.), *Eerdmans Dictionary of the Bible* (D. N. Freedman, A. C. Myers & A. B. Beck, Ed.) (1286). Grand Rapids, MI: W.B. Eerdmans.
23 J.H. Hertz, *The Pentateuch and Haftorahs*: (London, Soncino Press,1981), p.295
24 *The Holy Bible: English Standard Version*. 2001 (Je 33:3). Wheaton: Standard Bible Society.
25 *New American Standard Bible: 1995 update*. 1995 (Mt 11:28). LaHabra, CA: The Lockman Foundation.
26 *The Holy Bible: New Revised Standard Version*. 1989 (Is 43:1). Nashville: Thomas Nelson Publishers.
27 *The Holy Bible: King James Version*. 2009 (Electronic Edition of the 1900 Authorized Version.) (Jn 10:27). Bellingham, WA: Logos Research Systems, Inc.
28 Andy Stanley: *The Grace of God*. (Nashville, TN. Thomas Nelson, 2010)p. 58

29 *Nelson's new illustrated Bible dictionary*. 1995 (R. F. Youngblood, F. F. Bruce, R. K. Harrison & Thomas Nelson Publishers, Ed.). Nashville, TN: Thomas Nelson, Inc.

30 American Bible Society. (1992). *The Holy Bible: The Good News Translation* (2nd ed.) (Jn 14:21). New York: American Bible Society.

31 *The Holy Bible: New Revised Standard Version*. 1989 (Mt 7:24). Nashville: Thomas Nelson Publishers.

32 *New American Standard Bible: 1995 update*. 1995 (Mt 22:36-40). LaHabra, CA: The Lockman Foundation.

33 H. L. Willmington, *Willmington's Guide to the Bible;* (USA, Tyndale House Publishing, 1984), p. 940

34 Tyndale House Publishers. (2007). *Holy Bible: New Living Translation* (3rd ed.) (Is 1:11-19). Carol Stream, IL: Tyndale House Publishers.

35 W. T. Purkiser, *Exploring the Old Testament*:(Kanas City, Mo., Beacon Hill Press, 1955), p. 124

36 *The New King James Version*. 1982 (Mt 6:33-34). Nashville: Thomas Nelson.

37 *The New International Version*. 2011 (1 Jn 4:10-11). Grand Rapids, MI: Zondervan.

38 *The Everyday Bible: New Century Version*. 2005 (Mk 12:29-31). Nashville, TN: Thomas Nelson, Inc.

39 Alan Aldrige: *Religion in the Contemporary World*. (Malden, MA, Polity Press, 2007) p. 66

40 American Bible Society. (1992). *The Holy Bible: The Good News Translation* (2nd ed.) (Mt 15:8). New York: American Bible Society.

41 Peterson, E. H. (2005). *The Message: The Bible in Contemporary Language* (Ro 12:1-2). Colorado Springs, CO: NavPress.

42 *The Holy Bible: King James Version*. 2009 (Electronic Edition of the 1900 Authorized Version.) (Php 2:5). Bellingham, WA: Logos Research Systems, Inc.

43 *The Holy Bible: English Standard Version*. 2001 (Jn 14:23). Wheaton: Standard Bible Society.

44 Doug Stringer, *Living Life Well; The Spirit of the Ten Commandments*: (Houston, Tx, Prayer Point Press, 2010), p. 50

45 *The New King James Version*. 1982 (Lk 9:23). Nashville: Thomas Nelson.

46 *The New International Version*. 2011 (Mk 12:31). Grand Rapids, MI: Zondervan.

47 Anonymous

48 Dr. Laura Schlessinger, *The Ten Commandments; The Significance of God's Laws in Everyday Life*: (NY, Harper Collins, 1998),p.8

49 Tyndale House Publishers. (2007). *Holy Bible: New Living Translation* (3rd ed.) (Eph 5:22-32). Carol Stream, IL: Tyndale House Publishers.

50 Mark F. Rooker, *The Ten Commandment; Ethics For The Twenty-First Century*: (Nashville, TN, B&H publishing, 2010), pp. 28-29

51 http://pluto.matrix49.com/16065/?subpages/zzz_sermon_2004-03-28.shtml

52 http://www.preachersjournal.org/Sermons/The%20Ten%20Commandments%20Series/Which%20One%20(message%201).htm

53 http://en.wikipedia.org/wiki/Whatever_Gets_You_thru_the_Night

54 LeAnne Blackmore, *Obscure No More; Life-Shaping Lessons From the Often Overlooked*: (Cincinnati, Ohio, Standard Publishing, 2010),p.43

55 American Bible Society. (1992). *The Holy Bible: The Good News Translation* (2nd ed.) (Jn 14:6). New York: American Bible Society.

56 RELIGION ÐICS NEWSWEEKLY Transcript: Show #549 August 9, 2002

57 D. James Kennedy, *Why the Ten Commandments Matter*: (NY, Warner Faith, 2005), p.22

58 Anonymous

End Notes

59 Peterson, E. H. (2005). *The Message: The Bible in Contemporary Language* (Mt 6:24). Colorado Springs, CO: NavPress.

60 *The New International Version*. 2011 (Is 42:8). Grand Rapids, MI: Zondervan.

61 *The Holy Bible: New Revised Standard Version*. 1989 (Ex 20:4-6). Nashville: Thomas Nelson Publishers.

62 *The New International Version*. 2011 (1 Jn 5:21). Grand Rapids, MI: Zondervan.

63 *The New King James Version*. 1982 (Mt 5:18-19). Nashville: Thomas Nelson.

64 http://www.dumblaws.com/random-laws

65 American Bible Society. (1992). *The Holy Bible: The Good News Translation* (2nd ed.) (1 Jn 5:3-4). New York: American Bible Society.

66 *The Holy Bible: English Standard Version*. 2001 (Jn 14:15-16). Wheaton: Standard Bible Society.

67 American Bible Society. (1992). *The Holy Bible: The Good News Translation* (2nd ed.) (Dt 30:18-20). New York: American Bible Society.

68 *New American Standard Bible: 1995 update*. 1995 (Ps 34:3). LaHabra, CA: The Lockman Foundation.

69 William Barclay. *The Ten Commandments*. (Louisville, KY. Westminster John Knox Press, 1998),p.12

70 *The Holy Bible: King James Version*. 2009 (Electronic Edition of the 1900 Authorized Version.) (Ac 17:28). Bellingham, WA: Logos Research Systems, Inc.

71 Phil Moore, *Straight to the Heart of Moses:* (UK, Monarch Books, 2011),p.109

72 *The New King James Version*. 1982 (2 Co 5:6-8). Nashville: Thomas Nelson.

73 Peterson, E. H. (2005). *The Message: The Bible in Contemporary Language* (Ex 20:3-6). Colorado Springs, CO: NavPress.

74 Doug Stringer. *Living Well, The Spirit of the Ten Commandments*. (Houston, TX. Power Point Press, 2010),p. 53

75 R. Kent Hughes, *Righteousness From Heaven*: Wheaton, Ill., Crossway Books, 1991), p. 37

76 *The New International Version*. 2011 (Eze 14:6-7). Grand Rapids, MI: Zondervan.

77 *The New King James Version*. 1982 (Ex 12:37-38). Nashville: Thomas Nelson.

78 Tyndale House Publishers. (2007). *Holy Bible: New Living Translation* (3rd ed.) (Re 22:18-19). Carol Stream, IL: Tyndale House Publishers.

79 *The New King James Version*. 1982 (Jn 4:24). Nashville: Thomas Nelson.

80 Newman, B. M., & Nida, E. A. (1993). *A Handbook on the Gospel of John*. UBS Handbook Series (122). New York: United Bible Societies.

81 *The New International Version*. 2011 (Is 40:25). Grand Rapids, MI: Zondervan.

82 American Bible Society. (1992). *The Holy Bible: The Good News Translation* (2nd ed.) (Je 14:22). New York: American Bible Society.

83 American Bible Society. (1992). *The Holy Bible: The Good News Translation* (2nd ed.) (Ro 1:19-23). New York: American Bible Society.

84 *The New King James Version*. 1982 (Is 6:5). Nashville: Thomas Nelson.

85 Taylor, K. N. (1997). *The Living Bible, Paraphrased* (Mt 10:36-37). Wheaton, IL: Tyndale House.

86 American Bible Society. (1992). *The Holy Bible: The Good News Translation* (2nd ed.) (2 Ti 3:4-5). New York: American Bible Society.

87 *New American Standard Bible: 1995 update*. 1995 (1 Co 6:9-10). LaHabra, CA: The Lockman Foundation.

88 American Bible Society. (1992). *The Holy Bible: The Good News Translation* (2nd ed.) (Job 31:24-28). New York: American Bible Society.

89 *The New King James Version*. 1982 (Ps 107:8). Nashville: Thomas Nelson.

90 *New American Standard Bible: 1995 update*. 1995 (Jn 4:23-24). LaHabra, CA: The Lockman Foundation.
91 *New American Standard Bible: 1995 update*. 1995 (Ex 20:5). LaHabra, CA: The Lockman Foundation.
92 Osborn, N. D., & Hatton, H. (1999). *A Handbook on Exodus*. UBS Handbook Series (474). New York: United Bible Societies.
93 *The New International Version*. 2011 (Dt 32:21). Grand Rapids, MI: Zondervan.
94 American Bible Society. (1992). *The Holy Bible: The Good News Translation* (2nd ed.) (Ex 34:14-15). New York: American Bible Society.
95 *GOD'S WORD Translation*. 1995 (Is 48:11). Grand Rapids: Baker Publishing Group.
96 American Bible Society. (1992). *The Holy Bible: The Good News Translation* (2nd ed.) (Dt 4:24). New York: American Bible Society.
97 *GOD'S WORD Translation*. 1995 (Ex 20:5-6). Grand Rapids: Baker Publishing Group.
98 Stuart, D. K. (2006). *Vol. 2: Exodus*. The New American Commentary (454). Nashville: Broadman & Holman Publishers.
99 Arthur W. Pink. *The Ten Commandments*. (Memphis, TN. Bottom of the Hill Publishing, 2011), p. 24
100 *The Holy Bible: New Revised Standard Version*. 1989 (Ex 20:4-6). Nashville: Thomas Nelson Publishers.
101 American Bible Society. (1992). *The Holy Bible: The Good News Translation* (2nd ed.) (2 Ch 27:2). New York: American Bible Society.
102 *The Everyday Bible: New Century Version*. 2005 (2 Ki 15:34-35). Nashville, TN: Thomas Nelson, Inc.
103 American Bible Society. (1992). *The Holy Bible: The Good News Translation* (2nd ed.) (2 Ch 28:1). New York: American Bible Society.
104 *The Teacher's Bible Commentary*. 1972 (F. H. Paschall & H. H. Hobbs, Ed.) (244). Nashville: Broadman and Holman Publishers.
105 *The New International Version*. 2011 (2 Ch 28:3-4). Grand Rapids, MI: Zondervan.
106 American Bible Society. (1992). *The Holy Bible: The Good News Translation* (2nd ed.) (Ex 20:5-6). New York: American Bible Society.
107 Mark F. Rooker. *The Ten Commandments, Ethics for the Twenty-First Century*. (Nashville, TN. B&H Publishing,2010),p.46
108 *The Everyday Bible: New Century Version*. 2005 (2 Ti 1:4-6). Nashville, TN: Thomas Nelson, Inc.
109 *New American Standard Bible: 1995 update*. 1995 (Mt 6:33). LaHabra, CA: The Lockman Foundation.
110 *The Holy Bible: English Standard Version*. 2001 (Col 1:15-16). Wheaton: Standard Bible Society.
111 *The New International Version*. 2011 (Heb 1:3). Grand Rapids, MI: Zondervan.
112 *The Everyday Bible: New Century Version*. 2005 (Jn 14:9). Nashville, TN: Thomas Nelson, Inc.
113 Edmund P. Clowney, *How Jesus Transforms the Ten Commandments*. (Phillipsburg, New Jersey. P&R Publishing, 2007), p. 33
114 *The New International Version*. 2011 (Ex 20:7). Grand Rapids, MI: Zondervan.
115 Jill L. Levenson, *Shakespeare in Performance, Romeo and Juliet*. (Wolfeboro, NH. Manchester University Press, 1987), p. 114
116 Stuart, D. K. (2006). *Vol. 2: Exodus*. The New American Commentary (456). Nashville: Broadman & Holman Publishers.
117 *The Holy Bible: English Standard Version*. 2001 (Pr 22). Wheaton: Standard Bible Society.
118 http://bible.org/seriespage/overview-ten-commandments-exodus-201-17

END NOTES

119 Osborn, N. D., & Hatton, H. (1999). *A Handbook on Exodus*. UBS Handbook Series (476). New York: United Bible Societies.
120 American Bible Society. (1992). *The Holy Bible: The Good News Translation* (2nd ed.) (Le 24:10-16). New York: American Bible Society.
121 Tyndale House Publishers. (2007). *Holy Bible: New Living Translation* (3rd ed.) (Mt 6:8-9). Carol Stream, IL: Tyndale House Publishers.
122 D. James Kennedy, *Why the Ten Commandments Matter:* (NY, Warner Faith, 2005), p. 56
123 Laura Schlessinger, *The Ten Commandments; The Significance of God's Laws in Everyday Life:* (NY, Harper Collins Press, 1999), pp. 63-66
124 Raymond Culpeper, *Sermon on Prayer*: (Canton, Ohio, Camp meeting, 2001) I was there that night.
125 Edmund P. Clowney, *How Jesus Transformed The Ten Commandments*: (Phillipsburg, NJ. P&R Publishing, 2007), p. 40
126 http://www.biblebelievers.org.au/proph05.htm
127 http://www.truthofyahweh.org/elohim2.html
128 *The New King James Version*. 1982 (1 Sa 17:45). Nashville: Thomas Nelson.
129 American Bible Society. (1992). *The Holy Bible: The Good News Translation* (2nd ed.) (Jn 14:14). New York: American Bible Society.
130 *GOD'S WORD Translation*. 1995 (Col 3:17). Grand Rapids: Baker Publishing Group.
131 Doug Stringer, *Living Life Well; The Spirit of the Ten Commandments:* (Houston, TX. Prayer Point Press, 2010), p. 65
132 *The Holy Bible: English Standard Version*. 2001 (Pr 18:10). Wheaton: Standard Bible Society.
133 American Bible Society. (1992). *The Holy Bible: The Good News Translation* (2nd ed.) (Jn 16:23-24). New York: American Bible Society.
134 Confraternity of Christian Doctrine. Board of Trustees, Catholic Church. National Conference of Catholic Bishops, & United States Catholic Conference. Administrative Board. (1996). *The New American Bible: Translated from the original languages with critical use of all the ancient sources and the revised New Testament* (1 Jn 5:14-15). Confraternity of Christian Doctrine.
135 Tyndale House Publishers. (2007). *Holy Bible: New Living Translation* (3rd ed.) (Ps 8:1). Carol Stream, IL: Tyndale House Publishers.
136 J. I. Packer, *Keeping the Ten Commandments*: (Wheaton, IL. Crossway Books, 2007), p. 60
137 *Exodus Vol. II*. 1909 (H. D. M. Spence-Jones, Ed.). The Pulpit Commentary (132). London; New York: Funk & Wagnalls Company.
138 D. James Kennedy, *Why the Ten Commandments Matter:* (NY, Warner Faith, 2005), p. 60
139 http://www.hope-of-israel.org/tetragram.html
140 Edmund P. Clowney, *How Jesus Transformed the Ten Commandments*: (Phillipsburg, NJ. P&R Publishing, 2007), p. 40
141 William Barclay, *The Ten Commandments*: (Louisville, KY. Westminster John Knox Press, 1998), p. 16
142 J. I. Packer, *Keeping the Ten Commandments*: (Wheaton, IL. Crossway Books, 2007), p. 60-61
143 *GOD'S WORD Translation*. 1995 (Mt 12:36). Grand Rapids: Baker Publishing Group.
144 Laura Schlessinger, *The Ten Commandments; The Significance of God's Laws in Everyday Life*: (NY, Harper Collins Press, 1999), p. 70
145 Adrienna Dionna Turner. *The Day Begins With Christ*. (USA, Author House, 2009), p. 19
146 *The Holy Bible: The Contemporary English Version*. 1995 (Lk 6:45). Nashville: Thomas Nelson.
147 http://www.agapeindia.com/sermons/invain.htm
148 Michael Scott Horton, *The Law of Perfect Freedom*: (Moody Press, 1993), p. 107

149 Arthur W. Pink, *The Ten Commandments:* (Memphis, TN. Bottom of the Hill Publishing, 2011), p. 27

150 *GOD'S WORD Translation.* 1995 (Eph 5:3-4). Grand Rapids: Baker Publishing Group.

151 Mark F. Rooker, *The Ten Commandments; Ethics for the Twenty-First Century:* (Nashville, TN. B&H Publishing, 2010), p. 73

152 Peterson, E. H. (2005). *The Message: The Bible in Contemporary Language* (Eph 4:29). Colorado Springs, CO: NavPress.

153 Taylor, K. N. (1997). *The living Bible, Paraphrased* (Col 3:8). Wheaton, IL: Tyndale House.

154 Doug Stringer, *Living Life Well; The Spirit of the Ten Commandments*: (Houston, TX. Prayer Point Press, 2010), p. 69

155 Aaron Wolgamontt, *Blurred Vision*: (Bloomington, IN. WestBow Press, 2012), p. 5

156 *The New International Version.* 2011 (Is 48:1-2). Grand Rapids, MI: Zondervan.

157 *The Holy Bible: New Revised Standard Version.* 1989 (Lk 6:46). Nashville: Thomas Nelson Publishers.

158 *The New King James Version.* 1982 (Mt 15:8). Nashville: Thomas Nelson.

159 Edmund P. Clowney, *How Jesus Transformed the Ten Commandments*: (Phillipsburg, NJ. P&R Publishing, 2007), p. 41

160 American Bible Society. (1992). *The Holy Bible: The Good News Translation* (2nd ed.) (Mt 7:22-23). New York: American Bible Society.

161 Tyndale House Publishers. (2007). *Holy Bible: New Living Translation* (3rd ed.) (Mt 7:21). Carol Stream, IL: Tyndale House Publishers.

162 *The New International Version.* 2011 (Ac 19:15). Grand Rapids, MI: Zondervan.

163 R. Albert Mohler, Jr., *Words From the Fire.* (Chicago, Il, Moody Publisher, 2009)

164 J. H. Hertz, *The Pentateuch and Haftorahs:* (London, Soncino Press, 1960), p.

165 Mark F. Rooker, *The Ten Commandments; Ethics for the Twenty-First Century:* (Nashville, TN. B&H Publishing, 2010), pp. 65,66

166 Laura Schlessinger, *The Ten Commandments; The Significance of God's Laws in Everyday Life*: (NY, Harper Collins Press, 1999), p. 83

167 Mark F. Rooker, *The Ten Commandments: Ethics for the Twenty-First Century:* (Nashville, TN. B&H Publishing, 2010), p.62

168 Scotty Smith, *Objects of His Affection*: (West Monroe, Louisiana, Howard Publishing, 2001), p. 69

169 *The New International Version.* 2011 (2 Ti 2:19). Grand Rapids, MI: Zondervan.

170 Tyndale House Publishers. (2007). *Holy Bible: New Living Translation* (3rd ed.) (Ac 11:26). Carol Stream, IL: Tyndale House Publishers.

171 Gangel, K. O. (1998). *Vol. 5: Acts. Holman New Testament Commentary* (181). Nashville, TN: Broadman & Holman Publishers.

172 *The Everyday Bible: New Century Version.* 2005 (1 Co 6:19-20). Nashville, TN: Thomas Nelson, Inc.

173 Doug Stringer, *Living Life Well; The Spirit of the Ten Commandments:* (Houston, TX. Prayer Point Press, 2010), p. 64

174 Confraternity of Christian Doctrine. Board of Trustees, Catholic Church. National Conference of Catholic Bishops, & United States Catholic Conference. Administrative Board. (1996). *The New American Bible: Translated from the original languages with critical use of all the ancient sources and the revised New Testament* (Is 5:20). Confraternity of Christian Doctrine.

175 Tyndale House Publishers. (2007). *Holy Bible: New Living Translation* (3rd ed.) (Ro 2:21-24). Carol Stream, IL: Tyndale House Publishers.

176 American Bible Society. (1992). *The Holy Bible: The Good News Translation* (2nd ed.) (Tt 1:16). New York: American Bible Society.

177 Fred DeRuvo, *Under Grace.* (Scotts Valley, CA. Study-Grow-Know, 2011), p. 34

End Notes

178 *GOD'S WORD Translation*. 1995 (Col 3:17). Grand Rapids: Baker Publishing Group.

179 Edmund P. Clowney, *How Jesus Transformed the Ten Commandments*: (Phillipsburg, NJ. P&R Publishing, 2007), p. 44

180 *The Holy Bible: English Standard Version*. 2001 (Mal 3:16). Wheaton: Standard Bible Society.

181 http://answers.yahoo.com/question/index?qid=20080503222618AAMXsXz

182 *The Holy Bible: English Standard Version*. 2001 (Mk 8:38). Wheaton: Standard Bible Society.

183 *New American Standard Bible: 1995 update*. 1995 (Ps 9:10). LaHabra, CA: The Lockman Foundation.

184 *The Holy Bible: New Revised Standard Version*. 1989 (Ps 33:21). Nashville: Thomas Nelson Publishers.

185 American Bible Society. (1992). *The Holy Bible: The Good News Translation* (2nd ed.) (Is 50:10). New York: American Bible Society.

186 *The New International Version*. 2011 (Ps 20:7). Grand Rapids, MI: Zondervan.

187 http://www.gutenberg.org/files/13958/13958-0.txt

188 Edmund P. Clowney, *How Jesus Transformed the Ten Commandments:* (Phillipsburg, NJ. P&R Publishing, 2007), p. 48

189 American Bible Society. (1992). *The Holy Bible: The Good News Translation* (2nd ed.) (Php 2:9-11). New York: American Bible Society.

190 Confraternity of Christian Doctrine. Board of Trustees, Catholic Church. National Conference of Catholic Bishops, & United States Catholic Conference. Administrative Board. (1996). *The New American Bible: Translated from the original languages with critical use of all the ancient sources and the revised New Testament* (Ro 10:13). Confraternity of Christian Doctrine.

191 *The New King James Version*. 1982 (Ac 4:12). Nashville: Thomas Nelson.

192 Tyndale House Publishers. (2007). *Holy Bible: New Living Translation* (3rd ed.) (Mt 5:16). Carol Stream, IL: Tyndale House Publishers.

193 D. James Kennedy, *Why the Ten Commandments Matter:* (NY, Warner Faith, 2005), p. 67

194 Jean Calvin, *Institutes of the Christian Religion*: (Philadelphia, Presbyterian Board of Publication, 1921), pp. 347- 348

195 *The New International Version*. 2011 (Ex 20:8-11). Grand Rapids, MI: Zondervan.

196 Phil Cousineau, *Once and Future Myths; The Power of Ancient Stories in Our Lives*: (York Beach, ME, Conari Press, 2001), p. 81

197 Joseph Telushkin, *Biblical Literacy*: (Harper Collins e books), p.159

198 Stuart, D. K. (2006). *Vol. 2: Exodus*. The New American Commentary (458). Nashville: Broadman & Holman Publishers.

199 *The New International Version*. 2011 (Ge 2:1-3). Grand Rapids, MI: Zondervan.

200 *The Holy Bible: English Standard Version*. 2001 (Is 40:28). Wheaton: Standard Bible Society.

201 Bilkes, G. M. (2000). Selah. In D. N. Freedman, A. C. Myers & A. B. Beck (Eds.), *Eerdmans Dictionary of the Bible* (D. N. Freedman, A. C. Myers & A. B. Beck, Ed.) (1180). Grand Rapids, MI: W.B. Eerdmans.

202 *New American Standard Bible: 1995 update*. 1995 (Ex 31:13-17). LaHabra, CA: The Lockman Foundation.

203 *New American Standard Bible: 1995 update*. 1995 (Ex 35:2-3). LaHabra, CA: The Lockman Foundation.

204 http://articles.ochristian.com/article15616.shtml

205 William Barclay, *The Ten Commandments:* (Louisville, KY. Westminster John Knox Press, 1998), p.20

206 Mark F. Rooker, *The Ten Commandments; Ethics for the Twenty-First Century:* (Nashville, TN. B&H Publishing, 2010), p. 96

TIMELESS
The Ten Commandments Today

207 Abraham Joshua Heschel, *The Sabbath*: (The Noonday Press, 1951)
208 *The Holy Bible: English Standard Version*. 2001 (2 Co 5:17). Wheaton: Standard Bible Society.
209 *The Holy Bible: King James Version*. 2009 (Electronic Edition of the 1900 Authorized Version.) (Col 2:13-15). Bellingham, WA: Logos Research Systems, Inc.
210 Melick, R. R. (1991). *Vol. 32: Philippians, Colossians, Philemon. The New American Commentary* (263). Nashville: Broadman & Holman Publishers.
211 American Bible Society. (1992). *The Holy Bible: The Good News Translation* (2nd ed.) (Col 2:14-17). New York: American Bible Society.
212 Doug Stringer, *Living Life Well; The Spirit of the Ten Commandments*: (Houston, TX. Prayer Point Press, 2010), p. 82
213 *The New King James Version*. 1982 (Mt 11:28). Nashville: Thomas Nelson.
214 *The New International Version*. 2011 (Heb 4:1-11). Grand Rapids, MI: Zondervan.
215 *The New International Version*. 2011 (Ps 62:1). Grand Rapids, MI: Zondervan.
216 American Bible Society. (1992). *The Holy Bible: The Good News Translation* (2nd ed.) (Heb 10:12). New York: American Bible Society.
217 American Bible Society. (1992). *The Holy Bible: The Good News Translation* (2nd ed.) (Mk 16:9). New York: American Bible Society.
218 Taylor, K. N. (1997). *The Living Bible, Paraphrased* (Mk 16:12). Wheaton, IL: Tyndale House.
219 *The Everyday Bible: New Century Version*. 2005 (Jn 20:19-20). Nashville, TN: Thomas Nelson, Inc.
220 *GOD'S WORD Translation*. 1995 (Jn 20:21). Grand Rapids: Baker Publishing Group.
221 American Bible Society. (1992). *The Holy Bible: The Good News Translation* (2nd ed.) (Jn 20:22-23). New York: American Bible Society.
222 *The Holy Bible: English Standard Version*. 2001 (Ac 2:1-2). Wheaton: Standard Bible Society.
223 Peterson, E. H. (2005). *The Message: The Bible in Contemporary Language* (Re 1:9-12). Colorado Springs, CO: NavPress.
224 *The New International Version*. 2011 (Ac 20:7). Grand Rapids, MI: Zondervan.
225 *The New International Version*. 2011 (1 Co 16:2). Grand Rapids, MI: Zondervan.
226 J. I. Packer, *Keeping the Ten Commandments*: (Wheaton, IL. Crossway Books, 2007), p. 66
227 American Bible Society. (1992). *The Holy Bible: The Good News Translation* (2nd ed.) (Ex 20:8-10). New York: American Bible Society.
228 http://www.sermoncentral.com/sermons/wheres-your-treasure-t-michael-crews-sermon-on-finding-fulfillment-98854.asp?Page=3
229 James Merritt, *Homeland Security*: (Atlanta, GA, Touching Lives, 2010), Cd #4
230 http://library.generousgiving.org/page.asp?sec=8&page=579
231 D. James Kennedy, *Why the Ten Commandments Matter*: (NY, Warner Faith, 2005), p. 74
232 Ben Patterson, *He Has Made Me Glad*: (Downers Grove, IL, InterVarsity Press, 2005), p.122
233 Tyndale House Publishers. (2007). *Holy Bible: New Living Translation* (3rd ed.) (Mk 2:27). Carol Stream, IL: Tyndale House Publishers.
234 J. I. Packer, *God's Plan for You*: (Wheaton, IL, Crossway Books, 2001), p. 89
235 William Barclay, *The Ten Commandments*: (Louisville, KY. Westminster John Knox Press, 1998), p. 38
236 Philip Comfort, *Life Application Bible Commentary*; John: (USA, Livingston Corp., 1993), p.106
237 *GOD'S WORD Translation*. 1995 (Ex 20:8-11). Grand Rapids: Baker Publishing Group.
238 *The Holy Bible: The Contemporary English Version*. 1995 (Heb 10:24-25). Nashville: Thomas Nelson.

END NOTES

239 Christopher John Donato, *Perspectives on the Sabbath*: (Nashville, TN, P&H Publishing, 2011), p.129

240 Karen Lee Thorp, *Running Nowhere in Every Direction*: (Nav Press, 2005), p.113

241 Doug Stringer, *Living Life Well; The Spirit of the Ten Commandments*: (Houston, TX. Prayer Point Press, 2010), p. 79

242 Tyndale House Publishers. (2007). *Holy Bible: New Living Translation* (3rd ed.) (Ex 20:10). Carol Stream, IL: Tyndale House Publishers.

243 Barbara Brown Taylor, *Divine Subtraction*: (Christianity Today, November3, 1999)

244 *The Holy Bible: The Contemporary English Version*. 1995 (Is 58:13-14). Nashville: Thomas Nelson.

245 D. James Kennedy, *Why the Ten Commandments Matter*: (NY, Warner Faith, 2005), p.81

246 John Ortberg, *Teaching the Heart of the Old Testament*: (Grand Rapids, MI, Zondervan, 2010), p.301

247 *GOD'S WORD Translation*. 1995 (Ps 122:1). Grand Rapids: Baker Publishing Group.

248 Mark F. Rooker, *The Ten Commandments; Ethics for the Twenty-First Century*: (Nashville, TN. B&H Publishing, 2010), p.101

249 Confraternity of Christian Doctrine. Board of Trustees, Catholic Church. National Conference of Catholic Bishops, & United States Catholic Conference. Administrative Board. (1996). *The New American Bible: Translated from the original languages with critical use of all the ancient sources and the revised New Testament* (Ro 14:17). Confraternity of Christian Doctrine.

250 American Bible Society. (1992). *The Holy Bible: The Good News Translation* (2nd ed.) (Mt 11:28). New York: American Bible Society.

251 Taylor, K. N. (1997). *The Living Bible, Paraphrased* (Ex 20:12). Wheaton, IL: Tyndale House.

252 J. H. Hertz, *The Pentateuch and Haftorahs*: (London, Soncino Press, 1960), p. 299

253 Mark F. Rooker, *The Ten Commandments; Ethics for the Twenty-First Century*: (Nashville, TN. B&H Publishing, 2010), p.116

254 D. James Kennedy, *Why the Ten Commandments Matter*: (NY, Warner Faith, 2005), p.87

255 Laura Schlessinger, *The Ten Commandments; The Significance of God's Laws in Everyday Life*: (NY, Harper Collins Press, 1999), p. 139

256 William Barclay, *The Ten Commandments*: (Louisville, KY. Westminster John Knox Press, 1998), p. 42

257 Laura Schlessinger, *The Ten Commandments; The Significance of God's Laws in Everyday Life*: (NY, Harper Collins Press, 1999), p. 168

258 William Hernandez Requejo and John L. Graham, *Global Negotiation; The New Rule*: (NY, Palgrave Macmillen, 2008), p. 96

259 W. T. Purkiser, *Exploring the Old Testament:(* Kansas City MO, Beacon Hill Press, 1955), p. 124

260 J. H. Hertz, *The Pentateuch and Haftorahs*: (London, Soncino Press, 1960), p. 298

261 Joseph T. Lienhard, *Ancient Christian Commentary on Scripture*: (Downers Grove, IL, InterVarsity Press, 2001), p.106

262 Mark F. Rooker, *The Ten Commandments; Ethics for the Twenty-First Century*: (Nashville, TN. B&H Publishing, 2010), p.119

263 American Bible Society. (1992). *The Holy Bible: The Good News Translation* (2nd ed.) (Heb 13:17). New York: American Bible Society.

264 Webster, 1976

265 Mark F. Rooker, *The Ten Commandments; Ethics for the Twenty-First Century*: (Nashville, TN. B&H Publishing, 2010), pp.105-107

266 J. H. Hertz, *The Pentateuch and Haftorahs*: (London, Soncino Press, 1960), p. 299

267 http://en.wikipedia.org/wiki/Filial_piety

268 Osborn, N. D., & Hatton, H. (1999). *A Handbook on Exodus*. UBS handbook series; Helps for translators (478-479). New York: United Bible Societies.
269 *GOD'S WORD Translation*. 1995 (Pr 6:20). Grand Rapids: Baker Publishing Group.
270 *The Everyday Bible: New Century Version*. 2005 (Le 19:3). Nashville, TN: Thomas Nelson, Inc.
271 *The New International Version*. 2011 (Heb 5:4). Grand Rapids, MI: Zondervan.
272 *The New King James Version*. 1982 (Ro 12:9-10). Nashville: Thomas Nelson.
273 *The Holy Bible: New Revised Standard Version*. 1989 (1 Sa 2:30). Nashville: Thomas Nelson Publishers.
274 Doug Stringer, *Living Life Well; The Spirit of the Ten Commandments*: (Houston, TX. Prayer Point Press, 2010), p.90
275 Taylor, K. N. (1997). *The Living Bible, paraphrased* (1 Pe 2:17). Wheaton, IL: Tyndale House.
276 *The New International Version*. 2011 (Ro 13:6-7). Grand Rapids, MI: Zondervan.
277 Edmund P. Clowney, *How Jesus Transformed the Ten Commandments*: (Phillipsburg, NJ. P&R Publishing, 2007), p. 73
278 *GOD'S WORD Translation*. 1995 (Is 29:13). Grand Rapids: Baker Publishing Group.
279 American Bible Society. (1992). *The Holy Bible: The Good News Translation* (2nd ed.) (Eph 6:1-4). New York: American Bible Society.
280 Taylor, K. N. (1997). *The Living Bible, Paraphrased* (Dt 5:16). Wheaton, IL: Tyndale House.
281 American Bible Society. (1992). *The Holy Bible: The Good News Translation* (2nd ed.) (Is 41:10). New York: American Bible Society.
282 Author W. Pink, *The Ten Commandments:* (Memphis, TN. Bottom of the Hill Publishing, 2011), p.40
283 William Barclay, *The Ten Commandments:* (Louisville, KY. Westminster John Knox Press, 1998), p.44
284 *New American Standard Bible: 1995 update*. 1995 (Pr 3:27). LaHabra, CA: The Lockman Foundation.
285 Author W. Pink, *The Ten Commandments:* (Memphis, TN. Bottom of the Hill Publishing, 2011), p.37
286 *GOD'S WORD Translation*. 1995 (Eph 6:1). Grand Rapids: Baker Publishing Group.
287 *New American Standard Bible: 1995 update*. 1995 (Col 3:20). LaHabra, CA: The Lockman Foundation.
288 Michael G. Moriarity, *The Perfect 10; The Blessing of Following God's Commandments in a Post Modern World*: (Grand Rapids, MI, Zondervan Publishing House, 1999), pp. 118-119
289 Laura Schlessinger, *The Ten Commandments; The Significance of God's Laws in Everyday Life*: (NY, Harper Collins Press, 1999), p. 129
290 *The New International Version*. 2011 (Pr 23:24-25). Grand Rapids, MI: Zondervan.
291 American Bible Society. (1992). *The Holy Bible: The Good news Translation* (2nd ed.) (Pr 19:26). New York: American Bible Society.
292 Carol Tavris, Elliot Aronson, *Mistakes Were Made (But Not by Me):* (Orlando, FL, Harcourt Books, 2007), p. 230
293 *GOD'S WORD Translation*. 1995 (Pr 20:20). Grand Rapids: Baker Publishing Group.
294 American Bible Society. (1992). *The Holy Bible: The Good News Translation* (2nd ed.) (Pr 23:22). New York: American Bible Society.
295 Taylor, K. N. (1997). *The living Bible, Paraphrased* (Lk 2:51). Wheaton, IL: Tyndale House.
296 American Bible Society. (1992). *The Holy Bible: The Good News Translation* (2nd ed.) (Pr 13:24). New York: American Bible Society.
297 *The New International Version*. 2011 (Heb 12:7-11). Grand Rapids, MI: Zondervan.
298 D. James Kennedy, *Why the Ten Commandments Matter:* (NY, Warner Faith, 2005), p.94
299 http://devilsadvocatepaper.blogspot.com/2012/04/column-yolo-you-only-love-once.html

End Notes

300 American Bible Society. (1992). *The Holy Bible: The Good News Translation* (2nd ed.) (Pr 15:5). New York: American Bible Society.

301 D. James Kennedy, *Why the Ten Commandments Matter*: (NY, Warner Faith, 2005), p. 89

302 Osborn, N. D., & Hatton, H. (1999). *A Handbook on Exodus*. UBS handbook series; Helps for translators (478-479). New York: United Bible Societies.

303 R. Collins, *Christian Morality: Biblical Foundations*: (Notre Dame, IN, University of Notre Dame Press, 1986), pp. 73-75

304 http://www.christians.org/command/com05.html

305 J. I. Packer, *Keeping the Ten Commandments*: (Wheaton, IL. Crossway Books, 2007), p.72

306 Taylor, K. N. (1997). *The Living Bible, paraphrased* (Mt 15:3-9). Wheaton, IL: Tyndale House.

307 Mark F. Rooker, *The Ten Commandments; Ethics for the Twenty-First Century*: (Nashville, TN. B&H Publishing, 2010), p.115

308 *New American Standard Bible: 1995 update*. 1995 (Le 19:32). LaHabra, CA: The Lockman Foundation.

309 Laura Schlessinger, *The Ten Commandments; The Significance of God's Laws in Everyday Life*: (NY, Harper Collins Press, 1999), p. 166

310 D. James Kennedy, *Why the Ten Commandments Matter:* (NY, Warner Faith, 2005), p. 90

311 Derrel R. Watkins, *Religion and Aging:* (Binghamton, NY, Haworth Pastoral Press, 2001), p. 50

312 *The New International Version*. 2011 (1 Ti 5:3-8). Grand Rapids, MI: Zondervan.

313 American Bible Society. (1992). *The Holy Bible: The Good News Translation* (2nd ed.) (Jn 19:26-27). New York: American Bible Society.

314 Mark F. Rooker, *The Ten Commandments; Ethics for the Twenty-First Century*: (Nashville, TN. B&H Publishing, 2010), p. 115

315 Laura Schlessinger, *The Ten Commandments; The Significance of God's Laws in Everyday Life*: (NY, Harper Collins Press, 1999), p. 158

316 Doug Stringer, *Living Life Well; The Spirit of the Ten Commandments*: (Houston, TX. Prayer Point Press, 2010), p. 90

317 Taylor, K. N. (1997). *The living Bible,Pparaphrased* (Eph 4:26). Wheaton, IL: Tyndale House.

318 American Bible Society. (1992). *The Holy Bible: The Good News Translation* (2nd ed.) (Dt 5:16). New York: American Bible Society.

319 American Bible Society. (1992). *The Holy Bible: The Good News Translation* (2nd ed.) (Ex 20:13-14). New York: American Bible Society.

320 *The New King James Version*. 1982 (Ge 1:27-28). Nashville: Thomas Nelson.

321 Philip Graham Ryken, *Written in Stone; The Ten Commandments and Today's Moral Crisis:* (Wheaton, Ill. Good News Publishers, 2003), p. 138

322 Dr. D. James Kennedy, *Why the Ten Commandments Matter*. (NY, Warner Faith publishing, 2005), p. 103

323 American Bible Society. (1992). *The Holy Bible: The Good News Translation* (2nd ed.) (Jn 10:10). New York: American Bible Society.

324 Dr. Laura Schlessinger, *The Ten Commandments; The Significance of God's Laws in Everyday Life*: (NY, Harper Collins Publishers, 1998), p. 177

325 http://online.wsj.com/article/SB10001424052748703866704575224873880379734.html

326 *The New International Version*. 2011 (Jn 1:2-3). Grand Rapids, MI: Zondervan.

327 *The New King James Version*. 1982 (Ge 1:1-2). Nashville: Thomas Nelson.

328 Reyburn, W. D., & Fry, E. M. (1998). *A handbook on Genesis*. UBS Handbook Series (28-29). New York: United Bible Societies.

329 *The New International Version.* 2011 (Ge 2:7). Grand Rapids, MI: Zondervan.

330 Jamieson, R., Fausset, A. R., & Brown, D. (1997). *Commentary Critical and Explanatory on the Whole Bible* (Ge 2:7). Oak Harbor, WA: Logos Research Systems, Inc.

331 *The Holy Bible: New Revised Standard Version.* 1989 (Jn 14:6). Nashville: Thomas Nelson Publishers.

332 Tyndale House Publishers. (2007). *Holy Bible: New Living Translation* (3rd ed.) (Jn 10:9-10). Carol Stream, IL: Tyndale House Publishers.

333 *The New International Version.* 2011 (Jn 10:27-28). Grand Rapids, MI: Zondervan.

334 *The New King James Version.* 1982 (Jn 8:44). Nashville: Thomas Nelson.

335 Stuart, D. K. (2006). *Vol. 2: Exodus.* The New American Commentary (462). Nashville: Broadman & Holman Publishers.

336 Biblical Studies Press. (2006). *The NET Bible First Edition Notes* (Ex 20:13). Biblical Studies Press.

337 *The New International Version.* 2011 (Ge 9:6). Grand Rapids, MI: Zondervan.

338 Tyndale House Publishers. (2007). *Holy Bible: New Living Translation* (3rd ed.) (Ex 20:24). Carol Stream, IL: Tyndale House Publishers.

339 *The Holy Bible: English Standard Version.* 2001 (Mt 6:26). Wheaton: Standard Bible Society.

340 *New American Standard Bible: 1995 update.* 1995 (Ac 10:13-14). LaHabra, CA: The Lockman Foundation.

341 American Bible Society. (1992). *The Holy Bible: The Good News Translation* (2nd ed.) (Ex 21:12). New York: American Bible Society. lishing. 2010), pp. 132-133

342 Mark Rooker, The Ten Commandments; Ethics for the Twenty-First Century: (Nashville, TN. B&HPu

343 *GOD'S WORD Translation.* 1995 (Ex 22:2). Grand Rapids: Baker Publishing Group.

344 Tyndale House Publishers. (2007). *Holy Bible: New Living Translation* (3rd ed.) (Ec 3:8). Carol Stream, IL: Tyndale House Publishers.

345 http://www.winwisdom.com/quotes/malcolm-muggeridge/256718.aspx

346 http://en.wikipedia.org/wiki/Euthanasia_in_the_Netherlands

347 http://www.lifenews.com/2010/01/22/nat-5910/

348 J. I. Packer, *Keeping the Ten Commandments*: (Wheaton, Ill. Crossway Books, 2007), pp. 78-79

349 http://en.wikipedia.org/wiki/Roe_v._Wade

350 http://www.lwf.org/site/News2?page=NewsArticle&id=5813&news_iv_ctrl=0&abbr=for_

351 *New American Standard Bible: 1995 update.* 1995 (Pr 6:16-18). LaHabra, CA: The Lockman Foundation.

352 American Bible Society. (1992). *The Holy Bible: The Good News Translation* (2nd ed.) (Je 1:9). New York: American Bible Society.

353 *GOD'S WORD Translation.* 1995 (Is 5:20). Grand Rapids: Baker Publishing Group.

354 Tyndale House Publishers. (2007). *Holy Bible: New Living Translation* (3rd ed.) (Col 1:16). Carol Stream, IL: Tyndale House Publishers.

355 American Bible Society. (1992). *The Holy Bible: The Good News Translation* (2nd ed.) (1 Co 6:19-20). New York: American Bible Society.

356 *New American Standard Bible: 1995 update.* 1995 (Hab 2:12). LaHabra, CA: The Lockman Foundation.

357 Peterson, E. H. (2005). *The Message: The Bible in Contemporary Language* (Ps 82:2-5). Colorado Springs, CO: NavPress.

358 *The Holy Bible: King James Version.* 2009 (Electronic Edition of the 1900 Authorized Version.) (Jas 4:17). Bellingham, WA: Logos Research Systems, Inc.

END NOTES

359 American Bible Society. (1992). *The Holy Bible: The Good News Translation* (2nd ed.) (Jas 1:26-27). New York: American Bible Society.

360 *GOD'S WORD Translation*. 1995 (1 Jn 3:16-18). Grand Rapids: Baker Publishing Group.

361 Dr. Edmund P. Clowney, *How Jesus Transforms The Ten Commandments:* (Phillipsburg, NJ. P&R Publishing, 2007), p. 87

362 http://en.wikiquote.org/wiki/Martin_Niem%C3%B6ller

363 American Bible Society. (1992). *The Holy Bible: The Good News Translation* (2nd ed.) (Mt 5:21-22). New York: American Bible Society.

364 http://www.goodreads.com/quotes/310744-if-you-look-upon-ham-and-eggs-and-lust-you?auto_log-in_attempted=true

365 *The New International Version*. 2011 (1 Jn 3:15). Grand Rapids, MI: Zondervan.

366 http://www.brainyquote.com/quotes/authors/c/clarence_darrow.html

367 *GOD'S WORD Translation*. 1995 (Ro 14:10-11). Grand Rapids: Baker Publishing Group.

368 *The New International Version*. 2011 (Pr 3:2-4). Grand Rapids, MI: Zondervan.

369 American Bible Society. (1992). *The Holy Bible: The Good News Translation* (2nd ed.) (Pr 18:20-21). New York: American Bible Society.

370 Dr. Laura Schlessinger, *The Ten Commandments: The Significance of God's Laws in Everyday Life:* (NY, Harper Collins Publishers, 1998), pp. 200, 205

371 Peterson, E. H. (2005). *The Message: The Bible in Contemporary Language* (Mk 7:20-23). Colorado Springs, CO: NavPress.

372 *The New King James Version*. 1982 (Ac 8:1). Nashville: Thomas Nelson.

373 American Bible Society. (1992). *The Holy Bible: The Good News Translation* (2nd ed.) (Eze 3:17-21). New York: American Bible Society.

374 *The New King James Version*. 1982 (Jn 1:3-5). Nashville: Thomas Nelson.

375 *The Holy Bible: New Revised Standard Version*. 1989 (Jas 2:8). Nashville: Thomas Nelson Publishers.

376 *The Everyday Bible: New Century Version*. 2005 (Ro 5:4-5). Nashville, TN: Thomas Nelson, Inc.

377 *GOD'S WORD Translation*. 1995 (1 Jn 2:5). Grand Rapids: Baker Publishing Group.

378 Taylor, K. N. (1997). *The living Bible, paraphrased* (1 Pe 4:8). Wheaton, IL: Tyndale House.

379 American Bible Society. (1992). *The Holy Bible: The Good News Translation* (2nd ed.) (Lk 10:30-35). New York: American Bible Society.

380 Dr. D. James Kennedy, *Why the Ten Commandments Matter*: (NY, Warner Faith. 2005) p. 113

381 *The Holy Bible: English Standard Version*. 2001 (Ex 20:14-15). Wheaton: Standard Bible Society.

382 Dr. D. James Kennedy: *Why the Ten Commandments*. (NY. Warner Faith publishing, 2005) p. 116

383 McGee, J. V. (1997). *Thru the Bible Commentary* (electronic ed.) (Ex 20:14). Nashville: Thomas Nelson.

384 *The Holy Bible: King James Version*. 2009 (Electronic Edition of the 1900 Authorized Version.) (Ps 119:129-130). Bellingham, WA: Logos Research Systems, Inc.

385 *The Holy Bible: English Standard Version*. 2001 (Heb 13:4). Wheaton: Standard Bible Society.

386 American Bible Society. (1992). *The Holy Bible: The Good News Translation* (2nd ed.) (Ge 2:18-24). New York: American Bible Society.

387 *New American Standard Bible: 1995 update*. 1995 (Mk 10:9). LaHabra, CA: The Lockman Foundation.

388 *The New International Version*. 2011 (Mk 10:8). Grand Rapids, MI: Zondervan.

389 Tyndale House Publishers. (2007). *Holy Bible: New Living Translation* (3rd ed.) (Ge 1:28). Carol Stream, IL: Tyndale House Publishers.

390 *The Holy Bible: English Standard Version*. 2001 (1 Co 7:1-2). Wheaton: Standard Bible Society.

391 Achtemeier, P. J., & Society of Biblical Literature. (1985). *Harper's Bible dictionary* (1st ed.) (319). San Francisco: Harper & Row.

392 Trites, A. A. (2000). Fornication. In D. N. Freedman, A. C. Myers & A. B. Beck (Eds.), *Eerdmans Dictionary of the Bible* (D. N. Freedman, A. C. Myers & A. B. Beck, Ed.) (469). Grand Rapids, MI: W.B. Eerdmans.

393 *Exodus Vol. II*. 1909 (H. D. M. Spence-Jones, Ed.). The Pulpit Commentary (138). London; New York: Funk & Wagnalls Company.

394 Henry, M. (1994). *Matthew Henry's Commentary on the Whole Bible: Complete and unabridged in one volume* (Ex 20:12-17). Peabody: Hendrickson.

395 *New American Standard Bible: 1995 update*. 1995 (Mt 5:28). LaHabra, CA: The Lockman Foundation.

396 American Bible Society. (1992). *The Holy Bible: The Good News Translation* (2nd ed.) (Heb 13:4). New York: American Bible Society.

397 *The Holy Bible: King James Version*. 2009 (Electronic Edition of the 1900 Authorized Version.) (1 Co 5:11). Bellingham, WA: Logos Research Systems, Inc.

398 *The New King James Version*. 1982 (Col 3:5). Nashville: Thomas Nelson.

399 *The New King James Version*. 1982 (Mt 5:28). Nashville: Thomas Nelson.

400 Schmidt, Thomas E. 1995. *Straight & Narrow? Compassion & Clarity in the Homosexual Debate* (InterVarsity Press), pp. 102-103

401 Schmidt, Thomas E. 1995. *Straight & Narrow? Compassion & Clarity in the Homosexual Debate* (InterVarsity Press), p. 107

402 Ibid, p. 108

403 William Barclay, *The Ten Commandments*: (Louisville, Ky. Westminster John Knox Press, 1998), p. 143

404 Ibid, p. 147-148

405 American Bible Society. (1992). *The Holy Bible: The Good News Translation* (2nd ed.) (Pr 30:20). New York: American Bible Society.

406 *The New International Version*. 2011 (Job 24:15). Grand Rapids, MI: Zondervan.

407 *The Holy Bible: King James Version*. 2009 (Electronic Edition of the 1900 Authorized Version.) (Eze 18:20). Bellingham, WA: Logos Research Systems, Inc.

408 Jones, Stanton. *"My Genes Made Me Do It" Christianity Today* (1995)

409 http://www.msnbc.msn.com/id/17951664/ns/health-sexual_health/t/many-cheat-thrill-more-stay-true-love/

410 http://www.nytimes.com/1989/03/09/us/health-psychology-experts-find-extramarital-affairs-have-profound-impact.html?pagewanted=all&src=pm

411 Dr. Laura Schlessinger, *The Ten Commandments: The Significance of God's Laws in Everyday Life*: (NY, Harper Collins, 1998), p.211

412 *The New King James Version*. 1982 (Mt 5:14-16). Nashville: Thomas Nelson.

413 Jamieson, R., Fausset, A. R., & Brown, D. (1997). *Commentary Critical and Explanatory on the Whole Bible* (Mt 5:28). Oak Harbor, WA: Logos Research Systems, Inc.

414 http://en.wikipedia.org/wiki/Pornography_in_the_United_States

415 http://skyviewcounseling.com/PAGES/skyview_areas_of_speciality.html

416 *The Holy Bible: The Contemporary English Version*. 1995 (2 Sa 11:2-4). Nashville: Thomas Nelson.

417 *The Holy Bible: King James Version*. 2009 (Electronic Edition of the 1900 Authorized Version.) (1 Co 10:11-12). Bellingham, WA: Logos Research Systems, Inc.

418 *The New King James Version*. 1982 (Ps 101:3). Nashville: Thomas Nelson.

419 *The Holy Bible: English Standard Version*. 2001 (1 Pe 3:12). Wheaton: Standard Bible Society.

End Notes

420 *The New International Version.* 2011 (Pr 5:3). Grand Rapids, MI: Zondervan.
421 *The Holy Bible: English Standard Version.* 2001 (Pr 7:21). Wheaton: Standard Bible Society.
422 American Bible Society. (1992). *The Holy Bible: The Good News Translation* (2nd ed.) (Pr 6:25-26). New York: American Bible Society.
423 *The New International Version.* 2011 (Pr 7:26-27). Grand Rapids, MI: Zondervan.
424 https://en.wikiquote.org/wiki/Ted_Haggard
425 *The New King James Version.* 1982 (Pr 2:16-19). Nashville: Thomas Nelson.
426 *The New King James Version.* 1982 (1 Co 6:18). Nashville: Thomas Nelson.
427 Tyndale House Publishers. (2007). *Holy Bible: New Living Translation* (3rd ed.) (Pr 27:8). Carol Stream, IL: Tyndale House Publishers.
428 http://www.lwf.org/site/News2?abbr=for_&page=NewsArticle&id=10584
429 *New American Standard Bible: 1995 update.* 1995 (Ro 14:7). LaHabra, CA: The Lockman Foundation.
430 American Bible Society. (1992). *The Holy Bible: The Good News Translation* (2nd ed.) (1 Co 6:15). New York: American Bible Society.
431 William Barclay. *The Ten Commandments*: (Louisville, Ky. Westminster John Knox Press, 1998), pp. 120-124
432 Peterson, E. H. (2005). *The Message: The Bible in Contemporary Language* (Pr 6:31-32). Colorado Springs, CO: NavPress.
433 *The New King James Version.* 1982 (Ps 51:4). Nashville: Thomas Nelson.
434 *The Holy Bible: New Revised Standard Version.* 1989 (1 Co 6:9-10). Nashville: Thomas Nelson Publishers.
435 *American Standard Version.* 1995 (Eph 5:4-5). Oak Harbor, WA: Logos Research Systems, Inc.
436 *The New King James Version.* 1982 (Nu 32:23). Nashville: Thomas Nelson.
437 *GOD'S WORD Translation.* 1995 (Re 21:8). Grand Rapids: Baker Publishing Group.
438 Peterson, E. H. (2005). *The Message: The Bible in Contemporary Language* (Heb 12:5-8). Colorado Springs, CO: NavPress.
439 American Bible Society. (1992). *The Holy Bible: The Good News Translation* (2nd ed.) (Ps 119:9). New York: American Bible Society.
440 *The Holy Bible: The Contemporary English Version.* 1995 (Pr 5:15). Nashville: Thomas Nelson.
441 American Bible Society. (1992). *The Holy Bible: The Good News Translation* (2nd ed.) (Pr 6:26). New York: American Bible Society.
442 *GOD'S WORD Translation.* 1995 (1 Co 7:3-4). Grand Rapids: Baker Publishing Group.
443 http://www.hisneedsherneeds.com/his-needs-her-needs-list.html
444 *The Everyday Bible: New Century Version.* 2005 (1 Co 7:5). Nashville, TN: Thomas Nelson, Inc.
445 Rick Warren: *AFFAIR-PROOFING* YOUR *MARRIAGE Ten* ... - Purpose Driven Life www.purpose-driven.co.uk/media/.../AffairProofingYourMarriage.pd...
446 *The Holy Bible: English Standard Version.* 2001 (Jas 1:14-15). Wheaton: Standard Bible Society.
447 *The New King James Version.* 1982 (Je 17:9). Nashville: Thomas Nelson.
448 *The New International Version.* 2011 (2 Co 10:2-5). Grand Rapids, MI: Zondervan.
449 American Bible Society. (1992). *The Holy Bible: The Good News Translation* (2nd ed.) (Eph 5:3). New York: American Bible Society.
450 *The New International Version.* 2011 (Pr 6:27). Grand Rapids, MI: Zondervan.
451 Holbert, *The Ten Commandments*, 87. *Adultery Threatens Every Other commitment.* See R. A. Mohler jr., *Words from the Fire* (Moody, 2009), p.133
452 *Internet Surveys* and Usage Statistics - *Nua*/ www.nua.ie/surveys/

453 http://www.forbes.com/sites/julieruvolo/2011/05/20/the-internet-is-for-porn-so-lets-talk-about-it/
454 DR. Doug Stringer. *Living Life Well; The Spirit of the Ten Commandments.* (Houston, Prayer Point Press. 2010) p.114
455 http://www.forerunner.com/forerunner/X0332_Ted_Bundy.html
456 *The New International Version.* 2011 (2 Pe 2:14). Grand Rapids, MI: Zondervan.
457 *The New King James Version.* 1982 (Ps 101:3). Nashville: Thomas Nelson.
458 *The Holy Bible: King James Version.* 2009 (Electronic Edition of the 1900 Authorized Version.) (Ro 13:14). Bellingham, WA: Logos Research Systems, Inc.
459 *New American Standard Bible: 1995 update.* 1995 (1 Pe 2:11). LaHabra, CA: The Lockman Foundation.
460 *The Holy Bible: English Standard Version.* 2001 (1 Th 5:22-23). Wheaton: Standard Bible Society.
461 American Bible Society. (1992). *The Holy Bible: The Good News Translation* (2nd ed.) (Ps 51:3). New York: American Bible Society.
462 Tyndale House Publishers. (2007). *Holy Bible: New Living Translation* (3rd ed.) (Ps 95:7-8). Carol Stream, IL: Tyndale House Publishers.
463 *The New King James Version.* 1982 (1 Co 6:9-11). Nashville: Thomas Nelson.
464 *The Holy Bible: King James Version.* 2009 (Electronic Edition of the 1900 Authorized Version.) (1 Co 15:31). Bellingham, WA: Logos Research Systems, Inc.
465 *The Holy Bible: King James Version.* 2009 (Electronic Edition of the 1900 Authorized Version.) (Jn 15:5). Bellingham, WA: Logos Research Systems, Inc.
466 *The New King James Version.* 1982 (Eph 5:25). Nashville: Thomas Nelson.
467 American Bible Society. (1992). *The Holy Bible: The Good News Translation* (2nd ed.) (Pr 13:20). New York: American Bible Society.
468 *The New International Version.* 2011 (Ps 112:7). Grand Rapids, MI: Zondervan.
469 *The New King James Version.* 1982 (Jos 24:15). Nashville: Thomas Nelson.
470 *The New King James Version.* 1982 (1 Jn 1:9). Nashville: Thomas Nelson.
471 Wuest, K. S. (1997). *Wuest's Word Studies From the Greek New Testament: For the English Reader* (1 Jn 1:8-9). Grand Rapids: Eerdmans.
472 Dr. Doug Stringer. *Living Life Well; The Spirit of the Ten Commandments.* (Houston, TX. Prayer Point Press. 2010) p. 114
473 *The Holy Bible: King James Version.* 2009 (Electronic Edition of the 1900 Authorized Version.) (Ex 20:15-17). Bellingham, WA: Logos Research Systems, Inc.
474 Simeon, C. (1836). *Horae Homileticae Vol. 1: Genesis to Leviticus* (27). London: Samuel Holdsworth.
475 J. I. Packer. *Keeping The 10 Commandments.* (Wheaton, Il. Crossway Books. 2007) p. 90
476 American Bible Society. (1992). *The Holy Bible: The Good News Translation* (2nd ed.) (Eph 4:27-28). New York: American Bible Society.
477 Dr. D James Kennedy. *Why the Ten Commandments Matter.* (NY. Warner Faith publishing. 2005) p. 134
478 .http://www.sermoncentral.com/sermons/the-positive-side-of-the-ten-commandments-the-eighth-commandment-elmer-towns-sermon-on-commandments-steal-52300.asp
479 *The Holy Bible: English Standard Version.* 2001 (Ro 6:23). Wheaton: Standard Bible Society.
480 *The New International Version.* 2011 (Pr 14:34). Grand Rapids, MI: Zondervan.
481 *The Holy Bible: New Revised Standard Version.* 1989 (Ro 5:12). Nashville: Thomas Nelson Publishers.
482 *The New King James Version.* 1982 (Jos 7:21). Nashville: Thomas Nelson.

END NOTES

483 Howard, D. M., Jr. (1998). *Vol. 5: Joshua. The New American Commentary* (197). Nashville: Broadman & Holman Publishers.

484 Ellsworth, R. (2008). *Opening up Joshua.* Opening Up Commentary (74). Leominster: Day One Publications.

485 *US News and World Report,* Nov. 28, 1977

486 http://www.sermonnotebook.org/old%20testament/exodus_20_15.htm

487 http://www.sermonnotebook.org/old%20testament/exodus_20_15.htm

488 American Bible Society. (1992). *The Holy Bible: The Good News Translation* (2nd ed.) (Ro 13:8-10). New York: American Bible Society.

489 Dr. Laura Schlessinger. *The Ten Commandments, The Significance of God's Laws in Everyday Life.* (NY. Harper publishers, 1998.) p. 249

490 *The Everyday Bible: New Century Version.* 2005 (Pr 14:12). Nashville, TN: Thomas Nelson, Inc.

491 *The New King James Version.* 1982 (Is 5:20). Nashville: Thomas Nelson.

492 American Bible Society. (1992). *The Holy Bible: The Good News Translation* (2nd ed.) (Mt 7:13-14). New York: American Bible Society.

493 http://www.ebaumsworld.com/jokes/read/80596072/

494 *New American Standard Bible: 1995 update.* 1995 (Pr 15:3). LaHabra, CA: The Lockman Foundation.

495 *The Holy Bible: English Standard Version.* 2001 (1 Co 6:10). Wheaton: Standard Bible Society.

496 *http://www.identex.net/cost_of_crime.html*

497 http://news.google.com/newspapers?nid=1916&dat=19910806&id=DQ8hAAAAIBAJ&sjid=knYFAAAAIBAJ&pg=3451,721666

498 Taylor, K. N. (1997). *The Living Bible, Paraphrased* (Job 34:31-32). Wheaton, IL: Tyndale House.

499 http://www.mulhollandsecurity.com/articles/Business_Security/0034_shoplifting_facts_retail_theft_merchandise.html

500 James Patterson and Peter Kim. *"The Day America Told the Truth."* (Prentice Hall Press, 1991),

501 Peterson, E. H. (2005). *The Message: The Bible in Contemporary Language* (Col 3:22). Colorado Springs, CO: NavPress.

502 http://blog.nrf.com/2012/06/22/national-retail-security-survey-retail-shrinkage-totaled-34-5-billion-in-2011/

503 Adrian Rogers. *"A Perfect Ten for Homes That Win.* (Memphis, TN. Love Worth Finding Ministries. 1996) Tape #8

504 *The New International Version.* 2011 (Eph 4:28). Grand Rapids, MI: Zondervan.

505 Peterson, E. H. (2005). *The Message: The Bible in Contemporary Language* (Jas 5:4). Colorado Springs, CO: NavPress.

506 American Bible Society. (1992). *The Holy Bible: The Good News Translation* (2nd ed.) (Col 4:1). New York: American Bible Society.

507 *The New International Version.* 2011 (Lk 20:47). Grand Rapids, MI: Zondervan.

508 American Bible Society. (1992). *The Holy Bible: The Good News Translation* (2nd ed.) (Lk 20:25). New York: American Bible Society.

509 Tyndale House Publishers. (2007). *Holy Bible: New Living Translation* (3rd ed.) (Ro 13:6-7). Carol Stream, IL: Tyndale House Publishers.

510 *New American Standard Bible: 1995 update.* 1995 (Ro 13:8). LaHabra, CA: The Lockman Foundation.

511 http://www.glass-castle.com/clients/www-nocheating-org/adcouncil/research/cheatingfactsheet.html

512 *New American Standard Bible: 1995 update.* 1995 (Hab 2:6). LaHabra, CA: The Lockman Foundation.

513 American Bible Society. (1992). *The Holy Bible: The Good News Translation* (2nd ed.) (Am 8:5). New York: American Bible Society.
514 http://www.usnews.com/topics/subjects/digital_piracy
515 http://www.cerm.info/bible_studies/Exegetical/ten_command.html
516 Author W. Pink. *The Ten Commandments*. (Memphis, TN. Bottom of the Hill Publishing. 2011) p. 54
517 *The Everyday Bible: New Century Version*. 2005 (1 Co 6:19-20). Nashville, TN: Thomas Nelson, Inc.
518 *New American Standard Bible: 1995 update*. 1995 (Is 43:1). LaHabra, CA: The Lockman Foundation.
519 Taylor, K. N. (1997). *The Living Bible, Paraphrased* (Eph 5:15-16). Wheaton, IL: Tyndale House.
520 *The New King James Version*. 1982 (Eph 2:10). Nashville: Thomas Nelson.
521 American Bible Society. (1992). *The Holy Bible: The Good News Translation* (2nd ed.) (Mal 3:8-12). New York: American Bible Society.
522 *The New International Version*. 2011 (Eph 4:28). Grand Rapids, MI: Zondervan.
523 American Bible Society. (1992). *The Holy Bible: The Good News Translation* (2nd ed.) (Ps 51:2-4). New York: American Bible Society.
524 Peterson, E. H. (2005). *The Message: The Bible in Contemporary Language* (2 Th 3:10-13). Colorado Springs, CO: NavPress.
525 Dr. Laura Schlessinger. *The Ten Commandments, The Significance of God's Laws in Everyday Life*. (NY. Harper publishers, 1998.) p. 259
526 American Bible Society. (1992). *The Holy Bible: The Good News Translation* (2nd ed.) (Ec 5:18-19). New York: American Bible Society.
527 *The Holy Bible: King James Version*. 2009 (Electronic Edition of the 1900 Authorized Version.) (Ex 20:8-10). Bellingham, WA: Logos Research Systems, Inc.
528 James Merritt, *Homeland Security*: (Atlanta, GA, Touching Lives, 2010) CD #7
529 *The Everyday Bible: New Century Version*. 2005 (La 3:27). Nashville, TN: Thomas Nelson, Inc.
530 Peterson, E. H. (2005). *The Message: The Bible in Contemporary Language* (La 3:28-29). Colorado Springs, CO: NavPress.
531 http://www.goodreads.com/author/quotes/151350.John_Wesley
532 *The Holy Bible: English Standard Version*. 2001 (Ps 24:1). Wheaton: Standard Bible Society.
533 *New American Standard Bible: 1995 update*. 1995 (1 Co 4:2). LaHabra, CA: The Lockman Foundation.
534 Peterson, E. H. (2005). *The Message: The Bible in Contemporary Language* (1 Ti 6:17-19). Colorado Springs, CO: NavPress.
535 http://www.wisdomonwealth.org/Illustrations/
536 *The Holy Bible: King James Version*. 2009 (Electronic Edition of the 1900 Authorized Version.) (Php 4:19-20). Bellingham, WA: Logos Research Systems, Inc.
537 *The Everyday Bible: New Century Version*. 2005 (Mt 6:10-13). Nashville, TN: Thomas Nelson, Inc.
538 American Bible Society. (1992). *The Holy Bible: The Good News Translation* (2nd ed.) (Mt 6:28-34). New York: American Bible Society.
539 James Glentworth Butler DD. (NY. The Bible-Work, The OT; Exodus, chap. XII), Funk and Wagnalls, 1889. P. 195
540 Taylor, K. N. (1997). *The Living Bible, paraphrased* (Ex 20:12-18). Wheaton, IL: Tyndale House.
541 American Bible Society. (1992). *The Holy Bible: The Good News Translation* (2nd ed.) (Ps 58:3). New York: American Bible Society.
542 http://www.quotationspage.com/quote/27150.html
543 http://www.christianglobe.com/Illustrations/theDetails.asp?whichOne=l&whichFile=lie
544 http://en.wikiquote.org/wiki/Mort_Sahl#cite_note-DG-1

END NOTES

545 http://www.goodreads.com/quotes/tag/trust?auto_login_attempted=true
546 *The Holy Bible: English Standard Version.* 2001 (Jn 14:6). Wheaton: Standard Bible Society.
547 Sissela Bok, *Lying: Moral Choice in Public and Private Life*, (New York: Vintage books., 1989), p. 27
548 http://www.sciencedaily.com/releases/1999/12/991214072623.htm
549 http://edition.cnn.com/2002/fyi/teachers.ednews/04/05/highschool.cheating/
550 American Bible Society. (1992). *The Holy Bible: The Good News Translation* (2nd ed.) (Pr 12:22). New York: American Bible Society.
551 http://www.allphrasesandquotes.com/truth-and-lies/mirror-mirror-on-the-wall-you%E2%80%99re-not-pleasing-me-at-all-i-know-you-cannot-lie-forsooth-but-can%E2%80%99t-you-slightly-bend-the-truth/
552 (Bits & Pieces, December 9, 1993, pp. 12-13.)
553 *The New International Version.* 2011 (Pr 6:16-19). Grand Rapids, MI: Zondervan.
554 J. I. Packer, *Keeping the Ten Commandments*, (Wheaton, Ill: Crossway Books, 2007), p. 97
555 *New American Standard Bible: 1995 update.* 1995 (Ga 6:7). LaHabra, CA: The Lockman Foundation.
556 Stuart, D. K. (2006). *Vol. 2: Exodus. The New American Commentary* (465-466). Nashville: Broadman & Holman Publishers.
557 Dr. Laura Schlessinger, *The Ten Commandments*, (NY: Harper Collins, 1998), p. 275
558 *The New International Version.* 2011 (1 Jn 1:5). Grand Rapids, MI: Zondervan.
559 Jamieson, R., Fausset, A. R., & Brown, D. (1997). *Commentary Critical and Explanatory on the Whole Bible* (1 Jn 1:5). Oak Harbor, WA: Logos Research Systems, Inc.
560 Joseph T. Lienhard, (2001*) Ancient Christian Commentary on Scripture*: (Downers Grove, Ill.: Inter varsity Press) p. 107
561 American Bible Society. (1992). *The Holy Bible: The Good News Translation* (2nd ed.) (Pr 10:10). New York: American Bible Society.
562 *The New International Version.* 2011 (Dt 5:20). Grand Rapids, MI: Zondervan.
563 *New American Standard Bible: 1995 update.* 1995 (Jn 8:44). LaHabra, CA: The Lockman Foundation.
564 *Ibid.*
565 Soanes, C., & Stevenson, A. (2004). *Concise Oxford English Dictionary* (11th ed.). Oxford: Oxford University Press.
566 *The Everyday Bible: New Century Version.* 2005 (Ex 23:1). Nashville, TN: Thomas Nelson, Inc.
567 http://articles.nydailynews.com/2012-06-04/news/32037127_1_rusty-hardin-issa-roger-clemens
568 American Bible Society. (1992). *The Holy Bible: The Good News Translation* (2nd ed.) (Pr 25:18). New York: American Bible Society.
569 Mark F. Rooker, *The Ten Commandments*: (Nashville, TN: B & H Publishing, 2010) p. 158
570 *New American Standard Bible: 1995 update.* 1995 (Ps 101:5). LaHabra, CA: The Lockman Foundation.
571 *GOD'S WORD Translation.* 1995 (Ex 23:1). Grand Rapids: Baker Publishing Group.
572 *The New International Version.* 2011 (Le 19:16). Grand Rapids, MI: Zondervan.
573 http://community.seattletimes.nwsource.com/archive/?date=19940827&slug=1927370
574 *New American Standard Bible: 1995 update.* 1995 (1 Ti 5:13). LaHabra, CA: The Lockman Foundation.
575 *The New International Version.* 2011 (Pr 16:28). Grand Rapids, MI: Zondervan.
576 *Ibid.*
577 Taylor, K. N. (1997). *The Living Bible, Paraphrased* (Pr 15:14). Wheaton, IL: Tyndale House.
578 http://www.injesus.com/message-archives/christian-living/godwithusmin/daily-quote-law-of-the-nose-2

579 *The New International Version.* 2011 (Ps 55:21). Grand Rapids, MI: Zondervan.
580 *The Holy Bible: English Standard Version.* 2001 (Pr 26:28). Wheaton: Standard Bible Society.
581 Adrian Rogers, *A Perfect Ten for Homes That Win:* (Memphis, TN, Love Worth Finding, 1998), Tape #8
582 American Bible Society. (1992). *The Holy Bible: The Good news Translation* (2nd ed.) (Pr 27:5-6). New York: American Bible Society.
583 LEE IACOCCA, *U.S. News & World Report*, 1985
584 Arthur W. Pink, *The Ten Commandments*: (Memphis, TN: Bottom of the Hill publishing, 2011), p.62
585 *The New International Version.* 2011 (Le 5:1). Grand Rapids, MI: Zondervan.
586 http://thinkexist.com/quotation/in_the_end-we_will_remember_not_the_words_of_our/214890.html
587 *The Holy Bible: English Standard Version.* 2001 (Mt 12:34). Wheaton: Standard Bible Society.
588 Peterson, E. H. (2005). *The Message: The Bible in Contemporary Language* (Mt 15:16-20). Colorado Springs, CO: NavPress.
589 *New American Standard Bible: 1995 update.* 1995 (Is 57:11). LaHabra, CA: The Lockman Foundation.
590 *Ibid.*
591 Austin O'Malley, (1858-1932), American physician, humorist and author*: "Keystone of Thought."* http://www.discoverthebible.com/devotions/?s=There-Is-No-Lion-Only-Lying&g=a
592 http://quotationsbook.com/quote/23376/
593 American Bible Society. (1992). *The Holy Bible: The Good News Translation* (2nd ed.) (Ps 34:11-13). New York: American Bible Society.
594 Ibid. pg. 16
595 *New American Standard Bible: 1995 update.* 1995 (Ro 6:23). LaHabra, CA: The Lockman Foundation.
596 Mark F. Rooker, *The Ten Commandments:* (Nashville, TN: B & H Publishing, 2010) p. 161
597 *The Holy Bible: King James Version.* 2009 (Electronic Edition of the 1900 Authorized Version.) (Php 2:5-6). Bellingham, WA: Logos Research Systems, Inc.
598 *The Holy Bible: King James Version.* 2009 (Electronic Edition of the 1900 Authorized Version.) (Php 4:8). Bellingham, WA: Logos Research Systems, Inc.
599 American Bible Society. (1992). *The Holy Bible: The Good News Translation* (2nd ed.) (Eph 4:25). New York: American Bible Society.
600 American Bible Society. (1992). *The Holy Bible: The Good News Translation* (2nd ed.) (Eph 4:25). New York: American Bible Society.
601 *The Holy Bible: English Standard Version.* 2001 (Ac 4:12). Wheaton: Standard Bible Society.
602 *The Holy Bible: English Standard Version.* 2001. Wheaton: Standard Bible Society.
603 American Bible Society. (1992). *The Holy Bible: The Good News Translation* (2nd ed.) (Php 4:19-20). New York: American Bible Society.
604 Robert C. Shannon, *1000 Windows*, (Cincinnati, Ohio: Standard Publishing Company, 1997).
605 Dockery, D. S., Butler, T. C., Church, C. L., Scott, L. L., Ellis Smith, M. A., White, J. E., & Holman Bible Publishers (Nashville, T. (1992). *Holman Bible Handbook* (148). Nashville, TN: Holman Bible Publishers.
606 Bridges, R. F., & Weigle, L. A. (1994). *King James Bible Word Book* (electronic ed.) (89). Nashville: Thomas Nelson.
607 Draper, Charles W., Brand, Chad., & England, Archie. *Holman Illustrated Bible Dictionary*: (Nashville, TN, Holman Bible Publishers, 2003), p. 70

End Notes

608 *Webster's New Collegiate Dictionary*, G & C Merriam CO., (Cambridge, Mass: Riverside Press: 1953), p. 192

609 American Bible Society. (1992). *The Holy Bible: The Good News Translation* (2nd ed.) (Ps 37:4). New York: American Bible Society.

610 *The Holy Bible: English Standard Version*. 2001 (Ps 84:11). Wheaton: Standard Bible Society.

611 http://www.brainyquote.com/quotes/authors/e/epicurus.html

612 Tyndale House Publishers. (2007). *Holy Bible: New Living Translation* (3rd ed.) (1 Jn 2:15-17). Carol Stream, IL: Tyndale House Publishers.

613 *The New International Version*. 2011 (Lk 12:15). Grand Rapids, MI: Zondervan.

614 *GOD'S WORD Translation*. 1995 (Col 3:2). Grand Rapids: Baker Publishing Group.

615 *The Holy Bible: New Revised Standard Version*. 1989 (Mt 6:33). Nashville: Thomas Nelson Publishers.

616 *The New International Version*. 2011 (Ro 13:9). Grand Rapids, MI: Zondervan.

617 St. Thomas Aquinas, *St. Thomas Aquinas, Summa Theologica*: vol. 5 of 10. (Forgotten Books, 1947), p.425

618 J. Oswald Sanders, *Bible Men of Faith* (Chicago: Moody Press, 1974), p.13.

619 American Bible Society. (1992). *The Holy Bible: The Good News Translation* (2nd ed.) (Mt 15:19-20). New York: American Bible Society.

620 Tyndale House Publishers. (2007). *Holy Bible: New Living Translation* (3rd ed.) (Mk 4:18-19). Carol Stream, IL: Tyndale House Publishers.

621 Tyndale House Publishers. (2007). *Holy Bible: New Living Translation* (3rd ed.) (Lk 12:16-19). Carol Stream, IL: Tyndale House Publishers.

622 http://starwinar.wordpress.com/daily-short-story/just-a-little-bit-more/

623 http://www.preceptaustin.org/hebrews_135-7.htm

624 http://www.studyjesus.com/lifeofchrist/less57fr.htm

625 http://www.studyjesus.com/lifeofchrist/less57fr.htm

626 *The New King James Version*. 1982 (1 Th 2:5). Nashville: Thomas Nelson.

627 American Bible Society. (1992). *The Holy Bible: The Good News Translation* (2nd ed.) (Ro 7:7-8). New York: American Bible Society.

628 *New American Standard Bible: 1995 update*. 1995 (Mk 7:21-22). LaHabra, CA: The Lockman Foundation.

629 *GOD'S WORD Translation*. 1995 (Jn 8:44). Grand Rapids: Baker Publishing Group.

630 *GOD'S WORD Translation*. 1995 (Eze 28:15). Grand Rapids: Baker Publishing Group.

631 http://www.englishforums.com/English/CharlesKingsleyWish/lljnh/post.htm

632 http://thinkexist.com/quotation/if_i_am_what_i_have_and_if_i_lose_what_i_have_who/325790.html

633 *The Holy Bible: New Revised Standard Version*. 1989 (1 Ti 6:9-10). Nashville: Thomas Nelson Publishers.

634 *The New King James Version*. 1982 (Eph 5:5). Nashville: Thomas Nelson.

635 http://www.americansongwriter.com/2012/03/behind-the-song-i-cant-get-no-satisfaction/

636 News Week, March, 1996

637 http://www.goodreads.com/quotes/42553-too-many-people-spend-money-they-haven-t-earned-to-buy?auto_login_attempted=true

638 http://www.english-for-students.com/The-Greedy-Dog.html

639 James S. Hewett, *Illustrations Unlimited* (Wheaton: Tyndale House Publishers, Inc, 1988) p. 26.

640 *New American Standard Bible: 1995 update*. 1995 (Ro 12:15). LaHabra, CA: The Lockman Foundation.
641 *GOD'S WORD Translation*. 1995 (Ps 75:6-7). Grand Rapids: Baker Publishing Group.
642 MacArthur, John. (*The MacArthur NT Commentary: Ephesians)*, p. 154
643 *The New International Version*. 2011 (Jas 4:1-2). Grand Rapids, MI: Zondervan.
644 *The Holy Bible: King James Version*. 2009 (Electronic Edition of the 1900 Authorized Version.) (Jn 3:30-31). Bellingham, WA: Logos Research Systems, Inc.
645 *The Everyday Bible: New Century Version*. 2005 (1 Th 5:18). Nashville, TN: Thomas Nelson, Inc.
646 http://www.exploringcreativity.com/quotes6.html
647 *New American Standard Bible: 1995 update*. 1995 (Ex 13:3). LaHabra, CA: The Lockman Foundation.
648 American Bible Society. (1992). *The Holy Bible: The Good News Translation* (2nd ed.) (Php 3:20). New York: American Bible Society.
649 Tyndale House Publishers. (2007). *Holy Bible: New Living Translation* (3rd ed.) (Mt 6:19-21). Carol Stream, IL: Tyndale House Publishers.
650 Tyndale House Publishers. (2007). *Holy Bible: New Living Translation* (3rd ed.) (1 Ti 6:6-8). Carol Stream, IL: Tyndale House Publishers.
651 *New American Standard Bible: 1995 update*. 1995 (Php 4:11). LaHabra, CA: The Lockman Foundation.
652 *The New International Version*. 2011 (Ec 5:10). Grand Rapids, MI: Zondervan.
653 American Bible Society. (1992). *The Holy Bible: The Good News Translation* (2nd ed.) (Pr 23:4-5). New York: American Bible Society.
654 American Bible Society. (1992). *The Holy Bible: The Good News Translation* (2nd ed.) (Jn 4:13-14). New York: American Bible Society.
655 *GOD'S WORD Translation*. 1995 (Heb 13:5). Grand Rapids: Baker Publishing Group.
656 VICTORIA TIMES (SEPT 1990)
657 Tyndale House Publishers. (2007). *Holy Bible: New Living Translation* (3rd ed.) (Pr 11:25). Carol Stream, IL: Tyndale House Publishers.
658 *The New International Version*. 2011 (1 Ti 6:19). Grand Rapids, MI: Zondervan.
659 Bill Hybels, *"Power: Preaching for Total Commitment," Mastering Contemporary Preaching*: (Portland, OR: Multnomah Press, 1989), pp. 120-121
660 William Barclay, *The Ten Commandments*. (Louisville, Kentucky: Westminster Press, 1998), p. 192
661 M. Erickson, *Christian Theology*: (Grand Rapids, Baker, 1985), pp. 802-803
662 *The New International Version*. 2011 (2 Ti 3:16). Grand Rapids, MI: Zondervan.
663 http://www.truthinaction.org/sermon/GOSPEL%20AND%20THE%20LAW%20-THE_100250.pdf